THE
LIFE
INSURANCE
GAME

THE LIFE INSURANCE GAME

RONALD KESSLER

Holt, Rinehart and Winston New York

Published by Holt, Rinehart and Winston,
383 Madison Avenue, New York, New York 10017.
Published simultaneously in Canada by Holt, Rinehart and
Winston of Canada, Limited.

Library of Congress Cataloging in Publication Data
Kessler, Ronald.
The life insurance game.   029640
Includes index.   /6.95
1. Insurance, Life—United States.   I. Title.
HG8951.K47   1984   368.3'2'00973   84-6642
ISBN: 0-03-070507-X

First Edition

Design by Iris Weinstein
Printed in the United States of America
10 9 8 7 6 5 4 3 2 1

Grateful acknowledgment is made to the following
for permission to reprint excerpts from their
publications:

Fortune magazine, for reprint of life insurance
company data, June 13, 1983, © 1983 Time Inc.
All rights reserved.
Salomon Brothers Inc., for excerpts from "1983
Prospects for Financial Markets."

ISBN 0-03-070507-X

For Pam, Greg, and Rachel

CONTENTS

ACKNOWLEDGMENTS

This book began as a project for *The Washington Post*. I am grateful to Bob Signer, the editor who first approved the idea. Along the way, I received helpful ideas from editors Bob Woodward and Jane Amsterdam. Howard Simos, who at that time was managing editor and is now with the Nieman Foundation, supported going ahead with a book.

Throughout the effort, a number of people gave of their time unsparingly. They include Ray A. Philibert, senior vice-president of Computone Systems, Inc. of Atlanta; Irwin M. Borowski, formerly associate chief of enforcement of the Securities and Exchange Commission; William A. White, chief actuary of the New Jersey State Insurance Department; Christopher J. Vizas II, formerly special staff counsel of the Privacy Protection Study Commission; and J. Ross Hanson, a consulting actuary.

To my literary agent, Julian Bach, I owe a debt for his immediate enthusiasm about a book on this subject, and to Paul Bresnick of Holt, Rinehart and Winston for his deft guidance and skillful editing. After he left the publishing house, editor Bobbi Mark applied a strong and talented hand to completing the project.

My wife, Pamela Kessler; my children, Rachel and Greg Kessler; and my stepson, Mike Whitehead, encouraged me and provided the kind of support that is critical in undertaking a project of this magnitude.

Finally, I wish to thank the life insurance industry, more particularly the executives and public relations officers of some of the larger companies in the business; the American Council of Life Insurance, the chief trade and lobbying group; and the hundreds of agents, regulators, and other experts who gave of their time.

Acknowledgments

The American Council, in a memorandum distributed to its member companies, stated, "In keeping with our policy of providing information to the media, a number of our council staff people have been working with Mr. Kessler so that he will receive accurate material. The council has met his various requests by providing published information as appropriate. In addition, several council staff members have had long conversations with Mr. Kessler, and we can anticipate further dialogue as his work progresses."

The council, and others cited here, will not agree with everything in this book. But by opening themselves to my questioning, they demonstrated an awareness that they are accountable to the public.

In like fashion, I have tried to hold myself accountable by basing the information in this book solely on records or on-the-record interviews. In some instances, agents, while interviewed on-the-record, are not named because they merely reflect practices that are common within the industry. With the exception of the widows and consumers affected by the industry, and a handful of outside experts, every individual quoted is a member of the life insurance industry. Any critical findings have been presented to the companies, agents, or appropriate trade associations for their comment.

Books that have been helpful in developing the history of life insurance and its regulation include Merlo J. Pusey's *Charles Evans Hughes*, J. Owen Stalson's *Marketing Life Insurance*, William H. A. Carr's *From Three Cents a Week*, Marquis James's *The Metropolitan Life*, Carlyle Buley's *The American Life Convention*, and *Life Company Operations* published by the Life Office Management Association.

Unless otherwise noted, all rate comparisons come from computer terminals of Computone Systems, Inc. of Atlanta, which obtains the data from the companies, and represent rates paid by a thirty-two-year-old, nonsmoking male for $100,000 in coverage. Since the rates are not necessarily current, they are cited solely for purposes of comparing the relative differences among companies and policies.

THE
LIFE
INSURANCE
GAME

INTRODUCTION

■ American life insurance companies have more money than any other American financial institutions except those engaged in banking. Their investment decisions affect the economy and the growth of American cities and industries. Their buildings—the Empire State Building and Pan Am Building in New York, Prudential Center in Boston, Prudential Plaza in Chicago, and the Transamerica Building in San Francisco—dominate the skylines of American cities.

Two out of three Americans have life insurance coverage. They spend an average of a week each year working to pay for it. Each year, life insurance companies collect $50 billion in life insurance premium payments, write another thirty million policies, and add another $62 billion to their wealth, which stands at more than $600 billion.

Life insurance companies have accumulated an abundance of riches by offering "a piece of the Rock" or "an umbrella in stormy weather." They hold themselves out as protectors of widows and orphans, upholders of the American way. Without that bond of trust, people would not entrust their funds to them.

In fact, life insurance companies rarely go broke. They are generally more conservative in their investments and more financially stable than banks. For the most part, they pay off claims promptly and without dispute. And the overwhelming majority of their more than one million employees and agents are hardworking, honest individuals.

Yet the sole purpose of the million employees, the buildings that pierce the sky, and the trust that life insurance companies have built up is to pay death benefits to beneficiaries of life insurance policies—nothing more and nothing less. In that pursuit—the bottom line of an industry that accounts for a significant segment of the nation's economic activity—the nation's life insurance companies have failed.

For every dollar the nation's 2,100 life insurance companies receive as income from annual premium payments and investment earnings on individual policies, they pay out as death benefits an average of just fourteen cents. They also pay out as investment returns and similar benefits—which is not the reason for the industry's existence—another twenty-seven cents.

That leaves the policyholder with an average of forty-one cents for every dollar the companies get from him.

The companies do not give policyholders these figures, nor is there any practical way to obtain them. The figures, compiled internally by the American Council of Life Insurance, the chief industry trade and lobbying group, are not published in any statistical tract put out by the life insurance industry. In fact, for years, the industry has claimed its rate of return is irrelevant.

What these rates of return show is that the life insurance industry is not primarily providing life insurance protection. Instead, it makes investments for itself. Investment returns account for twice as much return on the dollar as death benefits. And those investment returns, even when combined with the death benefit returns, are so minuscule when compared with other financial products that the consumer would be far better off hiding his money under his mattress than entrusting it to a life insurance company.

This book will attempt to show just where the money really goes and why even the most sophisticated consumers—accountants, doctors, lawyers—repeatedly fall for the industry's line. In demonstrating how it is done, the book will trace your life insurance dollar from the time you hand it to your agent until what remains of it is finally paid to your beneficiary.

In doing that, the book will take you through the progression of stops in between: the misleading sales pitches, advertisements, and computer comparisons that are often employed to make the sale; the sale of new policies that ensnare consumers with claims of better returns when they are really the old policies in disguise; the investigations, undertaken before a policy is issued, into applicants' sex lives, character, and drinking habits; the investment of the funds and use of ingenious accounting systems to hide the industry's true profits; and the wining and dining of the industry's government regulators.

For the poor or the aged, there is a special route in the life insurance game to be explored. It provides even higher-priced policies than those sold to the more affluent.

At the end of this maze, the dollar received from the consumer has been whittled away by lavish agents' commissions and trips, needless turnover or churning of policies, and enhancement of the industry's already colossal reserves.

The game goes on because the companies involved in the life insurance game, as in no other financial industry, make the rules themselves. Much as securities firms sold stocks before the establishment of the Securities and Exchange Commission in 1933, insurance companies sell in an atmosphere almost totally free of effective regulation, rigorous competition, or honest disclosure.

Regulated by the states instead of the federal government, the industry holds itself aloof from the mainstream of the financial world. Its terminology and methods are so arcane that it takes months of study just to understand what life insurance people are talking about or even to know what the price of a policy is. Indeed, it is that inscrutability—the fact that no one can understand what is being sold—that is the industry's greatest weapon.

Like many systemic abuses, the game goes on largely unnoticed and neglected by official Washington or the press, as reflected in the degree of media coverage accorded the industry. As one example, only 116 stories referring to life insurance companies have appeared in *Newsweek* magazine in the last ten years, compared with 2,792 referring to banks.

Despite the importance of life insurance to the 150 million

Americans covered by it, no previous book has attempted to penetrate how the industry works by portraying the entire spectrum of its activities, based on specific examples and interviews with the principals—the agents, executives, regulators, consumers, and widows and widowers who are, in the end, the beneficiaries of the industry's product.

Through actual interviews with these insiders, this book will show how the industry has managed to retain whole life—a dinosaur in an age of computers—as its number-one seller; how agents are imbued with the belief that new policies promising market rates of return are better than the whole life policies they actually resemble; and how the industry preys on the poor and aged by selling them policies that cost two to four times as much as policies sold to others.

While some agents make hundreds of thousands of dollars in commissions a year, the abuses in the life insurance industry do not necessarily result in striking personal enrichment. There are no individual villains that one can point to. Rather, the abuses inevitably flow when human beings are left to tend huge sums of wealth with little or no check on their actions by the outside world.

The result is that the industry's vastly excessive funds—roughly half of it held by the ten largest companies—are hoarded to build even more buildings. That wealth is used to gain even more power. And the widows and orphans who are the entire reason for the industry's existence receive paltry benefits without even knowing how they got taken in the life insurance game.

I. THE GAME

■ The game starts with a call or a knock on your door. The agent has been trained in psychological techniques. He knows what responses—and nonresponses—to make to your every move. If you agree to meet with him, the chances are one in two you will buy a policy.

In most cases, you will not know what you bought or how much it actually costs. You will not compare policies from other companies. You will not understand just what the policy provides. Nor will you have any reasonable way of finding out. The agent himself may not understand the policy. But he will know one thing: that it pays a better commission than the one he does not recommend.

Even the actuaries who design the policies and life insurance executives themselves say they cannot tell what the effective price of a policy is so they can compare them. If two policies cannot be compared, the consumer cannot find out which is the better buy. That is the way the life insurance companies want it.

"Life insurance companies make the policies more complex to make it difficult to compare the price," said Francis E. Ferguson, chairman of Northwestern Mutual Life Insurance Company, the tenth largest in the country. "It's never really said," he said. "I don't think anybody [within the industry] in his right mind would say it."

This in itself is remarkable: an industry that collects $50 billion a year from American consumers who cannot tell the price of the product they are buying. If the price cannot be discerned, it is easy for one company to charge as much as double what another charges for exactly the same coverage and benefits. That is just what life insurance companies do. In some cases, the high-priced brands and the cheaper ones exist side-by-side in the same city.

Over time, a life insurance policy may cost as much as a house, and the difference between one company's policy and another's can amount to tens of thousands of dollars. Yet most consumers will never know they got a bad buy.

To find out how much a bank or money fund is paying for its money, you can call the institution or glance at newspaper advertisements. Then you can compare the interest rate with the average rates listed in the financial section of your newspaper. If one bank is paying nine percent interest a year, while its competitor down the street is paying twelve percent, you can expect that most people will patronize the one with the better rate. The one with the lower rate can be expected eventually to go out of business—which is almost what happened when money funds began drawing deposits away from savings and loan associations.

In the life insurance game, there are no interest rates. There are no price tags. There is no unit pricing. There are no advertisements listing prices, nor are there average rates listed in newspapers. You land on the company that your agent wants you to land on.

An industry study bears that out. "Not only do most people rely on the sales process [agent sales presentations] as their primary source of information about life insurance, in most instances they rely on the information provided by a single agent," according to the study by the American Council of Life Insurance and the Life Insurance Marketing and Research Association. In surveying fourteen thousand people who had had contact with a life insurance agent in the previous twelve months, the two industry trade groups concluded that only one in five of all the buyers ever attempted to compare price.

The study found those attempts were feeble at best. Usually, the buyers asked the same agent or a friend or relative, according to the study. If life insurance executives and actuaries themselves say they cannot compare prices, asking a friend or the same agent will be as helpful as a trip to the zoo.

As we shall see later, the companies and agents actively foster the impression that life insurance prices are all the same. If people can be convinced that there is no point to shopping for a better buy, the product can be sold with virtually no price competition. And if there is no price competition, why advertise prices?

When the companies do advertise, their claims cannot always be taken at face value. Take the case of Metropolitan Life Insurance Company, the second largest in the business. The New York-based company has been blanketing the country for some time with ads and commercials claiming its new policy provides up to a third more coverage for the same premium dollar as the company's old policy. The pitch, included in Sunday newspaper inserts and preceded by a massive introductory campaign within the company, features pictures of smiling, all-American families who are obviously sanguine because they know they are protected by life insurance.

In fact, Metropolitan's new policy is quite different. Metropolitan had, indeed, reduced its premium charge by up to a third. But the annual premium payment is only one ingredient in the mix that represents the actual, effective price of a policy.

The basic annual premium can be reduced substantially by dividends, which are really an overcharge of premiums and are returned a year later. Most policies also have cash values, which permit the consumer to receive a payment if he or she cashes in the policy before death. Finally, a variety of miscellaneous fees and special dividends must be taken into consideration when evaluating total price.

These assorted values vary with the age of the policyholder and change each year the policy is held. One company may have high premiums when the policy is first issued but lower ones in later years. Another company may charge low premiums but also pay low cash values or low dividends. To fairly compare two policies, the timing of these payments and values must be taken into account.

What Metropolitan's ads don't say is that the company, along with reducing premiums, also reduced dividends paid by its new policy. The net result is that the actual cost, at most coverage levels, is only slightly better than for the previous policy.

Richard R. Shinn, then chairman and chief executive officer of Metropolitan, saw nothing wrong with failing to disclose that dividends had been reduced. "The fact you don't see much difference in the net cost means we are treating our policyholders fairly [by distributing dividends evenly to old and new policyholders]," Shinn said.

Yet the fact is that the advertising of the second largest company in the business is plain wrong. Obscuring the prices means the industry can go on making such claims without challenge. And it permits the industry to go on offering a product whose return, if known, would probably put the companies out of business.

One reason the companies pay back forty-one cents on the dollar on individual life insurance policies is sheer waste. When you buy other types of insurance—covering your home or automobile—you call an agent, you tell him how much coverage you want, and you receive the policy in the mail. You can compare the prices because the regulators—the same ones who regulate life insurance—insist on a standard policy form.

But the methods for selling life insurance are quite different. Life insurance, according to a saying in the industry, is sold, not bought. You don't call the agent. The agent comes to you. Typically, he makes ten telephone calls before he gets an appointment. Only one in two appointments leads to a sale.

During the selling process, the agent may drive out to your home two or three times. The last trip will be to deliver the policy in person. He may take you to lunch or help you with your personal or financial problems. He sells a lot of snake oil. If bankers went through the same selling process to obtain an account, the nation's banks would go bankrupt.

Agents who sell a lot of policies may be rewarded with a trip to Hawaii—on top of commissions that range from 25 percent to as much as 130 percent of the first year's premium. There are additional commissions each year the policy is in force.

On top of these commissions, the managers of the companies get commissions called "overrides." These are payments for doing what managers of other companies do for a salary. Through such overrides, many managers make more than the presidents of Fortune 500 companies. One Prudential manager in Colorado, for example, made $274,525 in one year. His job: managing and training seventy agents, fewer employees than many stores have.

By the time everyone gets his cut, the commissions amount to well over one hundred percent of the first-year premium. In contrast, a stockbroker might get a commission of four percent, and part of it goes to his company.

Once the agent has made the sale and his charm has dimmed in memory, many people forget why they bought a policy or realize they made a bad decision. Life insurance is sold on the premise it will be there when you die, presumably in old age. In reality, most people drop their coverage by the age of sixty-five. In fact, one in four drop their policies within two years of buying them.

This turnover creates more waste. The companies have already invested in selling the product. They do not begin to recoup those selling expenses until several years after the policy is purchased. For example, at Northwestern Mutual, according to Ferguson, it costs $170 in sales costs to obtain the first year's premium of $100. So, unless a policy stays on the books for several years, the companies lose money by selling more policies.

Of course, if the companies lose, the consumer loses. The extra costs are just passed along in the form of higher prices. But there is also a special penalty exacted from the consumer.

The companies pay cash values to policyholders if they turn in their policies before death, but those benefits are paid only after the policy has been in force for a year or two. So the consumer winds up paying an extraordinarily high price for coverage and gets nothing back. If you withdraw a bank certificate of deposit before its maturity date, you will pay a penalty—but you will not lose all the interest accrued. Life insurance companies don't operate that way. They get away with it because virtually no one understands his own policy and its provisions.

It is the agent who makes out here. He gets his commission right up front. The consumer ends up a double loser: he gets no cash value back, and the price of his coverage gets inflated still more because the companies are losing money on so many policies that quickly lapse.

The greatest penalty is exacted from the widows and orphans who are the beneficiaries of life insurance policies. They lose the financial support of the family breadwinner. And they wind up with little to replace that financial support. The average death benefit actually paid out by all types of life insurance policies is $5,068, barely enough to pay for a funeral.

That is not the way it is supposed to work. If your house burns down, you expect your fire insurance to replace the house with one of similar quality. As it is designed and sold, life insurance will not replace your income or come anywhere close to replacing it. If you are a man, the average life insurance payment will replace four months of your salary. If you are a woman, it will replace six months of your salary. Even if a consumer has several policies, the average benefit is not enough to make a real difference.

If fire insurance paid off regardless of whether your house burned down, the coverage would be so costly that you could not afford enough to replace your home in the event of a real loss. The problem is that the life insurance companies promise something for everyone. The policies will pay off even if you don't die. By the time the life insurance companies foot the bill for the agents' commissions, the trips, and the extra payments even if you don't die, there is little left over to pay for a death benefit—which is, after all, the purpose of buying life insurance.

What remains is severely eroded by inflation. Assuming an annual inflation rate of six percent a year, $30,000 in life insurance coverage purchased today will be worth less than $10,000 in twenty years. That is one reason the average death benefit actually paid is so low. While their coverage is shrinking, consumers are losing the income they could obtain by investing their money instead of paying it as premiums to life insurance companies. Instead, the insurance companies get to use it to erect taller buildings. If you thought life insurance would take care of your survivors, go back to square one.

"The whole life insurance industry is an abuse of the public," said Donald G. Malik, who recently retired after twenty years as a San Francisco–based agent for Connecticut General Life Insurance Company, the eighth largest in the industry. "The salesmen browbeat the public and misrepresent when they get to them. An agent may have lunch with someone and see two people in a week, and make a good living." He added, "They sell policies that look good on the surface, but if you could compare and understand them, they screw you. . . . The nature of the product is such that, unless you had two weeks of training, you can't compare them.

"There is a deliberate attempt by agents and companies to confuse you," Malik said. "The way they write up the policies, you can't figure them out. Nobody will ever say that. These people are some of the sharpest in the world."

Malik, who now sells securities as well as life insurance, observed, "The misrepresentations that go on in this business would bring license suspensions or revocations if they were selling stock instead of life insurance. In the insurance industry, the agent laughs all the way to the bank."

Most of the differences between practices in the life insurance business and the rest of the financial world can be traced directly to the method of regulation. Insurance is regulated by the states. Nearly every other financial institution is regulated by the federal government.

This is no accident. In 1945 the insurance industry persuaded Congress to give it a special exemption from federal regulation. That meant the individual states would continue to regulate the industry, as they had been all along. As a result, companies with assets of tens of billions of dollars are supervised by state insurance departments that barely have enough people to answer their own telephones.

A third of the heads of the state insurance departments come from the industry, and a third leave for jobs in that industry. Given the backgrounds of the regulators and the paucity of state funding, it is hardly surprising that most of the laws proposed by these regulators are drafted by the industry.

Acknowledging that most of the bills introduced in state legislatures are "joint ventures" of the regulators and the industry, Richard V. Minck, executive vice-president of the American Council of Life Insurance, said, "The industry is complicated enough that you [the companies] really want to do a lot of the statutes yourself."

To say the regulators do nothing would be unfair. When agents steal from the companies, the regulators are quite vigilant, recovering the money for the companies. Indeed, they are pleased to act as the companies' bill collectors. On the other hand, consumers who are misled by agents into buying high-priced policies they can ill afford are thought to have been the victims of a "lack of communication."

Invariably, the few charges of misrepresentation brought by the regulators result from complaints by other companies. These companies complain when their policies are replaced by agents from competing companies. In the rest of the business world, that practice is known as "beating out a competitor." In the life insurance industry, it is known derisively as "twisting."

Over the years, "fair trade" laws that kept stores from offering discounts on appliances and other merchandise have been dropped. And the securities industry, in the 1960s, learned to live without the crutch of regulated commission rates after the Securities and Exchange Commission decided they stifle competition. Yet, in the life insurance industry, the regulators cling to "anti-rebate" laws that prevent the more competitive agents from offering lower prices to consumers by cutting their own commissions. Why operate in a free market when it is so much more profitable to keep prices high?

The companies not only make the rules, they also own the game. Responding to criticism in the late 1800s of abuses within the industry, a number of the companies turned themselves into mutuals.

Mutuals, which control two-thirds of the assets of the industry, have no stockholders, and are run by managements that are self-perpetuating.

The mutual companies cannot agree among themselves on just who owns them. Metropolitan's Shinn said mutual companies like Metropolitan are not owned by anyone. Robert A. Beck, chairman and chief executive officer of Prudential Insurance Company of America, the largest in the industry, said mutual companies like Prudential are owned by the policyholders.

But if that is true, there is little palpable evidence of it. In contrast to many of the larger mutual companies, life insurance companies owned by stockholders hold annual meetings where management can be criticized and rump groups organized. A Prudential policyholder would be hard put to find a forum for his complaints at Prudential's Newark, New Jersey, headquarters. Prudential, with $67 billion in assets, holds no annual meeting. Even if it did, it is unlikely a mere policyholder could bring any influence to bear on its practices or the type of product it offers.

2. THE DECK

■ With a little sleight-of-hand, it is possible to win at some games every time. In the life insurance game, that trick is called whole life insurance. If you understand it, the chances are good that you will never buy it. Unfortunately, this particular technique is so well-conceived that it may take months or even years before its true ramifications begin to jell in your mind. By that time, the consumer has usually paid in thousands of dollars that provided him with little insurance coverage and trifling investment returns.

Whole life—named to highlight the fact it can insure you for the whole of your life—was developed incrementally in this country and England. In 1762, the Equitable Society of England issued the first policy that would insure an individual for his entire life, so long as the premiums were paid each year. The Penn Mutual Life Insurance Company of Philadelphia, in 1848, was one of the first companies to pay a cash value upon surrender of a policy.

Whole life quickly became the bread-and-butter of the life insurance industry. It now accounts for nine in ten of its premium dollars.

On the surface, whole life sounds attractive. It promises to pay a death benefit if you die when the policy is in effect. It is also the policy that, if you decide to surrender it, promises to give you a payment in cash. You can borrow against the policy. It will do almost everything except wash your car.

What's more, the annual premiums for whole life remain constant as you grow older. No matter how bad inflation gets, the payments can never be increased.

"Deciding what type of life insurance you need can be compared to deciding whether to rent an apartment or own a home. Term insurance is like renting. And whole life is like owning," says a typical advertisement for Metropolitan Life Insurance Company's whole life policies.

In contrast, the other type of insurance—called term insurance—pays nothing if you live. It is pure insurance. Like fire insurance, it provides a benefit only in the event of a catastrophe—your death. The premiums for term insurance go up each year. By the age of sixty-five or seventy, the annual premiums become so expensive that they almost equal the death benefit provided by the coverage. As a result, most people drop their term insurance by then, and few companies even offer it beyond the age of seventy.

Robert A. Beck, a former agent who became chairman and chief executive officer of Prudential Insurance Company of America, likes to call whole life "permanent" insurance. That way, he said over his marble-topped table in the Newark headquarters of Prudential, he underscores the point that whole life will be there in old age.

"When making a buying decision, they can make a better decision if you say permanent insurance," said Beck, one of the most articulate, forceful, and confident proponents of whole life insurance. "You can keep it and borrow money for your children. I've borrowed on it. It makes it possible to keep a premium level."

Beck obviously believes in what he is saying. A former "whiz kid" at the Ford Motor Company, he became a Prudential agent in 1951 and moved steadily up. In 1973, at the age of forty-eight, he became president of the company.

Beck seems so open, sincere, and self-assured that one can barely resist agreeing with him. That impression was enhanced when Beck appeared on the "Phil Donahue Show" in 1979 with Thomas J. Wolff, then president of the National Association of Life Underwriters, the chief agents' group. Here was the chairman of a company with assets of tens of billions of dollars making himself vulnerable to attack from an obviously well-prepared and highly skeptical television moderator. Beck turned in a virtuoso performance, easily fielding questions later from the audience.

As we shall see, Beck brushed aside the fact that whole life insurance, in the early years, costs five to six times or even more each year than term insurance. Picture it: A thirty-two-year-old male pays $155 a year and gets $100,000 in term insurance coverage from Metropolitan Life Insurance Co. That same premium will buy only $8,055 in whole life coverage from Metropolitan—a difference, in this case, of twelvefold.

"Whole life," said Donald G. Malik, the San Francisco life insurance agent, "is just a lousy savings plan."

That becomes clear after one talks with Ray A. Philibert, another former agent who is senior vice-president of Computone Systems, Inc., an Atlanta-based computer service for the industry, who talks as fast as the computer he operates. Philibert has computed the actual rates of return of life insurance plans, just as banks and money funds compute rates of return on their financial products. But Thomas C. Newbill, the company's vice-president for marketing, explains that Computone provides services to agents and life insurance companies—not to consumers. There is no way to get Computone's rate data without buying a Computone terminal, which costs $3,000 and up. Even then, he said, many of the largest life insurance companies give their rate data to Computone only on condition it will not be disclosed to competing companies or agents. That means companies that want their rates kept confidential— including many of the largest in the industry—can keep the rates from the public through use of special access codes programmed into the Computone data base.

Even the National Association of Insurance Commissioners, which coordinates the system of state regulation, cannot see the rates provided by companies to Computone. "It can impede competition," Philibert said. "It could be restraint of trade."

In matters of life insurance, Philibert's credentials are impeccable. After majoring in life insurance at Tulane University, he entered the business as an agent in 1947. He soon became a district manager, branch manager, and vice-president for marketing of a life insurance company.

In 1966, he became vice-president of a national actuarial consulting firm based in Atlanta. Along the way, Philibert earned the equivalent of the doctoral degree of the life insurance industry, the prestigious Chartered Life Underwriter (CLU) designation. As the second-ranking officer of Computone, Philibert employs six actuaries, the high priests of the life insurance business. He is sought after as a speaker at life insurance industry conventions and meetings.

According to Philibert, the only difference among the policies offered by the major companies is price. "They [consumers] are kept in the hands of the agents, who are urged to sell their own company's product. He [the agent] has so much time to earn a living, and can't take the time to compare them even if he wanted to," he said.

The price disclosure provided by the companies is an empty gesture, Philibert said. These illustrations consist of a dizzying array of figures projecting the premiums and other values for each year the policy will be in force. Called "ledger statements," they fail to show a price that can be used to compare with similar, competing products. To fairly compare the values, that price should take into account the timing of the various payments and values, as well as the interest the consumer could be earning on the money he gives the insurance company.

Philibert said most agents still use what is called the "traditional" or "net cost" method for showing the price of a policy. Using that method, the total cost values and dividends promised are subtracted from the total premiums paid into the policy. Because that method fails to take into account the income lost by consumers when they let insurance companies use their funds, thirty-six states prohibit it as being misleading.

The importance of "the time value of money" can be appreciated by considering two methods of paying for a $10,000 car. In both cases, you get the car immediately. But in one case, you must pay the full price in cash upon delivery. In the second instance, you are not required to pay until twenty years later. Obviously, the car requiring the later payment is a far better value. Assuming an inflation rate of six percent a year, your $10,000 payment in twenty years will be worth only $3,118.

"The agent will say you get $27,000 [after the cash values and dividends are subtracted]," Philibert said. "In reality, it's cost you $60,000 in today's dollars because of the investment income you lost," he said. "That's the way the insurance companies make money."

As an agent, Philibert found selling life insurance frustrating because he could not tell the prices of the policies he was offering. He said most agents have no idea of how their own companies' rates compare. Rather, he said, they tend to think of them as "competitive"—an impression the companies actively encourage.

Explaining why life insurance companies keep their rates confidential in the Computone system, a vice-president of one company told Philibert he does not care if agents from other companies see his firm's rates. What he does not want is to have his agents see how low other companies' rates are by comparison.

"It's all a game," Philibert said.

Part of the game is making the public think it is getting honest price disclosure when it is not. Beginning with a speech before an industry group in the Chicago area on October 15, 1968, the late Sen. Philip A. Hart (D–Mich.), then chairman of the Senate Judiciary Committee's antitrust subcommittee, took the industry to task for failing to come up with an understandable price disclosure system. Reacting to pressure from Hart and others, industry leaders promised they would come up with a method that would take account of the cost of money and disclose prices fairly. Starting in 1976, the various states began passing laws that required the companies to provide these price disclosure figures to consumers.

We do not need to learn a lot about this method, except that no one understands it. That is hardly surprising. The figures developed for measuring the cost of a policy bear no relation either to annual percentage rates, or to dollars and cents normally used to portray the cost of other products.

The situation can be compared to a ketchup manufacturer who decides the price of his product shall never be displayed on grocers' shelves. Instead, he devises his own method for telling shoppers the price of his product. In order to know the price, shoppers will be expected to read a booklet that explains how the new price comparison method works.

Even if one understands the booklet—and almost nobody does—it will not tell the shopper how he can compare the manufacturer's price with prices of other brands of ketchup or, for that matter, with other condiments. The index numbers look so strange—they are expressed as dollars and cents but really are not—that even the store manager cannot explain what they mean.

Forget that virtually no one in the business feels he can understand the index numbers. Forget that the figures cannot be used to compare prices of different types of policies—precisely the reason they were needed in the first place. The companies wanted them implemented to still the growing criticism. But what if consumers did understand them? What if they actually could tell that one policy was outrageously more expensive than another policy?

Just in case, the state regulators added a clause to the provision that required companies to give out the figures. The clause says the figures must always be given to the consumer—*but only after he has bought the policy.* The consumer then has ten days to change his mind and get his money back.

"Once you've got the policy is not time to do comparison shopping," said Theodore T. Briggs, Maine's insurance commissioner, one of only two state commissioners who required disclosure before the sale in spite of the suggested law.

Philibert's solution to the joke that passes for life insurance price disclosure was to compute the annual percentage yields or rates of return offered by each policy. There is nothing novel about annual percentage yields. They tell us the interest we earn on our savings accounts and money funds, the dividend returns from our stocks and bonds, and the rate of interest we pay for our mortgage loans.

In fact, they are used to disclose the price of nearly every other financial product except life insurance.

What is pertinent here is that the companies do not want consumers to know what those yields are. When twenty companies were told that *The Washington Post* planned to list the yields of their policies for an article on life insurance, nearly twenty letters came back objecting to the method. The letters, mostly from actuaries, in some cases questioned the importance of price in buying life insurance coverage.

"[A] concern I have," wrote an actuary from Phoenix Mutual Life Insurance Company, "is that, once the numerical data is presented, the reader will be inclined to base his/her judgment on these numbers alone." In preparing a chart listing the effective prices of policies, he said, "some mention should be made of other factors, albeit somewhat intangible, that should be considered when contemplating a life insurance purchase." These factors include, he said, the strength of the company, the reputation of the company and its agent, and the policy provisions.

Can you imagine a bank or money fund seriously questioning whether its interest rates should be disclosed by themselves because people might not consider other factors—like stability and service—in deciding which bank to patronize? Phoenix Mutual is not a backwater company. It is the twenty-second largest in the industry and is based in Hartford, Connecticut, the property casualty insurance capital of the country.

One actuary, who approved of the rate of return method, James R. Montgomery III, the deputy insurance superintendent for the District of Columbia, thinks he knows why his colleagues oppose the method. "It's too simple," he said, with only a trace of a smile.

Perhaps. But there is more at stake here than professional pride. As we shall see in a later chapter, the Computone yields show that the return on a whole life policy, if surrendered for cash before death, vary from negative in the early years to three to five percent after the policy is held thirty or forty years. With nine out of ten of the companies' dollars coming from whole life, and most of the companies' vast assets accumulating from whole life premiums, the companies are not likely to adopt a price disclosure method that puts whole life in a poor light.

"The other companies are so committed to what they've been selling for a hundred years because it is so profitable, and they have a tremendous investment in their agents," said Robert W. Mac-Donald, president and chief executive officer of ITT Life Insurance Corporation, one of the few companies that has stopped selling whole life.

"It's one of the great marketing successes in the history of mankind," MacDonald said, referring to whole life. "It's an economic sacred cow. They've gotten people to view it as a mystical thing, and they don't question whether it's a good value or not."

In the larger scheme of things, it makes little difference if ITT Life has stopped selling whole life. Its premiums represent 0.06 percent of the industry's total. What does matter is what the top ten companies are doing. And they are all aggressively pushing whole life.

At the same time, the industry—taking heed of criticism of whole life in publications ranging from *Consumer Reports* to *The Wall Street Journal*—has succeeded in creating the impression that whole life has now been supplanted by other, more competitive policies. The fact is that whole life continues to account for four in five premium dollars paid for new policies.

"There is an old expression, 'The proof of the pudding is in the eating,'" Dale R. Gustafson, vice-president and chief actuary of Northwestern Mutual, told a consumer group in Columbus, Ohio. "We are finding insurance buyers nationwide to be most receptive. Sales are up over thirty percent ... and new premiums are up twenty-five percent. The biggest seller? Old-fashioned, participating [dividend paying] whole life insurance."

There is no more effective proponent of whole life than Beck, the chairman of Prudential. As the largest company in the business, Prudential takes in nearly $4 billion a year in life insurance premiums, or about one in twelve dollars paid to buy life insurance.

Sounding on the Donahue show like the missionary he is, Beck displayed his fine sense for when to move forward and when to draw back and listen. He expounded on the virtues of whole life while claiming term insurance has an important function as well. Term insurance is needed when people are young and cannot afford enough whole life coverage, he said. When they are older and have retired, they need whole life, Beck proselytized.

In fact, he claimed, more than half the insurance sold by Prudential is term insurance. Nor does Prudential pay a better commission for selling whole life insurance, he maintained.

"So we promote term insurance, we encourage people to buy term insurance, and when your needs are temporary or where you can't afford to buy as much permanent insurance as you might like, we encourage you to buy term insurance," Beck said. He added, ". . . I really want to state as strongly and unequivocally as I can that the financial motivation for the agent to sell whole life does not exist."

Beck was wrong on both counts. For selling $100,000 in insurance coverage, a Prudential agent gets an effective commission the first year of roughly thirty-five percent of the term insurance premium, or $78. For selling the same amount of whole life, he gets fifty percent of the first-year premium, or $740. In other words, he gets roughly nine times more for selling whole life than for selling term insurance.

Beck's claim that Prudential sells more term insurance than whole life does not tell the whole story, either. Beck compared the total coverage purchased rather than the total premium dollars represented by those purchases. Because a dollar buys five or six times more term insurance than whole life, comparing coverage magnifies term insurance sales. Only about one in five of Prudential's premium dollars is derived from term insurance.

When Donahue suggested that whole life provides a low rate of return, Beck deftly shifted gears. Normally, he maintains whole life insurance will pay for buying a house or a college education. Now he claimed that whole life is not an investment and should not be compared with one. "We claim we're dominantly selling insurance protection, that this cash value builds up in order to keep the premium level, but as a side benefit, the fact of the matter is the rate of return is a good rate of return," Beck said.

An investment is defined by the *Encyclopedic Dictionary of Business Finance*, published by Prentice-Hall, Inc., as the employment of current funds for the production of future income. One way an investment can be made is "by buying life insurance," the dictionary says.

In proving that whole life provides a good rate of return, Beck admitted on the show that it costs roughly six times more than term insurance initially. But he said that difference is wiped out as term insurance premiums increase. By the age of sixty, he said, term insurance rates have become very expensive. "At that time," he said, focusing on one example, "the cost of term insurance . . . is $1,500. The cost of permanent life policy after dividends is minus $148."

In making that comparison, Beck failed to take into account the time value or cost of money, as required by state insurance laws and regulations. Those regulations state, "A system or presentation which does not recognize the time value of money through the use of appropriate interest adjustments may not be used for comparing the cost of two or more life insurance policies." Such a comparison can be made if the consumer is told the time value of money was not taken into account.

If Beck had taken into account the time value of money, his comparison would have made the opposite point. It is true that, by the time the policyholder reaches the age of sixty, a whole life policy may actually cost nothing. The dividends in those later years usually exceed the required premium payments. It is also true that term insurance becomes very expensive by that age. But the consumer has fared far better with term insurance because he was able to use the savings in premiums between whole life and term in the early years to generate more income. Even if he did not save the difference, he was in a position to reduce interest payments on loans because of the availability of extra cash. By the same token, the insurance company fared far better with whole life because it invested those extra premium dollars.

Here is why: A thirty-two-year-old male who buys $100,000 in coverage from Metropolitan Life Insurance Company and invests the difference in premiums between the company's whole life and term coverage at eight percent a year would accumulate $79,327 in a side fund by the age of sixty-five. In the event of his death, his beneficiary would receive both the $100,000 term insurance death benefit and the $79,327 from the side fund—a total of $179,327.

By contrast, if he bought the whole life policy, his beneficiary would receive only the $100,000 death benefit. If he lived until the age of sixty-five and cashed in the policy, he would receive $53,100 from the whole life policy. Both the whole life cash values and the term insurance investment fund may or may not be taxable.

In other words, if he lives, he will do about fifty percent better with term insurance. If he dies, his beneficiary will do about eighty percent better.

Referring to Beck's appearance on the Donahue show, a Prudential spokesman said, "I believe if you are going to mention one passage on the show, you should clarify for your readers the fact that major portions of the program discussed price and rates of return."

If Prudential is "dominantly" selling life insurance protection, as claimed by Beck on the show, why do Beck and his agents sell the product by promising that it will pay for a new house, a college education, and maybe a new car? If they are selling life insurance, why does the company pay out $316 million in cash surrender payments, compared with only $260 million in death benefits on individual coverage? And why shouldn't consumers know what the yield is on those investment returns so they can make up their own minds about whether whole life provides a good return?

"I think people can do just as well looking at the rate of return each insurance company earns on its overall investment, because those investments are going to be passed on to the policyholders,"

Beck said. What he overlooked is that Prudential's expenses—including the cost of agents driving out to your home—are deducted before those investment yields are passed along to policyholders. By the time you get the funds, the yield from Prudential's investment portfolio has been slashed in half.

"I'll leave that to my technicians to go over," Beck said when that fact was pointed out. "The point I want to make is, I am, and we have been, totally supportive of all efforts to improve disclosure to the insurance-buying public. Disclosure that was not too costly to administer that it becomes a luxury for the insurance-buying public."

Why shouldn't that disclosure be in the form of percentage yields that everyone can understand? Echoing Beck, Joseph J. Melone, Prudential's executive vice-president for marketing, said, "Because the [life insurance] contract is not intended as an investment. You wouldn't buy whole life as an investment. There are just other alternatives that you could well wind up doing better with over time." Why shouldn't consumers know that fact? Melone said that such disclosure might distract from the purpose of life insurance—which is life insurance protection.

But if that is the purpose of life insurance, why shouldn't everyone buy straight term insurance, which is pure life insurance protection? Why are three out of four dollars collected by Prudential on new policies for whole life protection? Why is the life insurance industry not selling life insurance? What is wrong with it?

The answer is there is nothing wrong with it. Most people need more of it than they have. And they can get five to six times more of it by buying term insurance. If people want to invest and make a good return, they can open a bank account, an Individual Retirement Account (IRA), a money fund, or buy stocks or bonds.

Beck and others in the industry claim that people simply will not do that. "Theoretically, you can make the argument that you can invest, but almost no one invests the difference, so you don't end up with the savings," Beck said, referring to investing the difference in premiums between whole life and term insurance.

Here, Beck again switches themes. First, he says life insurance is not an investment. Now, he says it is a forced savings plan. Finally, he says Americans don't save. If that is confusing, how does one explain the fact that Americans do, in fact, save roughly $50 billion a year? Who fills the coffers of the nation's banks, savings and loan associations, and money funds? Who keeps the stock market going? And what moral right does the life insurance industry have to suggest that people should buy a low-yielding investment because they will probably squander their funds anyway?

The answer is that Beck's underlying theme is wrong. People do invest the difference in premiums between whole life and term insurance. A joint survey by the Life Insurance Marketing and Research Association and the American Council of Life Insurance found that eighty-nine percent of the people who bought term insurance had a savings account; twenty-five percent had savings certificates; thirty-four percent had government bonds; twenty-three percent had stocks; eleven percent had money market funds; six percent had annuities; and five percent had nongovernment bonds. The fact is that Americans save an average of six percent of their disposable income.

To be sure, people have a right to invest in a savings plan that gives them a poor return, or even to squander their money, so long as they have been adequately told what that return is. Under the present system of selling life insurance, they are not given that disclosure.

"The mainstay of life insurance marketing is that whole life insurance is protection and that savings is sort of incidental," said William C. Scheel, associate professor of finance and insurance at the University of Connecticut. "As soon as the public realizes it is savings, they'll ask nasty questions like, 'What is the rate of return, and how does it compare with others?'"

More tragically, with whole life, survivors are left virtually unprotected when the family breadwinner dies because their coverage has been so eroded by inflation, commissions to agents, and needless expenses. People need life insurance when their children are young and dependent on them for support. But when children are grown, the mortgage is paid off, and retirement benefits are coming in, life insurance is an expensive luxury. Life insurance should insure against catastrophic loss of income. A person living off retirement benefits has no income to insure against losing.

That is not the way life insurance is sold. The agent tells you that whole life will be there in your old age when you need it most. You can cash it in, or you can borrow against it. You will always get something out of it, he says.

If the agent honestly evaluated a young family's needs, he would be forced to sell term insurance. But term insurance, because of the commissions it pays, will barely pay for the agent's gasoline. The agent is not a crook or a scoundrel. He is a human being and a victim of the life insurance game. So, nine times out of ten, he will recommend whole life insurance. The customer will not know the agent gets a higher commission for selling whole life. He will not know he can get far more coverage with term insurance. Nine times out of ten, the customer will take the agent's advice and buy whole life.

"My advice is to buy term and buy more term," said William A. White, chief actuary of the New Jersey State Insurance Department, which regulates Prudential. "The damage done by the whole life people is [that] people are getting a less attractive investment program, but they also aren't getting as much insurance as they should get.

"The typical head of the family is limited by the amount of premium he can come up with," he said. "If a guy has $250 a year to spend, agents sell him $25,000 in whole life. You really need $200,000. The crime is the agent sells whole life and doesn't sell term insurance to meet the customer's needs."

3. THE PITCH

■ The agent from Aetna Life & Casualty Company of Hartford, Connecticut, is here to sell life insurance. A handsome man with a mustache, he confidently spreads some computer printouts on the dining-room table and suggests that the prospect's wife draw up a chair.

The agent has been with Aetna for twelve years. Aetna is the fourth-largest company in the business, with assets of $31 billion.

"We're dealing with the great variable—when will death occur?" he says. "It could be a week, a month, next year."

The agent has just the solution, a whole life policy from Aetna, along with an optional term policy. He boasts Aetna's rates are among the lowest in the industry. "You might find one or two lower in the 2,100 companies," he says.

In fact, Aetna's rates overall are among the highest in the industry. While Aetna's premiums appear lower initially, Northwestern Mutual Life Insurance Company's whole life policy yields twice as much as Aetna's by the thirty-eighth year, according to data compiled by Computone Systems, Inc. For the same cost, the Northwestern Mutual policy also pays twice as much in death benefits.

Asked later how he supports his claim, the Aetna agent says, "It's based on the brochures [from other brokers] and rates I get."

This is the way the game starts. Milkmen no longer deliver milk to your door, and doctors no longer make house calls, but life insurance is still sold by a force of some 250,000 agents who personally visit you in your home as many as two or three times before making a sale.

In this chapter, by visiting the offices of the five largest companies in the business, we will see how they do it. Together, these companies hold $240 billion in assets, or two in five of the industry's assets. Each year, they collect $27 billion in life insurance premiums, or more than half the total collected by the industry.

At each office, we will introduce ourselves as *Washington Post* reporters doing a story on life insurance. We will ask for an evaluation of our needs. We will fully disclose our finances if requested. We will then take notes on what the agents say.

What they say is critical, since their pitch is usually all the consumer will hear. According to a joint study by the American Council of Life Insurance and the Life Insurance Marketing and Research Association, in three out of four cases, the sale is made without any competition from another agent. "There is little evidence of comparison shopping among consumers," the joint industry study said flatly. "Clearly, the agent has a great impact on the consumer's choice of life insurance product."

Only one in twenty of the life insurance buyers surveyed tried to make price comparisons using the interest-adjusted index figures approved by regulators for that purpose. Whether many of them knew what the figures meant in the first place is questionable. Another survey of buyers in New Jersey found only seven percent were aware that the figures are lower if a policy is cheaper.

Surely, this gives one pause. Before we buy a house, rent an apartment, purchase a car, buy a television set, or invest in a money fund, we compare prices by calling or visiting different dealers or by checking ads. Why would consumers spend $50 billion a year for a product they blindly purchase without shopping for the best prices? And why do nine in ten consumers take the agent's recommendation and buy whole life?

Our sampling of agents provides the answer. Thirteen of the fifteen agents visited made statements that could be considered misleading. Six of the agents claimed his or her company had the cheapest rates, when it did not; six said the rates of all companies are about the same. Depending on which type of company they represented, four said that mutual companies or stockholder-owned companies are always cheapest.

Not surprisingly, all fifteen agents recommended whole life insurance, although several recommended term insurance in addition to whole life. For a person with a $120,000 home mortgage, they recommended additional coverage ranging from $60,000 to $165,000. Three of the six whose companies pay a higher commission for selling whole life insurance rather than term insurance claimed they get the same commission for selling both.

Thirteen of the agents claimed whole life is cheaper than term insurance, failing to take into account the money the consumer could make by investing the difference in premiums between the two policies. Several suggested that because whole life dividends and cash values eventually exceed the payments for the policy, whole life is actually free or returns a profit—statements prohibited by the insurance regulations of thirty-six states.

"Half the agents don't know what the truth is," said William E. Moulton, Jr., a Portsmouth, Virginia, life insurance agent. "They're programmed by the companies."

Because the agents are often unwitting pawns of the industry, we will not use their names in this chapter.

■

We begin at Prudential Insurance Company of America, the largest in the business. A Prudential publication called *Viewpoint* was lying on a table in the reception area. "Some argue that whole life is a poor investment. But whole life is not an investment," it says.

The receptionist directs us to an agent whose picture is displayed in the waiting room; he was one of the big sellers that month. A big man with a ready smile, he sat behind a cluttered desk and began spouting numbers.

"Many people have set a rule of thumb that you should have five times your annual income in life insurance," said the agent, who has been with Prudential for eighteen years. "If you have insurance, it eases the burden on those that remain."

He recommended a $20,000 whole life policy plus a special $50,000 term insurance policy called decreasing term insurance. While it does not develop cash values like whole life, it has whole life's chief drawback: the premiums start out high.

Explaining how the policies work, the agent rattled off a litany of seemingly incomprehensible figures. "The cost for twenty years is $7,732 for the whole life, and you get $11,120 in cash value at that time," he said. "The term costs $10,000 over twenty years, and provides $7,460 in dividends. You end up with $18,440 to pay off the house at that point. The insurance has cost you a gain of $1,000 over that time."

What could be a better deal? A product that actually costs you nothing. Yet in claiming the insurance would turn a profit rather than cost money, the agent made a statement considered misleading both by state regulators and Prudential, which says its agents are instructed to take into account the time value of money in every state.

Asked whether straight term insurance would be more suitable, he said, "Basically, term insurance is a money-making proposition for the insurance companies." A consumer could try to shop for lower prices, he said, but would find all the rates are about the same.

Asked if he gets a higher commission for selling whole life than term, he said, "The commission is the same for term and whole life." In fact, for selling $100,000 in coverage, he gets a commission of $78, compared with $740 for selling whole life.

Asked later why he said all rates are about the same, he said, "All major companies' prices are very much the same, just like you buy a newspaper for twenty-five cents, whether it's The Washington Post or USA Today. They are all within one percent." When it was pointed out that Northwestern Mutual Life Insurance Company provides a return about twenty percent better than Prudential's, he said, "To be quite honest, I haven't done a lot of this kind of comparison."

He said he would never compare prices using the interest-adjusted index figures recommended by regulators for that purpose. "You can show an interest-adjusted cost, but the customer can't relate to it," he said. "I think I've been asked about it twice in eighteen years." Indeed, he said, "[Price is] not something I get into that much. The most important thing is whether you trust the agent."

Asked why he said the commissions on whole life and term are identical when they are not, he said, "There is no great difference between thirty-five percent [for term insurance] and fifty percent on whole life."

The second Prudential agent, located in a different office, has been a life insurance agent for eleven years, the last four of them with Prudential. He is a member of the Million Dollar Round Table, which now requires sales of more than $2 million a year to qualify for membership.

A Prudential brochure distributed to agents happens to be lying on a table in the waiting room outside his office. Graphs depicted in the brochure show that the total outlay for a new Prudential whole life policy is far less than for term insurance. In one example, they show that, over time, a consumer would pay $50,447 for term coverage, compared with $19,977 for Prudential's Modified Life whole life policy.

In portraying those differences, Prudential had failed to take account of the cost or time value of money as required by insurance regulations in the majority of states. If it had, the chart would have made the opposite point: that term insurance is far cheaper than whole life at least until the age of seventy, when most people have no need for life insurance. Another chart on a different page contains a footnote in small type saying the time value of money has not been taken into account.

The agent explained that Prudential is a mutual company, which means it pays dividends to policyholders rather than stockholders. He said, "It's cheaper over the long run to deal with a mutual company," a statement which happens to be true in most cases. "On basic whole life, Prudential is very low on price. There might be one or two [other companies' policies] that you'll save a half a percent on. You aren't going to find that much variation in cost."

Turning to the types of insurance, he said whole life is superior because you can immediately borrow against the policy. "With whole life, you can borrow $1,000 in the first year . . . ," he said. In fact, no money can be borrowed until a Prudential policy has been in force at least two years.

The agent said the interest-adjusted index figures approved by regulators show whole life is better than term insurance, since the index numbers are lower for whole life than for term. In fact, just the opposite is true. "In the long run, it is cheaper to buy whole life," he said.

Even if the time value of money is taken into account, he said, whole life will beat term insurance after ten or twelve years. Asked for the specifics, he said he has a comparison but another agent borrowed it. He left to get it but returned empty-handed. "[He] won't give it out," was his explanation.

When it was later pointed out that Prudential's whole life policy is twenty percent more expensive than the policies of some companies like Northwestern Mutual, he said, "I think it's a half a percent difference, although I've never really looked at [a comparison]." If a shopper wants to find out what companies charge the lowest prices, "the first thing the guy has got to do is ask the agent." He said, "People buy the agent, just like they trust a doctor. You're wrong if you think you're buying a financial contract. You [the agent] become their friend, you become part of their family."

A Prudential agent who helps train other agents agreed to run through the sales presentation she teaches new agents. Propping up a large notebook on her desk, she said, "The people in the field use this tract."

The development manager, as she is called, asked what is the prospect's greatest asset. When she is told it is the ability to work, she said, "If your income is your greatest asset, it's important to look at the fact it can be disrupted by three things—death, disability, and old age. Living too long is a problem. When I saw people in Miami, I saw that I want to be financially stable when I am old."

She pointed to a funnel depicting an estate. Much of the money poured into it at the top gets siphoned off by funeral and medical costs, estate taxes, and debts by the time it drips out at the bottom. "Studies show the siphon draws off ten percent to fifty percent of our total estate," she said.

"Are you satisfied with your savings?" she asked. After getting the expected reply, she said, "What is your most important personal goal? Most people will say they want to buy a house. What do you feel your life insurance should do for you?" She ticked off various financial goals, asking how much money the prospect would like to meet them.   •

"If you had to pay off your debts, how much would you need? How much do you feel should be set aside for an emergency fund? Our furnace went, and it cost $3,200. Normally, they say one times your annual income should be set aside [for savings]. Do you want to pay off your mortgage?"

She added up the sums the prospect felt he could use to cover expected and unexpected expenses. She subtracted any benefits that would come from existing life insurance coverage. "I came up with a need of $112,000 on you and your spouse . . . ," she said. "What figure could you set aside for savings or something else?" She is told $100 a month.

Turning to specific plans and companies, she said mutual companies like Prudential pay dividends to their policyholders, while stockholder-owned life insurance companies pay dividends to their stockholders. "It's going to be cheaper [to buy from a mutual company] because the return is going to the policyholder," she said.

In either case, she indicated, the funds are safe. "Insurance is federally regulated; it's probably the most regulated industry around," she said. She later acknowledged that what she said was not true: insurance is regulated by the states. She explained she must have been thinking of a bill in Congress affecting life insurance companies.

Continuing with the presentation, she said there are two types of life insurance. "You have permanent and temporary insurance on the market. You have a definite death benefit with permanent [whole life] insurance. With term insurance, it's for a term."

She showed an illustration of a whole life policy. "At the age of sixty-five," she said, "the cash value is $65,000 that can be used to buy a piece of land in Florida . . . where else can you get protection and all your money back?" she said. She didn't mention that the cash value will be worth just $9,503 by the age of sixty-five, assuming inflation continues at six percent a year.

Referring back to a previous question, the agent said, "You said you could set aside $100 [for savings]. Normally, we say you can write a check for $100 now to cover the first payment and let the computer design the plan."

Asked about the interest-adjusted index figures required by regulators for portraying costs, she said she is not sure what they mean but would ask a more experienced agent. The top seller in the office said he does not know what they mean, either. "Maybe one person in eight years has asked me about the figures," he said.

Their manager, who directs the work of forty-two agents, correctly said the index figures are intended to take into account the cost of money while the consumer is letting the life insurance company use his money. Asked about Prudential's rates, he said, "At any given point in time, we may be a few cents higher or lower than someone else. We are extremely competitive. You're not going to find a large difference."

The pipe-smoking Prudential agent in a different office got right to the point. After taking down a few details of the prospect's finances, the agent, who has been with Prudential three years, concluded, "You really don't have any insurance." Explaining that group term insurance provided by employers ends when people retire, he said such people find themselves without insurance when they need it most.

"What happens if you leave the job?" he asked.

"Prudential is considerably cheaper than the other companies because of the investments they make," he said. If people want to confirm that, they can call other companies, he said. But he said he won't give out the full prices on the phone.

"I would give them the premium, but then they don't know the return [cash values]. We don't want a horde of calls coming in. They can schedule an appointment," he said.

The agent suggested $100,000 in Prudential whole life coverage. For just $51 a month, the policy will provide retirement income of $8,000 a year for life, he said.

"You put in $869 after five years and get back $1,174 [in cash surrender value]. You get more than you put in," he said, failing to take account of the time value or cost of money. "You put in $40,733, and at age sixty-five, you get back $98,000. How much has it cost you? Nothing. That's what I tell everybody. That's why I say you need $100,000 in whole life," he said.

When told of the number of agents who failed to take into account the time value of money, Richard V. Minck, executive vice-president of the American Council of Life Insurance, the chief industry trade and lobbying group, said, "If it's sold without the time value of money taken into account, it would, under the regulations of thirty-six states, be held to be misleading. . . . It's clear if you're buying an insurance policy, it's going to cost you something."

Later, the agent said he has never heard of the regulation requiring him to take into account the cost of money, even though he sells in states that have such a requirement.

Asked if he gets a higher percentage commission for selling whole life, he said, "The percentage commission is the same for whole life and term. I like whole life. With whole life, you get your money back, plus."

The agent we visit at Metropolitan Life Insurance Company just recently joined the company after spending most of his twenty years as an agent with Prudential. Metropolitan is the second-largest company, with assets of $56 billion.

A sales manager for Metropolitan, the agent is a member of the Million Dollar Round Table and a Chartered Life Underwriter (CLU), which means he has taken advanced training in insurance.

"My personal belief is that, if you love your family, you should be covered with seven times your annual gross income," he said. Writing on a yellow legal pad, he figured the visitor's total income until he retires will exceed $1 million. "It's your human life value," he said. Without explaining why, he concluded, "You need a minimum of $165,000 in more insurance."

Explaining that there are two types of life insurance, he said, "Mostly people buy term policies for temporary protection. There are other types called whole life. It not only protects, but it accumulates. The money is there for buying a house or a television or what-have-you." Buying whole life is like going to town in a Cadillac, he said. Term insurance is like taking the subway.

Drawing some more on the pad, he said a family is like a corporation with a balance sheet. "The only asset you have is you. The only way to create an asset if you die is life insurance."

"We believe you are better off with a whole life contract. Within eleven years, what you pay to the insurance company will be there for you to take. If you pay $10 a month or $1,300 in eleven years, we'll give it to you at eleven years if you want it. You're not throwing away money for term insurance," he said.

Later, he said there is nothing wrong with making such a statement, even though it doesn't take into account the time value of money. He said he knows of no state regulation that prohibits such comparisons.

"For whole life, we are the cheapest, not only for mutual companies but also for stock companies," he said. "We are also the cheapest in term insurance."

Metropolitan's term policies are among the cheapest, but its whole life policies after thirty-eight years are among the more expensive ones. They are a quarter to a third more expensive, for example, than the whole life policies sold by Massachusetts Mutual Life Insurance Company, based in Springfield, Massachusetts. Asked about his claim later, he said, "It depends on how many companies I look at. There might be a cheaper one. I don't know. He [the agent] can only talk about what he has seen."

Another Metropolitan agent has been with the company more than twenty years. He is considered one of the best agents in his office, selling more than $2 million in life insurance a year.

"Whole life is the best insurance you can buy," he said. When buying whole life, "You get back 1.5 times to 2 times more than you put into it. In twenty years, you could spend $37,800. The policy has actually cost you nothing, and you get back $77,900." Buying term insurance, on the other hand, ". . . will get you in a lot of trouble. You need permanent protection," he said.

He said people never invest the difference in premiums between whole life and term. "If the difference is $350 a year, what stockbroker is going to talk to you?" he said.

To invest the difference, however, it is not necessary to save the specific difference between the whole life and term premiums. Any saving by a consumer frees up more money for investing, or for paying off loans on which interest is being charged.

"You should not find a significant difference [in price] in any of the top ten companies. They may have a higher dividend, and we may have a higher cash value. You could spend a lot of time checking around and find at Prudential and New York Life, they aren't that different," the agent said. "It boils down to whom you want to deal with."

He pointed out that there is a high turnover rate among agents. But he said, "As far as reliability and stability, [Metropolitan] has been around more than one hundred years. I've been here more than twenty years." Besides, he pointed out, "Metropolitan has a ten-day free look." This refers to state laws that permit consumers to get their money back from any company within ten days of buying a policy if they are not satisfied.

Asked again about price, he said, "You're certainly not going to call 2,100 [life insurance] companies, because you don't have the time [to] see if you can get a dollar or two less."

Asked if he gets a higher percentage commission for selling

whole life than term, he said, "The term and whole life commissions are not that different." In fact, Metropolitan's whole life commission is fifty-five percent of the first-year premium, compared with twenty-five percent for term insurance. For selling a $100,000 policy, a Metropolitan agent earns a first-year commission of $652 on whole life, compared with $39 for selling a term policy providing the same coverage.

When it was later pointed out that life insurance rates vary substantially, he said, "I honestly don't know if they are all about the same. Everybody thinks their whole life is the best." He said a Metropolitan publication ranks competitors' policies by premium alone. Based on those comparisons, he said, "We're told [Metropolitan's whole life policy] ranked number one in the country right now on premium and overall cost."

He said he has never personally tried to compare costs using the interest-adjusted index number developed for that purpose, nor has he ever been asked about them by a customer. "They're something we don't fully understand," he said. "The average person doesn't understand them. I'm sure it's like Greek to them."

Asked why he said the commissions are the same for whole life and term when they are not, he said the statement could be true if one compares a small amount of whole life coverage with a much larger amount of term coverage. But he conceded the term commission is so insignificant in comparison with the whole life commission, "A lot of agents won't broadcast [Metropolitan's term policy] because the commission is so low."

Reflecting the views of his agents, Richard R. Shinn, until recently the chairman and chief executive officer of Metropolitan, said consumers are interested in more than price. "In many ways, they are buying the confidence and credibility of the individual [agent] and the company he represents," he said. "I happen to think that when you buy from a big company—within a reasonable amount—you get about the same price."

An agent from Equitable Life Assurance Society of the United States escorted the visitor into an office with a green blackboard.

The agent, formerly in another business, stayed with Equitable three years. Several months after being interviewed, he returned to his original career because he found he was not making enough money. Equitable, with assets of $41 billion, is the third-largest in the industry.

In making his presentation, the agent drew lines and arrows on a pad of paper. Showing off his work, he said term insurance is far more expensive than whole life. "It's a rental policy," he said, referring to term insurance. "At the eleventh year, with whole life, it'll give you a chunk [of cash] for all the premiums. The cost is zero."

Arranging for a home visit, he arrived ten minutes early, lugging a briefcase crammed with computer printouts. Bringing out a sheaf of them, he reeled off the figures from long rows of numbers. "Column seven shows you get $42,793 more than you paid in [with whole life]," he said. "At the end of twenty years, on [whole life], you get a profit, and with term, [you get] $16,000 and a thank you."

Later, he said he had never heard of the state insurance regulation that prohibits such statements. He said he feels the cost of money is an important consideration. However, "We don't discuss the time value of money with a twenty-two-year-old kid who is going to spend the money on Schlitz. He is going to throw it away."

With the prospect's wife sitting in, he volunteered that he sometimes has difficulty selling new Equitable policies because one or another state has not yet approved them. When that happens, he said, he arranges to deliver the policy in a state where the policy has been approved.

"I've met with a guy in his office and driven two blocks up and have a cup of coffee [in another state where the policy has been approved for sale]," he said.

Asked about price, he said, "We have a stock answer that our training school tells us to say when people ask about prices. There are 2,100 companies in the country, and no two are alike. Where do you stop and where do you start? You buy from an agent you feel comfortable with."

Warming to the subject, he said, "If this is the amount I can do in a few minutes, think of how I could confuse you in an hour. As a consumer, you really don't have a chance. The only thing you can go on is what the salesman is telling you, and he's paid by commission. It's a question of whether I'm honest to begin with." He said most customers quickly realize they cannot compare price; moreover, he said he cannot think of any who have tried.

While misrepresentations are against the law, he said, "The problem is it's hard to police. The insurance commissioners can't police it. It's a self-policing industry, to a large extent."

Before considering whether to act on a complaint of misrepresentation, he said, a supervisor will check to see how much sales an agent is bringing in. "If I sell $2 million and they hear I'm fudging, they're not going to get too upset. If I sold $10,000, they might care. That's true of everybody in the world," he said.

In an interview, Coy G. Eklund, then chairman and chief executive officer of Equitable, said he knows of no reason why whole life could not be described as "free," even if an agent failed to account for the cost or time value of money.

Another Equitable agent ushered the visitor into a conference room. WINNERS LOOK LIKE WINNERS, an orange sign on the wall said.

An agent two years, she began filling out a "capital needs analysis" designed to make the prospect recognize a need for more life insurance. "Your estate has to go through probate," she said. "Have you thought about whether you'll need to support your parents? Disability insurance? Social Security benefits? If you were to die prematurely, have you made provision for burial? It's got to cost $5,000 to $8,000. Then you need a plot," she said.

Adding up the figures, she said she sees a preliminary need for at least $55,000 more in life insurance. "Maybe we're talking about $100,000 [more]. How much can you comfortably pay?" she said.

She suggests a home visit so she can meet "your better half." Sitting on the living room sofa, she pulled out the analysis. "By the time I get through, your insurance agent knows you like a doctor," she said.

Focusing on the wife's needs, she said, "Has there been provision to bury you? A lot of people experience a death and then find out how much it's going to cost. They'll put you in a wood box, and then a metal box." Inexplicably citing a different burial cost, she said, "Let's say it will cost $4,000."

Taking out her calculator, she totaled the figures, coming up with a need for at least $60,000 more in coverage. "At this point, we've hit a need," she said. "Do you feel the figures are real?" When told they are, she said, "I'm going to show you some concepts."

She brought out some computer printouts and spread them on the dining-room table. "In the long run, it's a heck of a lot cheaper [to buy whole life] than term insurance," she said. "If you're planning to keep it for ten to fifteen years, there's probably a better way [than buying term insurance]."

She suggested an Equitable variable life policy, a variety of whole life insurance. Under the plan, the policyholder decides if he wants his cash value to build up in a stock market account or money fund. Pointing to the stock market option on the printouts she said, "This thing made fifty percent last year."

She mentioned that a portion of that fifty percent return goes to pay for expenses. What she didn't say is that after these expenses are deducted, the twelve percent returns promised in the policy literature are whittled down to four or five percent—about what other whole life policies pay.

"I'm a new person to you, and I'm throwing all these figures at you," she said. To give the prospect time to think, she said she could take an application for the policy now. When it is issued in four or five weeks, the prospect could get his money back if he has decided against buying it. "Yes, you are insurable today," she said, indicating that might not be true if the prospect delays.

She left policy comparisons that do not list the interest-adjusted index figures approved by regulators for comparing costs. These are the figures that look like dollars and cents comparisons but really are not and that no one in the business understands. She is not any different.

Saying she could supply them, she admitted, "I can't tell you what the interest-adjusted figures mean. No one compares [prices] with them. A CPA or engineer every now and then will ask about it." Confirming this, her manager later said, "Generally speaking, the majority of the people we deal with don't look at price."

Another Equitable agent has been with the company fourteen years. A CLU, he became an agent after managing a supermarket.

Focusing on the visitor's mortgage, he said, "If the mortgage is taken care of, it will reduce the outflow of funds. Your wife could either pay off the mortgage or leave the funds on deposit. In about fifty percent of the cases, it's in the individual's best interests to pay off the mortgage."

The best solution would be whole life, he said. "It costs less in the long run than term insurance. At age sixty-five, what would you be happier with? A stack of receipts for $21,000 for term insurance and no insurance [coverage], or $28,800 in dividends and a cash value of $46,000 and coverage for life of $100,000?"

Later, he said he has never heard of the insurance law prohibiting such statements that fail to take into account the time value of money. In any case, he said, the time value of money has "very little relevance."

Claiming Equitable has very competitive rates, he acknowledged it would be difficult for a consumer to determine that for himself. He said one might go to the Library of Congress and look up a publication called *Best's Flitcraft Compend*, published by A. M. Best Company. This 592-page book lists the rates of some policies of major companies at selected age brackets. Many other policies are not listed, however.

"It's tough to understand what is printed there," he said. While the book lists some interest-adjusted index figures, "It's a bag of worms to understand. . . . If you want to understand how they are arrived at, it takes three hours of study."

Next, we visit an Aetna agent, who maintained that his company, which is owned by stockholders, charges less. "As a general rule, with the competitive companies, Aetna's whole life is one of the lowest in the interest-adjusted surrender and payments index cost comparisons, taking into account the cost of money," said the agent, who has been with the company seven years.

"Dollar for dollar, you're going to be higher at Prudential, because they charge the premium and then they may return the dividends. If you want to buy it at the cheapest price, nonpartici-pating [nondividend-paying policies issued by stockholder-owned companies like Aetna] is the way to go," he said.

In fact, after thirty-eight years, a Prudential whole life policy is sixteen percent to seventy-two percent cheaper than an Aetna whole life policy, depending on whether you die or cash it in.

Kenneth P. Veit, an Aetna actuary and, until recently, vice-presi-dent in charge of life insurance, said Aetna, when comparing other companies' rates, has a hard time. The company uses one of its actuaries who is aided by a computer working just to compare what other companies are charging.

"Even for us it is difficult to compare policy prices. What does the consumer do?" he said.

But John H. Filer, chairman and chief executive officer of Aetna, brushed aside the difficulties. "Go to an agent," he advised, saying the agent will tell the consumer anything he needs to know about prices of other companies.

Filer acknowledged such comparisons will show Aetna is not "low-priced," but he said, "I think you do have a guarantee from a company that's been in business [more than 120] years and ought to last another [120] years, a quality organization, a reputation for honesty and fair play."

Before coming out to the prospect's house, an agent from New York Life Insurance Company wanted to know how much the prospect can spend on life insurance. New York Life, which has assets of $23 million, is the fifth largest in the business. This particular agent has been with New York Life seventeen years and is a member of the elite Million Dollar Round Table.

As promised, he came to the prospect's house one evening,

loaded with colored felt pens and drawing paper. He used the pens to draw lines comparing whole life with term insurance.

"A term policy is like renting a house; you don't own it," he said. So the prospect can afford enough coverage, he suggested a whole life policy combined with a term policy.

"I don't want to say whole life is better," he said. "The question is, will you invest the difference [between whole life and term premiums]?" Asked how New York Life rates compare, he said, "We are not the lowest. We take pride in the fact that no matter where you move, you'll have a New York Life office and agent."

In response to a question, he said, "Yes, I do get a higher commission on whole life," explaining that whole life premiums are higher. Unlike most companies, New York Life pays the same percentage commission for sales of both products. However, the company still credits agents with retirement benefits based only on whole life sales.

The agent said he has little use for the interest-adjusted index figures required by regulators. "When you buy your car and refrigerator, you don't look at interest-adjusted figures," he said.

He later sent packets of articles extolling whole life. "If it is such a bad product as you seem to imply, how come it has survived for almost three hundred years?" he said in a four-page, typewritten letter.

Another New York Life agent, who has been with the company for ten years, took down some figures on a yellow pad. "It seems you need at least $100,000 in additional coverage," he said.

"Do you want it to be for a short period or until you die? You pay all this money out for term, and there's no value there. So if we look at the permanent form of protection, it gives you more flexibility. You can pay for it in as little as ten years," he said.

What he didn't say is that paying for life insurance with large premiums in the first few years is the most costly way of buying life insurance. The company gets to earn interest on your larger payments, while you lose the income you could be making on your own money. Meanwhile, the agent obtains a higher commission, since he gets a percentage of the larger, first-year premium.

In this case, the New York Life agent brought out some comparisons meant to show that whole life costs less than term insurance. A footnote said the figures do not take into account the time value of money. Asked about the meaning of the footnote, he said, "There are certain arguments about the time value of money. Do we go through the same calculation if we buy food? I try not to involve myself in the argument."

"If you find out, let me know," he said when asked if he is required by state insurance rules to take into account the time value of money.

A response to a New York Life mail solicitation brought a visit from an agent who has been with the company twenty-three years. A member of the Million Dollar Round Table, he recommended $130,000 in whole life coverage at a cost of $2,561 a year.

Asked how New York Life rates compare, he said, "There isn't much of a spread in the price because of the competition among the companies. You're talking about a $50 [a year] spread on a yearly premium of $2,500." When asked for support for that statement, he said he would mail it. When the documentation did not arrive, he was asked a second time for the information. It never came.

According to the Computone figures, the first-year premium for a $100,000 policy from one of the largest companies can vary by as much as $693.

The last agent, also from New York Life, offered to provide any information that would be helpful. "You have probably heard of the much-maligned whole life insurance," he said. "Some of the criticism has come from your colleagues. . . . Usually, these people don't know what they're doing."

An agent with the company for twenty-eight years, he displayed computer printouts showing whole life can be slightly cheaper than term insurance after a number of years, so long as the policyholder is in a high tax bracket and borrows against the policy in four out of seven consecutive years. This rather complicated procedure takes advantage of tax rules to lower the after-tax cost of whole life.

"There is no equity on term insurance," he said. "You have a big, fat outlay." Turning to an illustration, he said, "You are $38,000 ahead with whole life at age sixty-four. Under term, it would have cost you $24,000." Pointing to the whole life plan, he said, "There you get a check for $38,000."

Calling the interest-adjusted figures approved by the regulators "meaningless," he said he knows of no insurance department restriction against claiming a whole life policy has produced a profit when comparing it with a term policy.

"[Life insurance] is sold not by price but by the agent," he said. Life insurance is "not generally purchased on the basis of cold, calculating, quantitative facts."

Asked why people should buy life insurance with a savings feature, when no other types of insurance are sold that way, he said, "I would simply point out that the savings feature on whole life is purely incidental. It is not a savings." But he later said, "A large percentage of the buying public would not save a penny if it were not for their insurance. It is a blessing for many people who face sudden emergencies."

■

How many agents purposely misstate the truth and how many do not know it in the first place? That is hard to say. Clearly, agents know what their commissions are. When they get a higher percentage of a much larger premium for selling whole life than for selling term, there is little question that they are aware of one of the most crucial facts of their existence. And when they make a claim, only to admit under questioning that it is wrong, it is safe to say the claim in most cases was deliberately misleading.

On the other hand, the amount of misinformation received and spread by agents cannot be underestimated. With no effective regulation and few consumers who can understand what they are saying, there is little incentive for agents to hew strictly to the facts—or to know them in the first place.

4. THE AGENTS

■ "I'll tell some fibs, all right," the agent said in the car on the way to the potential customer's town house. "I know exactly what my range is and what the [premium] numbers are. He doesn't know that. I'm going to be as amazed as he is. You do have an ax to grind," he continued, "but he's going to be better off when I walk out the door."

Since he is not affiliated with any one company, the independent agent will say he has come to analyze the man's need and offer a choice of companies and policies. He will say he has no preference for any one policy or company. In fact, though, he has already determined which company's policy he will sell. It is the one that pays him a higher commission. And the premiums will come out at just about what he thinks the prospect will be willing to pay.

In a business where it takes twenty calls to make one sale, it takes a particular style to succeed. Some agents are flamboyant, drive Corvettes, and wear suede jackets. Some, like this agent, are practitioners of the hard sell, and dispense with the time-consuming task of analyzing individuals' financial needs. Still others project to their prospects that they care or impress them with their analytical abilities.

Most agents are driven by commissions, and they never lose sight of a basic reality: they make a far higher percentage commission for selling whole life than for selling term insurance. And, regardless of the type of policy, the higher the premium, the more commission they receive.

In this chapter, we will look at the different styles and techniques that are used by agents by focusing on three of them and how they do their jobs. The three agents we will examine represent a range of income levels.

The first agent, who makes about $40,000 a year, once qualified as a member of the Million Dollar Round Table but has not qualified recently. Another agent makes well over $100,000 a year and sells more than $8 million in life insurance a year. Because he has met the selling requirements for more than ten years in a row, he is a life member of the Million Dollar Round Table. A third agent represents a minority of agents who are beginning to charge fees for their services. He makes $79,000 a year.

Agents usually receive their training from life insurance companies. The companies prefer to hire trainees rather than experienced agents from other companies. That tradition is kept intact by the commission structure. If an agent leaves a company to go to another, he usually loses any right to collect commissions from his existing customers.

The new agents are assigned to "agencies," which are just like branch offices. The difference is they are run by managers who get a percentage of their agents' sales. The managers, in turn, are responsible for training agents and developing new business for the company.

In many states, the new agents may begin selling with a ninety-day temporary insurance license. Eventually, they must pass tests to obtain a permanent license. The test tends to emphasize knowledge of the technical jargon of the industry, rather than the more vital questions of why people need life insurance or how they can get the best value for their dollar.

While in training, the agents receive a subsidy from the company. Metropolitan Life Insurance Company, for example, pays $400 a week for thirteen weeks. Agents then receive a tenth of the commissions they make on new sales each week.

As a rule, life insurance agents are not unionized. The companies have a philosophy about recruiting: "Throw them against the wall and see which ones stick." No one really knows beforehand if an agent will be able to sell. Practically all applicants are taken with the hope that a few will have a knack for it.

An 1867 article in the *Western Insurance Review* is probably as true today, as far as it goes, as it was then. The author noted that it was often puzzling to see how some agents who appear highly qualified fall flat, while others with "nothing to recommend them build up in a short time a large business and earn a handsome competence." The author of the article suggested the reason for success is perseverance and refusal to accept defeat, according to a synopsis in *Marketing Life Insurance.*

Most agents sell all their friends and relatives and then, seeing they are making no headway, go on to other businesses. After four years, four out of five new agents have left, creating a tremendous drain on life insurance company resources.

The more successful agents like people. They tend to be confident, enthusiastic, and hardworking. They organize their time well.

For those who succeed, the rewards are great. The top achievers—the biggest-selling four percent—become members of the Million Dollar Round Table, an organization based in Des Plaines, Illinois. To join, agents must write at least $2 million in new coverage a year. The threshold increases each year with inflation. Some 20,000 agents from forty-four countries belong to the Million Dollar Round Table, which holds a meeting every year where members hear tips from the top sellers. A Louis Harris survey of Million Dollar Round Table members found their median income is more than $70,000. One in twelve makes $150,000 a year or more.

■

The first agent we meet has an impressive certificate hanging on the wall of his three-room suite showing he has passed the difficult courses required to become a chartered life underwriter. He has also taught classes conducted by the Washington-based Life Underwriter Training Council.

Like most agents, he began his career as a recruit of a life insurance company, Metropolitan Life. He left Metropolitan to join Acacia Mutual Life Insurance Company of Washington. Now, after eight years in the business, he is no longer associated with Acacia and calls himself an independent agent.

There is less to that designation than meets the eye. As an independent agent, he can, in theory, sell a policy of any company and is therefore impartial. In practice, most independent agents sell primarily for one company. The point is borne out by the survey of Million Dollar Round Table members, which found nearly four out of five place more than half their business with one company.

The reason is simple math. "You [generally] get fifty-five percent [of the first year premium] ... but if you write it with one place, you get seventy percent," the agent said. "That is the reason the majority of the business is put in one company."

Even agents who are affiliated with a single company like to create the impression they are independent. "A lot of guys have cards that only say [the name of an independent company] because a lot of people have bugaboos about dealing with someone affiliated with New England Life," said Donald Shaw, a former New England Mutual Life Insurance Company agent. "They seem more independent if they are brokers," he said.

To develop new customers, some agents knock on doors. Some comb through the obituary columns of newspapers and try to sell the recently bereaved. This agent said he finds it difficult to take the rejection that comes with making cold calls, so he mails solicitations to people who have just bought new homes. Usually, these people are more receptive to buying life insurance.

The agent gets the names and addresses from local real estate directories. He works twelve-hour days and sends out 100 to 200 computer-prepared letters to new homeowners each week.

"Would you be interested in saving up to sixty percent on your mortgage insurance?" his letter reads. It compares a monthly premium of $38 for $75,000 in insurance coverage from Prudential Insurance Company of America with a monthly premium of just $12 for the same amount of coverage from the agent.

The letter does not say that he is comparing two different types of policies. The Prudential policy is a decreasing term policy, which has the worst features of whole life because it starts out with high premiums that bring a decreasing amount of coverage.

The agent said he knows he is comparing "an apple and an orange" but explained, "The idea of the letter is to show there's a colossal difference. It's not quite fair . . . all I'm trying to do is get them to talk to me."

The letters ask people to return a card if they want more information or a visit. He said he calls all the recipients even if they do not respond.

In calling, he practices techniques he learned from a psychological training course offered to agents by Acacia Mutual Life Insurance Company. Taught by Dr. Edwin O. Timmons, a former professor of psychology at Louisiana State University in Baton Rouge, it uses videotaped training sessions and workbooks that teach agents the best ways to approach people.

In one videotaped presentation, the bearded Dr. Timmons appears behind a desk. "Why do we encounter hostility?" he says, and he lists some of the reasons: stereotypes, fear, resentment that a stranger is encroaching on valuable time. The solution, Dr. Timmons suggests, is building a "bridge of trust" by finding out what prospects like to talk about. Instead of saying he would like to sell a policy, the agent can propose an appointment by suggesting he would like to "share some ideas."

According to Dr. Timmons, ". . . all the agent really is selling is trust; that's all. I have life insurance policies, but I never have read them and never intend to read them. I just have to trust the guy who sold them to me. He sold me something for which I keep giving his company money, and I never will see anything for it. The agent has to sell trust."

In teaching the course, Dr. Timmons tells agents they have to be "congruent" with themselves, meaning their words should match the "music" or manner in which they say the words.

"Listen to the prospect," Dr. Timmons advises. "Don't threaten his sense of self-worthiness. Assume that he means well. Don't tell him what he ought to do. Allow him to use his own personal values, not yours. Don't tell him what he needs. Make him feel like some-body; accept him," he said.

"If I can become congruent with myself," he continued, "not just in insurance sales but in life itself, other people will tend to trust me, and we'll be moving toward our win-win ballgame." A win-win ballgame, of course, is an encounter where both sides come away feeling they won.

Demonstrating how he uses Dr. Timmons's methods, the agent first goes through what he calls a "process." He goes to the bathroom, returns to his office, leans back in his chair, and opens a large Pepsi. Leaning back forces him to talk slower. He smiles into the tele-phone receiver, giving his voice a more amiable quality. He does not call after 9:00 P.M.

"I used to think I had to educate people, but they don't remem-ber a lot of it," he said. "It doesn't affect their decision. So why make it hard for them?"

He does not argue if the prospect wants less coverage than he should have. "If a guy said $25,000, that's not going to be a shot in the bucket. But his widow is going to be $25,000 better off," he said.

He begins dialing a recipient of one of his letters. "Good evening, is Mr. Anthony in?" he asked. Introducing himself as the agent who sent him the letter, he said, "Do you have a moment to talk, sir? [Pause.] Would it be appropriate if I call you tomorrow at 7:00 P.M.?"

Hanging up, he said the prospect could not talk then but agreed to speak with him the next night. "Two things happened," he said. "I asked if it was appropriate to talk, and is it appropriate to call?" He got a positive response. "I bet I get an appointment," he said.

Asking people's permission to talk with them is crucial. If they agree, they have lent their support to what he is trying to do. Quot-ing Dr. Timmons, the agent said people support what they help create.

In talking with prospects, the agent tries to choose his words carefully. He searches for what he calls "round words," which are positive and nonthreatening, and he lards his conversation with other words like "money saving" and "competitive bid."

"They all connote an image," he said.

If he encounters an objection, he engages in what the course calls "sponging." He will say, "I can understand why you say that." According to the agent, "If you come back with a positive, then we are communicating."

If a potential customer says he is too busy to talk because he is painting the basement, he has his computer programmed to spit out the person's telephone number when he said he will be finished. When he calls back, "I say, 'Have you finished painting the basement?' You can almost hear the amazement on the other end."

At first, the agent sold a new kind of policy introduced by E. F. Hutton Life Insurance Company of La Jolla, California. Called universal life, it is a type of whole life policy that we will learn more about in a later chapter. Rather than having a fixed ratio between cash values and death benefits, the amounts of the benefits and the size of the premiums can be varied at the request of the customer. The highly publicized policy develops cash values based on fluctuating market rates of interest.

More recently, he switched to Jefferson National Life Insurance Company of Indianapolis, Indiana. "I wanted a bigger first-year commission and extra money based on production commitments," he said. "At Jefferson, they'd give you that and bonuses."

At the time, Jefferson National had no universal life policy, but that did not concern him. He said he sells the company's adjustable policy as if it were universal life. The policy uses a different method for achieving the same end.

"It's not really universal," he said. "I call it universal because, why confuse somebody? If you've read six articles about universal, and we watch it perform, you can't tell the difference," he said. "I think it's equal [to Hutton's universal life]; besides, it pays me more."

In fact, the Adjustable I and II policies he has been selling generally provide less coverage for the same price than the Hutton policy.

The agent believes there is nothing wrong with pushing a policy that gives him a higher commission if the customer ends up with more coverage than he had before. "I tell my students [in an industry training course for new agents], if you've left the guy better off than when you walked in, it's okay," he said.

In preparing to visit a prospect in his town house, the agent explained that the man had answered one of his solicitation letters. He had been listed in a real estate directory as the new owner of a home with a $60,000 mortgage. After setting up an appointment, the agent mailed him articles about universal life from *The Wall Street Journal* and *Money* magazine.

In preparation for the visit, the agent had also opened a file on him. It contained the calculation of the premiums that would be required to buy the term insurance he had promised in his letter. The agent explained it was a meaningless gesture. "The only reason I'm doing this [figuring the cost of term insurance] is so I'll have the numbers, even though I'm going to sell adjustable life," he said.

Adjustable life pays him a commission of ninety percent of the first year's premium, compared with twenty percent to forty-five percent for term insurance. In addition, he pointed out, the adjustable life premium is higher than the term insurance premium.

When customers insist on term insurance, "I would rather not make the sale than sell a term policy that gives me a $35 commission," he said. In fact, he said, "A lady said she wanted a [term] policy for $12 a month. I could have gone down to $8 a month for the same coverage, but she said, 'Don't you have anything lower?' and I said no."

Loading his computer terminal into the car just before the appointment, the agent said, "What I'll do here today is sit down and tell him a little about myself . . . I'm going to ask some questions that are throwaway questions. I don't need to have the answers, and it sets the stage. Then I'll probably come back to those responses when I am ready to close. Then we'll talk about what he wants to do. I usually tell him I'm here to help him do what he wants to do."

He said the "razzle-dazzle" of the computer helps make the sale. "Here's this poor fellow who works all day long at the office, and you've given him a plan with his name on it and his age that he's given you. All of a sudden the paper [printout] comes out. It's magic."

The Louis Harris survey of Million Dollar Round Table members found about a third considered computer services to be the most important support they had in their business. Continuing education ranked just above computer help in importance.

"He's going to tell me his needs, and how much he wants to spend, and he wants term. I'm going to sell him universal, but he doesn't know it because I've figured out the range [of premiums]," the agent said. In his file on the new homeowner, he had already noted the amount of premiums needed to cover the $60,000 mortgage with adjustable life. If the homeowner died, the money would be available either to pay off the mortgage, put into an investment, or pay bills. If he balks at the premium, the agent said he will be able to lower it and still provide $60,000 in coverage. The cash value will then become lower.

"Sometimes they'll say all I want is term. You agree with him. You ask if he knows about universal life. If he wants to hear about it, you tell him. If the whole life or universal life sale isn't there, don't push it, because at some point it will be there," he said.

The agent arrived at the prospect's beige-carpeted home in the afternoon. Rock music was playing on the stereo. The new homeowner, an assistant restaurant manager, agreed to let a visitor sit in on the meeting. Offering coffee, the twenty-four-year-old man sat down at the dining-room table, where he placed his existing policy from another company.

As promised, the agent began by telling about himself.

"I've been in the insurance business eight years. I was with Metropolitan, and then went to Acacia, and then went out on my own," he said. "The real reason I left was they say you can sell only our product. If you work for Metropolitan, you don't sell Prudential. The first thing that happens is a guy comes in with a better product, and you lose the case. I like to keep eating. I felt it was better for me [to be an independent agent], and better for the client."

As an independent, he said, "What I am able to do is tell you if you want a brown one or a pink one, I can go to the company and get it," he said. "I represent the twenty majors. That's where I'm coming from."

"Okay," the man said with a touch of impatience. "I want the best buy for my money."

"What I like to do is find out what you want to do. What are you trying to do? What's your budget? And after I find out what you want to do—because I really don't know—then I'll show you the pros and cons of two or three plans and let you pick it. Does that sound reasonable to you?" he asked.

The man agreed it did.

The agent asked for the balance outstanding on the new mortgage. He did not write down the answer. He already had it in his file.

Explaining that there are two types of life insurance, he said, "There's term insurance, which is just exactly—I make the analogy—like renting a house. With term insurance, you say, 'I want $100,000,' and the company says, '[You pay] $10 a month.' At the end of the period, you want to renew it, and the landlord says, 'I'm going to raise your rent from $400 to $425 a month.' When you move out, all you have is a batch of receipts. But it served its purpose. You got protection at a low dollar outlay."

The man is sitting with his arms crossed.

"Let's talk about whole life," the agent continued. "It's designed to meet the premiums when you're older. With term, the insurance stops by age seventy. That's when you need it."

"Right," the man said.

The agent said higher interest rates and inflation have made whole life less attractive, so an Atlanta actuary designed universal life, which responds to current market rates and offers more flexibility because premium payments can be adjusted up or down.

The man is listening intently.

"What does that mean to you?" the agent asked. "It means if you put money in you get interest at current rates—now twelve percent. The rate fluctuates with the marketplace.

"Let me be quiet and let you ask questions," he said.

"You recommend universal?" the man asked somewhat tentatively.

"I haven't said yet," he said, gauging his prospect's reaction.

"Term is a definite no for me," the man said.

"Yes, on the permanent side, yes, I'm recommending universal, definitely, just because of the way the numbers work out," he said finally.

Offering to show the numbers, the agent asked the man to dial the telephone number that connects the computer terminal to Jefferson National's computer. As the machine sputtered, the man observed that he took a course in life insurance at Indiana University, where he obtained a bachelor of science degree in management administration and marketing. But he said he recalls little from the course, which was taught in the department headed by Joseph M. Belth, a leading advocate of better cost-disclosure in life insurance.

Double-checking with the man on the spelling of his name, the agent typed it into the computer. "What are your thoughts on budget?" he asked.

He said he could pay $25 to $30 a month. "If it meant getting the coverage, I could go higher," he added.

"Let's call it $30 a month," he said, punching the number into the computer. The agent already knew that $25 a month would give him $60,000 in coverage. Any additional payments would provide more cash values and increase his commission.

As prearranged, the computer showed that $30 a month will just pay for the $60,000 in coverage.

"Sounds good," the man said as he looked at the printout. "Like I told you, I'm checking around. You brought me some things I didn't know about." He paused. "Do you have trouble selling insurance because of a low return?" he asked.

"Not with this," the agent said. "That's why universal life is such a neat product." He related an anecdote about another customer who thought he could get a better return at a bank. Telling him universal life cash values are not taxable, the agent told him he would have to get a fifteen percent return from the bank to match an after-tax return of twelve percent from universal life. "You don't give any to Uncle Sam," he told the customer. "The guy said, 'Who do I write my check to?'"

The anecdote made the point even if it was not true. Just like the cash values offered by whole life, the cash values provided by universal life are taxable when they are received, but not each year as they accumulate.

"If that's paying me four percent, and this twelve percent, I'll take that," the prospect responded, pointing first to his whole life policy and then to the computer printout. He said he will get back to the agent after checking with the agent who sold him his existing whole life policy.

Starting his car outside the man's home, the agent observed, "One of the things I didn't do was try to close. There wasn't a close there. I have to feel there's an honest shot. The biggest drawback is his wife wasn't there."

But the agent said he was satisfied that he played his cards well. "Did you notice how the premium came out at $30? I knew where I could play the game down to. I already figured the lowest I could go was $25," he said. "He didn't want to have anything to do with term the way I described it. I made term insurance sound terrible, didn't I? It is, unless you need it, and that's all the dollars you can afford. I tried not to tell him too much."

On the way back to his office, he pointed out that his comparison of the values of the adjustable or universal life policy he was selling and the man's existing whole life policy might be considered unfair. He pointed out that the cash values paid by the man's existing whole life policy are guaranteed, while the adjustable or universal life returns are not. But he said, "Guarantees shouldn't be involved, because they just get in the way and cause confusion."

What's important, he felt, is that the numbers impressed the man. But he pointed out the numbers by themselves do not tell the whole story. To fairly present the cost of a policy, the time value or cost of money must be taken into account, he said. "Most people have no conception of the time value of money. It makes all the difference in the world. The agent says such a deal—you pay $20,000 and you get $50,000 [back]. But if you figured the true rate of return . . ."

Referring back to what he told the prospect earlier about a twelve percent return on adjustable life's cash value, he said, "Is the true rate of return twelve percent? No way." Explaining that twelve percent is a gross rate of return, he said the insurance companies deduct from that yield their expenses, the cost of insurance, and commissions to agents.

"The real question," he said, "is what is the average rate of return? The [typical] agent has no way to figure it out. I know the answer. It's four percent. I wouldn't tell him that."

Rollins W. "Bill" Miller, Jr., is a successful and respected life insurance agent. He writes better than $8,million in new premiums a year, and he makes well over $100,000 a year. When the National Association of Life Underwriters, the chief agents' group, points with pride to one of its members, Miller is one of the agents they cite. "He's in the upper strata. He's in the top one percent," said Jack E. Bobo, executive director of the agents' organization.

Miller started as an IBM Corporation salesman and joined New York Life Insurance Company more than thirty years ago. Just recently, he retired from the company to sell as an independent agent.

At sixty-one, Miller could play the Robert Young role in *Father Knows Best*. He projects concern. If you overspent your allowance, you would want Miller to tell you not to worry.

"Where are you going? What do you want out of life?" he asks prospects. He does not seem to want to sell life insurance. He wants to hear your life story.

"People need people to listen to them," he says in his low, slightly husky voice. "Whether it is someone struggling for a living or not, they have targets of where they want to go," Miller says. "You form a close relationship with these people, and they tell you things their doctors don't know."

"They [clients] know I'm nonjudgmental," he said. "To me, the balancing factor is human relations. Technical knowledge is number two."

Indeed it is. The survey of Million Dollar Round Table members found they considered the most important personal attributes needed for successful selling are self-confidence and the ability to build goodwill among customers. Detailed knowledge of their own and their competitors' products ranked well below these personal characteristics in importance.

Miller wears a pinstriped suit, carries a black leather briefcase, and has graying hair. His office is decorated with Oriental rugs. A copy of *The Wall Street Journal* is displayed on a coffee table. You would not blink if someone told you Miller, tanned and standing erect, is chairman of General Motors Corporation. Still, he is deferential. "I don't want to infringe on your time," he says when setting up an appointment.

Miller doesn't like to talk about his condominium in St. Thomas, his Mercedes, his sailboat, or the apartment houses he owns with his wife, Jane, the only woman he ever dated. "It's embarrassing, really. I don't consider myself a big hitter," he says. But, when still a New York Life agent, Miller did say that he stops in to have a chat with the president of the company whenever he is in New York; that he gets his information directly from vice-presidents in the home office; and that he is a life member of the Million Dollar Round Table, having exceeded the membership requirement for more than ten consecutive years.

Miller rattles off information about estate planning, taxes, computers, and accounting. His knowledge is vast. In life or death, you would want Bill Miller on your side.

Like most members of the Million Dollar Round Table, Miller sells mostly to businesses. He tells owners of small companies he can give them a competitive edge by providing attractive fringe benefits to help lure executives from other companies.

Miller uses his memberships in an old-line country club and several city clubs to meet businessmen. Sometimes, it takes two years before a key introduction is made and he gets to meet with the chief executive. Before such a meeting, Miller spends months learning about the company.

Businessmen and individuals have the same concerns, he said. "What goes through people's minds," Miller said, "is does this man care about my problems, does he know what he's talking about, and can he be trusted?"

Miller does not let his own value system interfere. If a client wears a polka dot tie and a striped shirt, "it may be distasteful, but it's his tie," he said. Sometimes, customers are having marital difficulties and do not want to provide for their wives. He understands and may suggest a trust for their children.

Like most life insurance salesmen, Miller talks of prospective clients who died before they had a chance to apply for a policy. On the other hand, he recalls holding the hand of a terminal cancer patient who was secure in the knowledge he had already purchased life insurance from Miller. Usually, Miller delivers the death benefit checks personally.

"Sometimes the responsibility is awesome," he said. "You stay awake at night saying, 'Did I do my best? Did I cover all his needs?' You never do enough. . . . If you want to know what stress is, have a widow and her children looking at you because, of all the people the husband knew, you were closest to him. It's a terrible thing to live with. Kids never have a chance to go to college, or conversely, can go to medical school, as a result of what the man did." If they had the foresight to buy enough life insurance, he said, their widows do not have to have their hands out.

Miller has spent most of his career recommending whole life insurance. "Individuals should buy whole life if they have insurance needs beyond five or six years," he said. "It will have a lower net cost over fifteen to twenty years." But when questioned further, he said you would come out better with term insurance if the savings in premiums are invested. More recently, Miller has been selling the universal life policy of E. F. Hutton Insurance Company.

Inevitably, Miller, a born-again Christian, meets with a lot of rejection. It does not bother him. "It's like a missionary trying to get someone to believe in God," he said. "If someone throws sand in your eyes, you walk away and wipe your eyes."

■

David M. Adelberg is a life insurance agent, tax planner, legal expert, and accounting expert all rolled into one. He is what is known as a financial planner, a relatively new concept that permits life insurance agents to give their clients better and—in theory, at least—impartial advice.

Adelberg has been an agent with Sun Life Assurance Company of Canada for eight years. He sells policies of other companies as well. If a customer wants a visit from Adelberg in his home, he charges an hourly fee of $75. Even office visits incur a charge after the first visit, unless he receives a commission from the sale of insurance.

"After all," Adelberg said, "how many doctors or lawyers go to their clients' homes, except in an emergency?" Adelberg sees his way of doing business as a way of reducing the cost of selling life insurance. He said agents who make special trips to people's houses to make the sale, then make a second trip to deliver the policy, are wasting everyone's time.

Besides selling life insurance, Adelberg sells mutual funds, Individual Retirement Accounts (IRAs), real estate partnership shares, and other investments. Only about half his income of $79,000 a year comes from insurance commissions.

In furthering his business, Adelberg does not sell his personality, his good looks, or his tennis game. What he sells is his knowledge and analytical ability.

His professional credentials are impressive. He is a member of the Million Dollar Round Table; chairman of the Northern Virginia Life Underwriters Training Council, which oversees training of new agents; and is registered to sell securities. Adelberg is also a Chartered Life Underwriter and a Chartered Financial Consultant. Both certificates are issued by the American College in Bryn Mawr, Pennsylvania, an accredited college that specializes in insurance.

The tree-shaded campus of the American College provides in-depth training in accounting and finance, economics, business insurance, estate planning, taxes, and insurance. In the college's fifty-seven-year history, more than 50,000 agents have earned the CLU designation, which is akin to a certified public accountant's diploma. As a rule, CLUs tend to be more knowledgeable and sophisticated than the average life insurance agent.

Adelberg contrasts himself with most life insurance agents, whom he describes as generally misinformed. "I believe if the life insurance industry were willing to be regulated as the securities industry is regulated, it would be a lot better off," he said. "There is no nonsense with the sale of securities. If you put something down on paper and it's wrong, that's your license for life. That, unfortunately, is not the way life insurance works."

Adelberg said consumers have no hope of understanding life insurance "under the best of circumstances." Their agents, in many cases, are just as ignorant, he said. "I know agents who say something and you say, 'Are you sure?' They say, 'No.'"

Adelberg takes pride in educating clients. If a client says he wants to invest in a municipal bond, he asks impertinent questions, like whether the client knows what a municipal bond is. Sometimes, the curly-haired Adelberg's frank approach gets him in trouble with his company or with other agents. "I am not emotional with clients," he said. "I refer to the replacement value of your wife. There is a cost to replacing services that a spouse provides."

Adelberg believes whole life is no longer a viable product and recommends mostly universal life insurance, which he says is better than term insurance. For Adelberg, the argument of universal whole life versus term insurance is somewhat academic. With a commission of about $300 for selling $100,000 in universal life coverage, compared with $61 for selling the same amount of term insurance, there is no contest from the agent's standpoint.

Referring to the term insurance commission, he said frankly, "I can't sell insurance with that commission." In fact, Adelberg stated flatly, "You can't stay in business with that commission."

5. THE POOR

■ We will now explore a route in the life insurance game reserved for the poor and the powerless. In this separate world within the life insurance industry, there are no office visits and no computers, no analyses of financial needs and no names to drop. Instead, we have people who cannot feed their children paying for policies that cost two to four times what standard policies cost. They continue to pay because their agents—who are most likely the only financial experts they ever get to meet—have persuaded them they need the protection, and they know no better. Once the sale is made, the nightmare intensifies: agents often collect more than is due or cancel the policies and issue new ones so they can get even more commissions.

Virginia E. Williams lives in a low-income housing project in Washington. Until just recently, she was paying $1,640 a year for thirty life insurance policies. With policies on herself, her husband, her six children, and one of her daughter's children, she had coverage that ranged from $2,000 to $5,000 on each family member. She was paying half as much for the policies as she pays for renting her tiny apartment, where three children and a grandchild sleep in one bedroom not much bigger than a walk-in closet.

Agents of Southwestern General Life Insurance Company of Dallas had sold Williams the policies by telling her they would provide for her children. Williams herself knew little about the policies, what they provide, or how much they cost.

"I don't know why I was paying it," said the forty-seven-year-old Williams, a black woman who finished the sixth grade. "It didn't make sense, but I didn't know any better. Nobody told me any better."

Williams's policies are called industrial life insurance policies. What makes them different from other whole life insurance policies is mainly the price. They are roughly two to four times more expensive. Industrial insurance is a special route in the life insurance game. It is reserved for impoverished people like Williams.

Looking at the practices of this segment of the life insurance industry is like going back in time to the days of Charles Dickens. With *Oliver Twist*, the British author began a series of indictments of his society for abusing the poor. Largely untouched by the industrial, financial, and regulatory progress that has taken place since that time, the industrial life insurance business is an enclave within the life insurance industry subject to its own rules, jargon, and unique set of values.

Companies that specialize in this type of insurance readily acknowledge that it's more expensive than the ordinary life insurance sold to the more affluent. But they say it is more expensive because payments for the policies are usually collected in person by agents. The companies argue that many poor people would never have any coverage if their agents did not collect from people in their homes.

While it is true that many of the agents collect in person, an increasing number encourage their customers to mail in their payments, just as they mail in payments for telephone and electric service. Even allowing for the extra cost of home visits that are actually made, the industry's own figures show industrial coverage is far more profitable to the companies than ordinary life insurance. In effect, these figures from the American Council of Life Insurance demolish the companies' argument that the higher prices are justified by the increased costs.

There is nothing new about the abuses. In 1905, Louis Brandeis, who went on to become a Supreme Court justice, singled out industrial life insurance as "legalized robbery" because of its high expenses, high lapse or dropout rates, and selling abuses. More recently, industrial insurance has come under attack from "60 Minutes" and the *Nashville Tennessean*, which ran a classic exposé on the subject by Carolyn Shoulders and Linda Solomon in 1978.

Loading them up with as many as thirty policies when one policy with greater coverage would be far cheaper, the industry preys on people like Virginia Williams. What they are doing is something like selling dozens of one-ounce boxes of soap powder without telling the customer the product comes in five-pound boxes at a lower unit cost, then suggesting the whole house should be filled with soap because of a threatened cutoff of supply. Because life insurance is so mysterious, many customers have no way of knowing they are being cheated.

Since they usually cannot afford the coverage to begin with, the admittedly gullible clients of industrial companies find themselves on a treadmill. When they cannot make a payment, the agent issues a new policy at an even higher rate. In the process, any cash values and other rights built up within the old policy are wiped out. The agents collect greater commissions because the customer has advanced in age: the rates are higher, so the commission is higher. When they cannot afford the new, higher payments, the customers again fall behind. Once again, their policies are rewritten, this time at even higher rates.

Most customers subsist like that for much of their lives. Williams was an exception. She dropped her industrial policies only because the Southwestern General manager who supervised her agent happened to leave the company to sell ordinary policies. Telling her she could do far better, he sold her five times more coverage for about half of what she had been paying. That fact, of course, is the bottom line. Multiply her experience by the millions of industrial policyholders and you have an idea of the magnitude of the extent to which the companies soak the poor.

To William E. Moulton, Jr., a Portsmouth, Virginia, life insurance agent who counsels poor people with industrial policies, cases like

Williams's illuminate a shameful national scandal that exists because of the absence of effective regulation by the states. "The American public is being defrauded legally and illegally," he said. "The reason the American public has been ripped-off is that the insurance regulators condone it."

Many states effectively encourage agents to load people up with multiple policies by placing a cap on the maximum industrial coverage that can be sold. Usually, the cap is $1,000 per policy. Originally, the limit was placed on industrial coverage because the policies were thought to be too expensive. Therefore, the coverage had to be limited. Today, the limitation on coverage means agents have to write multiple policies because one will not adequately cover the cost of a funeral.

A primary reason the coverage is so expensive is that the insurance commissioners have set up industrial insurance as a special category of insurance. They have required the companies to use mortality tables that show death rates as much as twice as high as the actual death rates for the United States population as a whole. Consequently, the premiums must be higher to cover the extra risk that is assumed. As the immense profits from the industrial business demonstrate, those estimates of death rates are grotesquely out of line.

Industrial life insurance got its start in this country in 1875 with the founding of Prudential Insurance Company of America. John F. Dryden, Prudential's founder, had borrowed the idea from the Prudential Assurance Company of Great Britain, started twenty-five years earlier. In those days, standard life insurance coverage was unavailable to the poor. There was even a prejudice that the poor would insure their children and then murder them for the money.

For three to five cents a week, the American Prudential enabled working-class people to obtain coverage previously available only to the rich. It was called "industrial" insurance because it was sold primarily to factory workers.

By investing the funds, Prudential turned the pennies into billions of dollars, becoming the largest life insurance company in the world. Metropolitan Life Insurance Company became the second-largest, also by selling industrial coverage.

As life insurance became available at lower rates, industrial policies were no longer tenable, and both companies stopped sales of new policies in the late 1960s. They also voluntarily increased existing industrial coverage free of charge.

"We thought it was the right thing to do for the consumer," said Beck, the chairman of Prudential.

Today, the rest of the life insurance industry would rather industrial insurance go away. Executives of companies that sell ordinary insurance either do not know or do not want to know that it is still being sold.

"I don't think it exists much anymore, does it?" asked John H. Filer, chairman and chief executive officer of Aetna Life & Casualty Company, the nation's fourth-largest life insurance company, when the subject of industrial insurance was raised. Recalling that his grandfather sold such policies, Filer pointed out it was once the only way many people could buy life insurance. Probably today, he said in his Hartford, Connecticut, office, ". . . there are better ways to buy life insurance."

But industrial life insurance is alive and well. While the total coverage has been declining slightly over the years, industrial insurance continues to collect $1.5 billion a year in premium payments, according to the American Council of Life Insurance, the chief industry trade group.

Some companies like Southwestern General have recently stopped selling new industrial policies, but they generally continue to collect on existing ones. Many sell other policies with different names that also require home collections by agents. Known as monthly debit ordinary policies, these are less expensive than industrial insurance but usually far more expensive than standard life insurance.

Collectively, policies requiring home collections are known as home service or debit policies. In all, there are 102 million of them in force. An estimated 90,000 agents specialize in this type of life insurance.

In comparing industrial rates with ordinary life insurance rates, the industrial companies point out that ordinary policies usually cannot be obtained for just $1,000 in coverage. While that is true, it obscures the fact that industrial policies are usually sold in multiples on the same individual. With the money a customer is paying for several industrial policies, he could get substantially more coverage from an ordinary policy.

Based on the same $150 in annual payments, for example, a person with $4,222 in industrial coverage from Southwestern General could buy $8,269 in coverage from Phoenix Mutual Life Insurance Company of Hartford, Connecticut. After keeping it twenty-two years, the Southwestern General customer would obtain a cash payment if he surrendered the policy of $1,397. The Phoenix Mutual customer would receive $8,269.

Taking into account the time value of money, the differences are even more stark. The rate of return on the death benefit would be about four times greater with the Phoenix Mutual policy, according to calculations on a Computone Systems, Inc. computer terminal. The rate of return if the policy is surrendered for cash would be 1.4 percent a year on the Phoenix Mutual policy, compared with a negative return for the Southwestern General policy.

For the sake of comparison, a term policy from Phoenix Mutual, for the same $150 in annual premiums, would provide $44,500 in coverage, or about ten times more than the Southwestern General industrial policy. All the comparisons include extra charges for making payments monthly and other policy provisions that normally come with industrial insurance.

While Southwestern is no longer selling new industrial policies, it continues to collect on the ones it has already sold.

G. Mason Connell, Jr., president of the Life Insurers Conference, a Richmond-based trade association composed primarily of home service companies, said industrial prices are only "slightly" higher than regular policies. He said that difference can be attributed to the fact that agents often collect in person, coverage is sold in small amounts, and many poor people have higher mortality rates. He noted that a committee of state regulators recently concluded that home service insurance serves a "useful social function" and that door-to-door collections do not necessarily raise the price of the coverage.

If that is true, it does not explain why industrial coverage recently turned a profit after taxes of twenty percent of the total income received by life insurance companies, or almost three times the profit margin of standard life insurance, according to filings with state regulators compiled by the American Council of Life Insurance.

"It's an organized system of exploitation," said Francis B. Stevens, an Antioch School of Law professor who has tried to help people who cannot collect death benefits on their industrial policies.

Usually, the idea of shopping for lower rates—or doing without life insurance entirely—never crosses policyholders' minds. Even if it did, the state insurance departments require no price disclosure that would permit them to make consistent comparisons. Indeed, the normally inscrutable price disclosure figures that must be given when ordinary insurance is sold are not required when industrial coverage is sold.

Many industrial agents say they did not realize they were bleeding the hungry, or if they did, the companies had convinced them they could not make it selling ordinary life insurance. Virginia Williams's agent, Zalmer J. Nichols, said the companies teach agents to mislead their customers.

"We wouldn't say how much it costs a month. You tell them how much it costs a week. It sounds good that way. You pick up [the money] when they get paid," Nichols said.

A key reason for buying industrial insurance is to pay for a funeral. According to many industrial agents, in selling industrial policies, the companies prey on the fears of the poor that they will be buried in "potter's fields," cemeteries where the indigent are buried by local governments. Yet the customers of industrial companies often are on welfare, which will pay for their burial. The companies teach agents to get around that, however.

"They taught me to say [that if buried by the city], you'll be buried in a plastic sack that they'll throw in the ground," Nichols said. "These people are uneducated."

"People like to talk about you," Cora Brown said, explaining why she bought her industrial policies. "I don't want them to say my son died and there was no money to bury him."

Inez Smith, a fifty-nine-year-old nurse in Norfolk, Virginia, finds it is difficult to pay $80 a month for twenty-two industrial policies that provide coverage of $500 to $2,000 on herself, her husband, and each of her nine children. One or two years of premium payments would equal the total benefits she would obtain if any one of her family members died now. Nevertheless, she said, "I've had it so long, and if I drop out now, it would be a waste. It's hard to get good insurance."

Often, customers do not know just how much coverage they have, how much they're paying, or what they're supposed to pay. "I'm paying $17.50 a month," Grace D. Covington, who lives in a low-income housing project, said when asked how much she pays for her eight industrial policies. But, after consulting the policies, she found she is paying $42.95 a month. Covington is spending ten percent of her welfare income for life insurance. What is it for? She shrugs, "I don't know. For my children."

In some cases, agents take advantage of customers' ignorance of how much they should be paying by collecting more than is due, according to former industrial agents. In these cases, the agents either pocket the money themselves, use it to cover temporarily other customers' payments, or give it to the company to apply against future payments, providing the companies with interest-free loans. It is easy for the agents to confuse customers, since the only record of payment they are given is a booklet where the agents scribble notations of payments.

Describing his training as an agent with Charlotte Liberty Mutual Insurance Company of Charlotte, North Carolina, Robert Lee testified before the Senate Judiciary's antitrust subcommittee in 1979, ". . . on my first day I was told, you just used a pencil . . . I assumed from what [the manager] told me it was because I was new and I would make mistakes that would have to be erased. But later on I found out that was not the reason at all. It was to actually erase things out of the book, to erase the marks we put on when we collected."

If the agent collects more than he should, he may record the true amount or he may show it in code. Either way, the policyholder has no reasonable way of figuring out that the amounts collected do not correspond to what has been paid. If questions are asked, the agent usually has a ready explanation.

"I've seen it written for a year in advance," said William F. Sullivan, a former assistant manager of Interstate Life Insurance Company of Chattanooga, Tennessee. The company has since been acquired by another. "These people get to trust the agent . . . he's the only financial person they know.

"It's wrong," he continued. "A lot of agents feel the same way, but they're scared to buck the companies. . . . People with a little education would never buy that type of policy. They would say it's ridiculous."

The debit book of Delphia Wilson of Leitchfield, Kentucky, shows that her agent has been charging an extra week's premium each month. Wilson, who is seventy-two and lives on Social Security payments, has no way of knowing. She has a speech impediment and can hardly communicate her most rudimentary needs.

Her agent said, "Nobody is trying to beat her." John T. Acree, III, the chairman of Lincoln Income Life Insurance Company of Louisville, Kentucky, said the extra money is credited to her policy with the company. After receiving an inquiry, he dispatched a vice-president to talk with her. He reported, said Acree, that she said she wants to pay ahead.

According to former agents, another common practice is purposely allowing a policyholder to fall behind in payments so new policies can be written at higher rates. Besides paying more, the policyholders lose any cash values they may have accumulated in the first year or two of coverage. They also lose an important protection. If a policyholder dies within two years of purchasing his policy, the insurance company may refuse to pay the death claim if it can prove that he lied about important information on his application. If, for example, he failed to list previous hospitalizations, his beneficiary may get no death benefit.

After two years, the policyholder is protected by what is known as the "incontestability clause." This prevents the insurance company from challenging a death claim even if the information on the application is wrong. A policyholder whose policy has been reissued must wait another two years before he is protected by this clause.

John D. Wilson, a former industrial agent with Citizens Home Insurance Company of Richmond, Virginia, said, "When they take you out [for training as a new agent], they say, 'There's a woman you can make some money on. I made some money. I'll show you . . . here's one four weeks behind, and if you don't go by there to collect, it will lapse.'

"If you can get a policy to lapse, you can rewrite it, and they're off the hook for the cash value and the two-year incontestability clause," said Wilson, referring to the company's right to challenge a claim. "The poor people out there have been bled to death."

Until it was acquired a few years ago by Independent Life Insurance Company of Jacksonville, Florida, Citizen's Home's rate book told agents in boldface type: "WRITE all that you can! COLLECT all that you can! LAPSE all that you can!"

At Charlotte Liberty Mutual Insurance Company, the practice of purposely lapsing policies was called "rolling," according to the Senate testimony of former agent Robert Lee. Lee told Senator Howard M. Metzenbaum (D–Ohio), chairman of the subcommittee, ". . . if a person was paying $10 a month and you wanted to increase your sales, you would say [to the policyholder], 'Well, this policy is ten or twelve years old. Why don't you get the cash value of this and take out another one?' And you would not tell the person that the premiums would be at the attained [current] age."

A chief reason for the high cost of industrial insurance is its high lapse rate—as much as seventy percent of new policies are canceled within a year. In comparison, the average industry rate for ordinary insurance is about nine percent.

"It comes down to the individual agent," Connell of the Life Insurers Conference said of the abuses. "I've heard stories of agents intentionally lapsing policies. It may very well be true in some instances. I can't say they're all pure as snow. We've seen some congressmen that are not honest, either."

■

Virginia E. Williams's black-tiled living room barely has room for a tiny Christmas tree. The sofas have holes in them, and they are covered with slip covers that have holes in them, too. The walls are covered with grime. In the winter, the walls sweat because there is no insulation, and the family wears sweaters and jackets in the house most of the time.

For three years, the toilet upstairs has leaked into the kitchen downstairs. Despite repeated complaints, the public housing authority will not fix it. Cockroaches crawl brazenly on the kitchen walls. A gas burner is kept on to compensate for the lack of adequate heating.

Williams has six children. Four of them and a one-year-old grandchild live with her. The three girls, ages twelve, eighteen, and nineteen, and the grandchild sleep in one room. A twenty-one-year-old son sleeps in another room. An additional child who is not living with Williams is insured as well.

Williams drives an ice cream truck, which costs $332 a month in loan payments alone. She may make $100 or more in a day, but her supplies often cost that much. Williams often does not come home until nine or ten in the evening, and she lives in constant fear of being robbed. Just recently, some boys with sawed-off shotguns held up someone in front of her truck.

Williams's husband is a construction worker who works sporadically. After the loan payments are made and new tires are bought, it is not clear how much they actually take home. However, they find they often cannot make the rental payment when it is due.

After former Southwestern General manager Zalmer Nichols explained to her that she was being taken advantage of, Williams began cashing in her thirty industrial policies. In many cases, she had bought policies, fallen behind in payments, and bought new ones to replace them. Most of the policies could not be cashed in because they had not yet accumulated enough in cash values.

Sitting at a picnic table that serves as the family's dining-room table, Williams said she did not know she could get more coverage at a lower price. Fingering the policies not yet cashed in, she displayed three policies costing $83.72 a year on DeWayne Adams, three costing $126.72 on Towanda Williams, three costing $150.60 a year on Dennen Williams, three costing $134 a year on Maria R. Williams, three costing $163.88 a year on Tyrone Williams, two costing $110.52 a year on Johnnice Williams, two costing $202.72 a year on John Williams, two costing $120.60 a year on William Dorsey, and three costing $258.72 a year on herself.

Now, she and her children each have roughly five times more coverage for $843 a year, compared with the $1,640 a year she was paying. Nichols said he tried to get her to buy coverage only on herself and her husband, since they have the income that would need replacing in the event of a death. "But she said as long as she is alive, she was going to have them covered. That was her responsibility," he said. "The agents prey on that fear. They'll try to cover everyone."

After cashing in six of the old policies, Williams got a letter from the then president of Southwestern General. In the letter, he urged Williams to reconsider cashing in her policies and return the $317.54 he was enclosing.

"In addition to the important insurance protection it [the coverage] provides, the value of your money increases each year, causing your net cost to decrease," he said. In making that statement, he had failed to take account of the cost or time value of money.

Referring to the poor people like Williams who buy such policies, he said in a telephone interview, "In a lot of instances, it's the only savings they have. . . . If we stripped them of that, it would take away their dignity and [ability to pay] for their last expenses themselves." He said agents should not load up customers with multiple policies. If they do, they should discuss rearranging the coverage with their customers so they will have just one policy. But he said many people like to have small policies. "It's inbred in the people who buy that type of insurance," he said.

Southwestern General's letter did not refer to its return on its industrial coverage. In a recent year, it earned income of seventeen percent after taxes on industrial policies, compared with nine percent for ordinary insurance. Asked about that, the then company president said the results are affected by the many older industrial policies that are not paying commissions to agents. Whatever the reason, Southwestern General makes twice as much selling industrial policies to poor people as it does selling to the more affluent.

After Nichols and two other Southwestern agents left the company, they began replacing their former customers' policies with ordinary insurance policies. Nichols and the two other agents, Clifford F. Powell and Daniel E. Baynard, then filed suit against the company, claiming its employees were spreading stories about them among their customers. The suit has since been settled.

As industrial agents, Powell and Baynard, both black, say they were taught to rip-off other blacks. They both entered the business for the money. Baynard began his career with Southwestern General in 1977 after serving in the Navy as an X-ray technician. At the time, he was making $9,000 a year. By putting in twelve-hour days, he quickly began making $16,500 selling industrial policies.

"At my third year in the business, I started asking questions," Baynard said. "But I was making a lot of money."

Powell started with Southwestern General in 1970. He, too, realized that what he was doing was wrong, but he said he feared he could not do as well selling ordinary insurance.

"You get locked into the security. You have to follow through. They brainwash you to death that you can't survive [selling ordinary insurance]," Powell said.

Both men left in 1981 to join Acacia Mutual Life Insurance Company of Washington.

While industrial agents, the two men said they learned how to collect more than is due, a practice known as collecting "blind advances." The policyholder is told to pay $5 for every $4 in premiums actually owed. The $4 figure is recorded in the debit book, while the agent records the $5 payment in his receipt book.

"Safety First—Keep Your Premiums Paid in Advance," Southwestern General's debit book suggests to policyholders.

Usually, customers do whatever the agent suggests. "People love their agent," Powell said. "If that man has been collecting for twenty years, you're going to have trust in him," he said.

Nichols, who was Powell's and Baynard's boss, takes some pride in having learned to perform all the tricks of the industrial life insurance business better than anyone else. He started as an industrial agent in 1974 with American National Insurance Company in Galveston, Texas. He moved to Southwestern General in 1979, becoming district manager in Waco, Texas.

As an industrial agent, Nichols said, he learned to perform all the abuses. "I moved up in it," he said. "I did it all." He said the system forces agents to write what he calls "inferior insurance." "What you have to do is make increases [let policies lapse and write new ones at higher prices], and a lot of people lapse because they can't afford it." If a policy lapses, a portion of the agent's commission is taken back, even if he did not write the original policy. That forces agents to keep looking for new first-year commissions, according to Nichols.

When "60 Minutes" ran an expose of industrial life insurance, he said, customers asked him if the policies they had bought from him were industrial. "I said, 'No, it was a different company.'"

■

Eva Mae Charlton has been paralyzed from the waist down since suffering a stroke twenty years ago. She has a tenth-grade education. Until several years ago, she was paying $672 a year for industrial life insurance policies from Citizens Home Insurance Company of Richmond. The $56 a month she was paying for insurance came out of the $171 a month she receives in welfare payments.

Charlton had policies on her own life, her children's lives, and on their children's lives. In many cases, she had several policies on the same person. Altogether, she had seventeen policies which she first began buying in 1967.

After paying a third of her income for life insurance, she had $115 a month left for feeding her daughter and three grandchildren. Often, she makes do by serving beans and bread for dinner. Her telephone has been disconnected for lack of payment.

"The agent said you got grandchildren you can insure," the fifty-six-year-old woman explained in her cramped Portsmouth, Virginia apartment. "I felt it was my duty at the time."

More recently, Citizens Home canceled all but one of her policies, because, according to Citizens Home, she had not been paying the weekly premiums. The result was that the cash values she had built up were canceled, even though Charlton said she always made the required payments to her agent.

Through her daughter, Charlton heard of Moulton, the Portsmouth, Virginia, agent who helps the poor to collect what meager money they can from the policies before replacing them.

Charlton's nearly illegible debit books show regular payments up to the time they were canceled. What they do not show is the numbers of the policies for which those payments were made. In fact, they list no policy numbers, depriving Charlton of any evidence that she had been paying for her insurance.

In a telephone call, Charlton's agent hung up when asked about her payment books.

Alexander H. Ware, Jr., then president of Citizens Home, said his agents do not lapse policies intentionally. Ware declined to discuss Charlton's case. Before he sold the company to another insurance concern, Ware earned a salary of $61,080 and received another $75,675 in stock dividends, according to documents filed by the company with the Virginia bureau of insurance. Ware sold the company to Independent Life and Accident Insurance Company of Jacksonville, Florida, for $16 million in cash.

Moulton asked the Virginia bureau of insurance to investigate Charlton's case. He alleged the new policies were issued without her knowledge, and that the signature on the applications had been forged, since she can barely sign her name. In a letter, then Virginia Insurance Commissioner James W. Newman, Jr., assured Charlton, "I will have a member of my staff investigate this matter." But the department has taken no action, and Charlton is still out the money she paid for the policies. Because of her age and disability, she cannot buy new policies.

"There's no way we can force the companies to give the money back," said Newman. "It's up to a court to handle." He said the practice of selling too many policies to one person is not illegal, and it is not for the court to intervene.

Newman has since resigned to join an insurance trade association.

■

Nineteen-year-old Michelle Noble is the unmarried mother of a five-year-old son. She has no job and is on welfare, which gives her $213 a month plus about $100 in food stamps. She lives with her grandmother in a two-bedroom apartment. Her son sleeps in her grandmother's room.

Recently, an agent for United Insurance Company of America, based in Chicago, sold her two home service policies called monthly debit ordinary. "I didn't shop around. He [the agent] came around. I thought about it for a few days. He was sort of talking fast," she said.

She is paying $22 a month for the two policies, one covering her life and one covering her son's life. After looking up the policies, she said she gets coverage of $5,000.

For that same payment, she could get $100,000 in term insurance coverage from Metropolitan Life Insurance Company and still have money left over during the next twenty years.

She feels the money is worth it. "It would help bury my son," she said. "Mainly, it would see he has a funeral."

■

Twenty-three-year-old Paulette said she went without food to help pay for thirteen life insurance policies sold to her by an agent of

Mutual Life Insurance Company of Washington, D.C. Paulette has three children. She lives in a two-bedroom apartment in a low-income housing project that smells of urine and is frequented by heroin addicts.

Her receipt book shows she had eleven policies costing $31.60 a month and another two that cost $4.60 a month. She had three policies covering one son; three covering the other son; two covering her daughter; and five on her own life. Her $36.20 monthly payment represented about half the $78 in rent she pays each month.

Altogether, Paulette was paying about eight percent of her total welfare income for life insurance. One policy was a fifteen-year-payment policy that cost $3.50 a month and gave her $1,000 in protection. A fifteen-pay policy means all the premiums are paid in the first fifteen years. To the policyholder, it sounds like a great deal. You pay for fifteen years, and then the coverage is free until you die.

In fact, because of the high up-front payments, this is one of the most expensive policies available. The money is paid in with valuable current dollars and is paid out in death benefits years later with dollars worth far less because of inflation. Taking account of the time value of money, the Mutual Benefit policy by the age of sixty-nine provides a negative return of −4.5 percent if it is surrendered for cash. In contrast, a policy of Phoenix Mutual Life Insurance Company of Hartford, Connecticut, provides a return if paid monthly of 3.7 percent.

After paying for three years, Paulette decided to cancel the policies when an agent from another company came around and claimed he could give her more insurance.

"It's for the kids to have something to fall back on," she said when asked why she was considering new coverage.

During the time she was paying $434 a year for her Mutual Benefit policies, Paulette could have bought $200,000 in straight term insurance protection for the same money, compared with a maximum of $3,000 in coverage she actually had.

After turning in the Mutual Benefit policies, she got back only a few hundred dollars in cash surrender values.

"It was tough," she said. "I had to go without food. The food stamps of $110 a month don't come until the seventh of the month, and he [the agent] collects on the first. I couldn't have soap powder. I would stretch my budget."

■

James Willie Jennings, an unemployed construction worker, has been paying $970 a year for eleven life insurance policies on himself, his wife, and three children. His payments represent forty percent of the rent he pays for his cramped, low-income housing-project apartment. For his money, Jennings get coverage of $1,000 to $5,000 on each of five family members.

"I feel I need it," he said. "I would use it for a funeral."

In fact, his thirty-two-year-old daughter died during an operation, and he collected $1,000 from one policy on her life. Since she was insured where she worked and had no children, there was no need for the life insurance. Jennings said he used the payment to help pay his own bills.

With the annual premiums he is paying, and the $599 in cash values he has built up, Jennings would almost have enough in two years to pay for a funeral without carrying life insurance. But no one has suggested that to Jennings.

An agent from another company advised Jennings that he could get more coverage at less cost by dropping his industrial policies. But Jennings said his agent insisted that could not be done.

"The [Southwestern General] agent said if I change insurance, I'd have to have a checking account," said Jennings, who had only a sixth-grade education. Jennings uses a money order to pay his rent. His agent told him only personal checks are accepted for payment of life insurance premiums.

■

William Moulton sold new and used cars before becoming an industrial life insurance agent in 1963. A big man who sounds like Jerry Lee Lewis, Moulton had sold industrial insurance for six different companies before he began questioning what he was doing. In particular, he recalls thinking it was strange being told to collect from policyholders in advance, without giving them a receipt.

"Of course, when this was taught to me, I asked several agents about this because it did not make good sense to me. And they told me that is the way the practice was," Moulton said. "I questioned the manager and assistant manager several times, and [they] said, 'Bill, you don't have to worry because the money is turned over to the insurance company. This is the way we do it.' So as an insurance agent I was taught by the industrial companies, I was programmed by the companies like so many other insurance agents today. They do not know that what they are doing is wrong. They really believe that this is what should be done because this is the way the industry has taught them."

Indeed, Moulton said he was not aware the rates were so high, or that he was being taught to "steal from people legally." In talking with another agent, Moulton had come to realize by 1973 that what he was doing was wrong and that other agents were also violating insurance laws and regulations. He decided to do something about it.

After fruitlessly exchanging thirty letters with the Virginia bureau of insurance and a company involved, Moulton took his charges to the Federal Bureau of Investigation, unaware the federal government is precluded by a special congressional exemption from regulating the life insurance business.

When he got no results, Moulton returned to the Virginia insurance authorities. Bringing along copies of debit books, he pinpointed which agents were collecting money they should not have been collecting. Three years later, the insurance department decided "widespread" violations had been occurring. It warned the companies to halt them or action would be taken.

Two years after that, the bureau disclosed that Southwestern General, as an outgrowth of the original investigation, had agreed to a cease-and-desist order barring it from engaging in further violations of the insurance laws. As part of the settlement, Southwestern General agreed to pay $10,500. In addition, twelve agents and managers agreed to pay $50 for each violation.

"We don't try to bankrupt the agents," explained then Virginia Insurance Commissioner James W. Newman, Jr.

Today, Moulton, wearing a large diamond ring and a suede sports jacket, acts as a sort of Robin Hood of the insurance industry. Thumbing his nose at the companies and the insurance departments, he intercedes on behalf of poor people like Charlton, analyzing their policies and writing letters to the companies to try to get their money back.

If they need insurance, he sells them policies at standard rates. "I make money on other people's greed," he says in his booming voice. If they do not need life insurance, or if it would be too expensive, he tells them to get rid of their policies and put their money in a bank account. "One thing I tell them is they don't need insurance on the kids. They need the money to live on," Moulton said.

The companies he sells for do not want their names brought into a controversy, he said. Historically, the life insurance industry has frowned upon replacing existing policies, a practice known as "twisting." Said Moulton, "The agents are trained not to replace policies. . . . The bureau of insurance tells companies you're hurting your industry [by replacing them]."

Newman, while still Virginia insurance commissioner, admitted, "If these people would shop around, they can do better, no question. . . . They can call [the companies] on the phone. Look them up in the phone book." But, echoing the industry watchword, he said, "Life insurance is sold, not bought."

■

William F. Smith, seventy, had fourteen industrial life insurance policies from United Insurance Company of America. In late 1981, Smith, who had worked as a laborer for a local water company for twenty-three years, had both his legs amputated during a one-month hospital stay, the result of complications from arteriosclerosis.

According to Smith's claim in a subsequent court suit filed on his behalf against United, Smith's agent continued to collect from him for at least two months before telling him that the two $1,000 policies written on his life provided benefits for the loss of limbs. The agent gave Smith a claim form, together with a section that had to be filled out by Smith's doctors. Smith gave the completed form to the agent on March 15, 1982.

"During the next four months, while continuing to collect premiums from Mr. Smith, [the agent] twice requested the Smiths and their doctors to complete additional claim forms, including some that had previously been submitted," according to allegations in a complaint filed by Smith's lawyer, who is representing him free of charge.

"With regard to the first such request, [the agent] explained variously that the original form submitted to him on March 15, 1982, had been misplaced, or that, contrary to his initial representation, at least two forms were required," the papers say.

According to affidavits submitted in the suit, Smith's lawyer, in a letter to the agent, urged him to expedite the claim. "The Smiths, who are longstanding customers of your company, have had a traumatic experience in regard to the operations that prompted them to file this claim. I am sure that you and your company would not want to aggravate this situation," the letter from the lawyer said.

Nevertheless, United then lost the second form, according to the agent's deposition testimony. The agent called Smith's wife on July 12, 1982, saying she would have to return to her husband's doctors yet a third time and ask them to complete the same forms, since Smith himself can neither read nor write. United did not accept the final papers until mid-July 1982, after "repeated phone calls to [the agent] and the national claim office by counsel for Mr. Smith," according to motion papers submitted by Smith's lawyer.

Yet the Smiths' problems had only begun. The Chicago-based company informed Smith that United believed it was only obliged to pay for the loss of one limb, not two, because, according to the complaint, the legs had been lost in two separate operations. Quoting from the policies, Smith's lawyer argued that the policies say they will pay the full amount of the insurance "[u]pon receipt of due proof" that the insured has suffered "the loss by severance of both hands or both feet." Since Smith submitted proof that he had lost his legs in a single claim, the policy requires payment for loss of both legs, the lawyer said.

In late July, United informed the Smiths that it was about to mail them two checks for $500, representing benefits from the two policies for the loss of one leg. A month passed without the checks or any word from United. In September, the agent told Smith that he had the checks at his office. On September 7, Smith's lawyer wrote to the agent, requesting the checks. Finally, on September 13, United sent the checks to Smith's lawyer.

In response to the suit, United admitted that it had lost the original set of claim forms submitted by the Smiths. It admitted it had requested a second set and then requested a third set after losing the second set. The company also admitted that the third set had not been submitted to United's national office until repeated telephone calls had been made by Smith's lawyer to the agent and to the company. United denied, however, any subsequent delays, and it denied that it is obligated to pay more than the $1,000 it already sent Smith as payment for his loss. Yet there is enough in United's admissions to illustrate just how backward the industrial life insurance companies are when it comes to making good on their promises and how insensitive they can be to human suffering.

United has since settled the case by paying the Smiths $10,000.

■

James R. Montgomery III, deputy superintendent of insurance for the District of Columbia, said industrial companies sometimes make additional money by strictly interpreting the clause in life insurance policies that permits them to challenge a death claim up to two years after a policy is issued.

When applying for insurance, he said, consumers are asked to answer questions about their health. Paid on commission, the agent has "every incentive" to answer "no, no, no" to questions asking if the policyholder had previous health problems, Montgomery said. When the policyholder dies and a death claim is presented, the companies investigate and find out the answers were not filled out truthfully. At that point, it's the agent's word against the dead man's, and the companies deny the claim.

"The people are semiliterate. The deceased is six feet under the ground. Who is going to say the agent lied?" Montgomery said. He has asked the District of Columbia government for a legal opinion on whether he can declare the clauses as written to be illegal but has yet to receive an answer.

"The regulations are not enforced at all," according to Moulton. "If the commissioner started fining them, they'd get another commissioner."

By setting up industrial life as a separate class of insurance, the states actually give it preferred treatment. Legal Services of Nashville, Tennessee, found thirteen requirements that apply to ordinary insurance but not to industrial insurance. For example, agents are prohibited from selling ordinary insurance but not industrial policies until they have passed their state licensing examination.

Moulton feels many of the abuses would be eliminated if insurance departments banned cash collections. After all, power and telephone companies do not collect in cash, except through banks that issue valid receipts. By establishing strict limits on commissions and laying down other rules in 1966, New York State virtually abolished industrial life insurance in that state. The rules prevent agents from selling several industrial policies within a short time span to the same individual and from charging more for industrial insurance than the cost of ordinary life insurance.

Montgomery, calling industrial insurance "legalized discrimination," has proposed eliminating the legal distinctions between industrial and ordinary insurance altogether. That way, the standards that apply to the sale of standard insurance would also apply to industrial insurance, bringing the cost down. "If anybody ever needed low-cost life insurance, it's people at the lower socioeconomic level," he said.

But Montgomery, who has served as chairman of the National

Association of Insurance Commissioners' cost disclosure committee, said there is little chance of those reforms coming about. He
said that coming up with sweeping changes that would properly
disclose what consumers are getting from industrial and other types
of life insurance policies would require more expertise and political
clout than state insurance departments possess.

6. THE NEW POLICIES

■ "Yields on whole life insurance are low. It isn't a good investment. I can show you twenty textbooks that refer to the 'savings' element in whole life insurance. They're wrong: it isn't savings. And there isn't any question about it, annual renewable term insurance is the cheapest form of life insurance."

So said M. Gordon Gaddy, a longish-haired young man from San Mateo County, California, in a 1979 *Wall Street Journal* article. More recently, Gaddy has been taking out advertisements in the *Journal* and life insurance industry publications warning that the life insurance industry will "self-destruct" if it does not offer policies with better returns.

LIFE INSURANCE IS THE ONLY INDUSTRY THAT TRIES TO KEEP PEOPLE FROM TRADING IN THEIR OBSOLETE PRODUCT FOR A NEW, IMPROVED VERSION, the headline on one such ad read.

As the *Journal* article pointed out, Gaddy is hardly a Federal Trade Commission official, nor is he a Ralph Nader–style consumer advocate. He is president and chief operating officer of American Express Company's Fireman's Fund American Life Insurance Companies.

But in the life insurance game, what you see is rarely what you get. As we shall find out in this chapter, life insurance companies commonly sell "new" policies as answers to the abuses of the "old" whole life insurance. In reality, they are selling the same old whole life policies that, in some cases, are among the most expensive available. The consumer caught in this particular snare thinks he has gotten a good buy. In fact, he has become a victim of yet another ruse in the life insurance game.

Gaddy's product is a prime example. His unconventional approach has earned him the ire of many in the life insurance industry, as well as steadily increasing sales. If he knocks the industry in general, and whole life in particular, he must be offering a very desirable policy, or so one might think.

But rather than offering a cheaper term insurance policy, Gaddy's policy—called deposit term—is actually a whole life policy combined with an annuity. Moreover, while the annuity is attractive enough, the whole life policy is among the most expensive policies sold. One reason is it requires a steep initial payment in the first year. Taking account of the time value of money, a thirty-two-year-old male who buys Gaddy's policy winds up paying far more than for almost any other term insurance policy available. After thirty-eight years, the policyholder has paid about as much as he would have for a whole life policy of Prudential Insurance Company of America or Metropolitan Life Insurance Company. At that point, the Fireman's Fund policy pays a cash surrender value, but it is so insignificant that it actually represents a negative rate of return.

If Gaddy has accomplished anything, it is to unite critics and defenders of the industry. Herbert S. Denenberg, the former Pennsylvania insurance commissioner who turned life insurance sales practices into front-page stories in the early 1970s, said the Fireman's Fund policy ". . . is structured to lead to misrepresentation and misunderstanding, is a likely tool of fraud and deception, and is another sorry example of life insurance by confusion and by proliferation and profusion of policy forms. It should not be approved for sale."

New England Mutual Life Insurance Company of Boston, in a memorandum distributed to its agents, said, "We think deposit term, as currently constituted, is often sold on a misleading basis and in many instances proves to be detrimental to the financial well-being of consumers."

Brushing aside the criticism, Gaddy said in an interview that an evaluation of what is called the company's LifeCycle package should include the annuity. "You have to look at both parts," he said.

What Gaddy is suggesting is that two separate financial products should be evaluated as if they are one. Most other companies would be glad to sell an annuity tacked onto a life insurance policy. It would bring them more money, and it would make their policies look better. The fact is, any policy would come out looking better if an annuity were added to it. Gaddy's point is akin to saying you should compare the nutrients in a dry cereal by including the vitamins and minerals in the milk it is served with—while neglecting to add milk to the competitor's product.

In describing the policy, Gaddy repeatedly refers to it as a term policy, even though he admits, when questioned on the point, that it's really a whole life policy. In the life insurance industry, it is possible to call a whole life policy a term insurance policy, just as it is possible to temper criticisms leveled against an old policy by calling it a new policy.

In this chapter, we will examine how that works by looking at three widely publicized new policies. One, sold by Academy Life Insurance Company and other companies, is known as a group policy that is sold primarily to older people. The second is a term insurance policy sold by some 70,000 agents who work for A. L. Williams. The third is universal life insurance, sold by a growing number of companies as an answer to the criticisms of whole life insurance.

■

You have probably seen Academy Life's commercials on television. A succession of public personalities—from singer Burl Ives and actor Harry Morgan to John S. D. Eisenhower, the late President's only son—have solicited business for the company.

In one commercial, Bob Barker, master of ceremonies for the Miss Universe Pageant and host of CBS's "The Price is Right," sits on a white sofa. Conveying the impression that he—like you, the listener—has been through a lot, he holds up a savings account passbook.

"Hello, I'm Bob Barker," he says. "If you're between the ages of forty-five and seventy-five, could I take just a moment of your time? Most of us work hard, all of our lives, to make our *savings* worth something, and the last thing we ever want is for our death, or the death of our spouse, to deplete or even *wipe out* our savings.

"Since life insurance can become so expensive, or even impossible to get as we get older, a lot of folks just can't afford the life insurance they need. That's why the National Alliance of Senior Citizens, a nonprofit organization, is now sponsoring a group life insurance plan specifically for people forty-five to seventy-five. But this plan is unique, in several very important ways.

"First, you can't be turned down or canceled on the basis of your health. Second, neither your current health, nor your future health, will have any bearing on the premium you pay. Third, your premium will *never* go up. Fourth, this policy builds cash values you can withdraw should you ever need them.

"And most important, instead of paying interest rates of three to five percent like most other whole life policies, this policy pays current high interest rates. Right now, it's paying twelve percent. So you have the comfort of knowing that even your life insurance is earning interest at today's high rates. Best of all, you can get this coverage for only *five dollars a month*."

The announcer cuts in to give listeners a toll-free number they can call to get a free information kit. "Operators are standing by," the announcer says.

The kit comes in a big brown envelope with red and green writing. A glassine window displays the "current interest rate" of twelve percent. Inside is a "personal message" from Barker, an assortment of enrollment forms and brochures, and a letter from W. Benjamin Weaver, president of Academy Life.

"Congratulations!" it says. "Because you meet certain requirements, you are guaranteed you cannot be turned down for a new group whole life insurance plan called High Interest Life. That's right, this guarantee is being extended to you because you're between the ages of 45–75."

One burgundy-colored folder says it should only be opened "if you've decided not to enroll in High Interest Life." It contains a letter from Eisenhower, who makes $33,999 a year as chairman of Academy Life, urging the consumer to reconsider.

"I can't stress enough how important adequate life insurance protection is to you and your family," he says. Another message from Eisenhower says the policy is a good way to fight inflation: "The only thing that goes up is your cash value, which builds at higher interest rates than most life insurance policies."

Still another brochure explains that a $1 annual membership fee in the National Alliance of Senior Citizens will be added on to the cost of the life insurance. The Falls Church, Virginia, group offers discounts to members on such items as travel, prescription drugs, and car rentals. By sponsoring Academy Life's policies, the group has made $700,000 in about two years, according to Curt Clinkscales, national director of the group.

The kit's literature says many life insurance companies have strict requirements about who can qualify for coverage. Often, questions about an applicant's previous hospitalizations and ailments are asked, and a physical examination by a doctor is required. Even then, one brochure says, the applicant may be rejected or charged an extra premium because of his medical condition. With the Academy Life policy, that cannot happen.

The brochure does not explain how Academy Life is able to accept all health risks. However, a footnote to one chart gives a clue. It says death benefits in the first year of coverage are only ten percent of the amount purchased. If you die in the second year of coverage, the death benefit is twenty-five percent of the full amount.

In other words, the consumer gets virtually no coverage in the first or second year the policy is in effect. That's fine if he is aware of it. But a footnote in a sales brochure is hardly adequate disclosure.

This type of coverage is known as a guaranteed issue, graded death benefit policy. It is not sold by most of the more established life insurance companies.

A brochure explaining a similar Academy Life policy offered through the National Alliance of Senior Citizens is more explicit than the one for the first policy. It says the reduction in death benefits in the first two years "allows Academy Life to guarantee your acceptance, no matter what health conditions you may have."

What the material does not say is that the Academy Life policies are, in fact, quite high-priced. Taking Academy's word that the cost of guaranteeing acceptance is covered by reducing the death benefits initially, the consumer gets coverage that is considerably more expensive than other traditional whole life policies paid on a monthly basis.

For example, a forty-five-year-old male who pays $17 a month for the second Academy Life policy aimed at senior citizens gets coverage of $3,387. For the same price, he could get coverage of $7,813 with a standard policy from Phoenix Mutual Life Insurance Company of Hartford, Connecticut. If he turns in the policy after fifteen years, he gets $946 in cash from Academy, compared with $2,226 from Phoenix Mutual.

Despite the promises of a twelve percent return, there is no guarantee the first policy would pay any more than the second. The policy itself said only that "excess interest" will be credited to the policy. It does not define what "excess interest" is, nor does it illustrate how much money twelve percent would pay.

The company decides if it has "excess interest." By the time a policyholder turns in his policy, the rate could have been lowered to four percent. Even if the policy continues to pay at the rate of twelve percent, the cash value would amount to only $1,716 after fifteen years, according to the company—still below the amount Phoenix Mutual pays.

That might seem odd. A return of twelve percent sounds hefty. Yet the cash values paid are still below those of a Phoenix Mutual whole life policy. The reason is the 12 percent return is not a 12 percent return. It's really a negative return. For example, if the policy is turned in for cash after fifteen years, the return on premiums paid is −8.2 percent a year, according to calculations performed with a Computone computer terminal.

The twelve percent advertised rate is actually a gross return. Before the consumer gets the money, the company subtracts its expenses for selling and providing the insurance. That only makes sense. The company could not pay a twelve percent return on your premiums and still pay all its selling expenses and death benefits.

As it happens, Academy's expenses are considerable. The company's filings with state insurance commissioners do not break down the financial results of each policy sold. However, they give overall results of group insurance sales. In a recent year, according to those statements, Academy paid out as benefits less than twenty percent of its income from sales of group life insurance policies. That compares with an industry average for group insurance of sixty-five percent, according to figures compiled by the American Council of Life Insurance. In other words, the average company pays out three times more than Academy for each dollar received.

Many of Academy's overall expenses are paid to companies affiliated with Academy Life's parent company, Academy Insurance Group Inc. of Valley Forge, Pennsylvania. The parent company, whose stock is traded over-the-counter, earned an after-tax profit recently of $9.8 million on total income of $71.3 million.

In a recent year, Academy paid out $4.9 million to Unicom Administrative Services, Inc., a subsidiary of the parent company that does billing and accounting; $8.6 million to Ammest Life Insurance Company, a second subsidiary, for reinsuring some of Academy's coverage; and $3.5 million as commissions on sales to Ammest Services, Inc., another subsidiary.

In addition to related-party payments, Academy paid $6.3 million to R. M. Marketing Inc. of Valley Forge, which does Academy's advertising, and $7 million to Insurance Marketing Associates of Valley Forge. These companies are not connected with Academy Life or its parent company.

It is not clear who owns Insurance Marketing. It has no telephone listing in Valley Forge, and Academy would not divulge any information about it. R. M. Marketing, on the other hand, has its offices a floor above Academy's in a templelike, ten-story office building.

Weaver, who makes $223,279 a year as president of Academy and executive vice-president and chief operating officer of the parent company, said he would answer questions about the company's policies only in writing. In several lengthy letters, he said Academy saves money by not using agents and is providing insurance coverage that many people otherwise could not obtain at any price. For that reason, he said, Academy's policies cannot be compared fairly with other companies' policies.

In his response, he said Academy is making life insurance "available to people in lower income groups who are no longer adequately being served by other life insurance companies."

Weaver had an actuarial firm respond to the question of whether Academy's policies are high in cost. The firm concluded that the Academy policies will actually produce a thirty-four percent higher payout than the Phoenix Mutual policies for the same price. It based that conclusion on Academy's estimates of death rates and costs, rather than the actual prices and values of the policies. Moreover, the firm said reducing the death benefits in the first two years of coverage does not cover the cost of taking all health risks.

Weaver is right that some people—about two percent of all applicants—are rejected for life insurance and could benefit from Academy's policies. Another five percent of all applicants must pay a higher premium. A terminal cancer patient who dies within six months of buying an Academy Life policy would provide his beneficiary with a death benefit of $339, or about triple the $102 premium paid to Academy during the six-month period.

But what about the vast majority of people who are in good health? Claiming it is giving them "group rates," Academy actually pays benefits that are one-half the benefits they could receive with the same premium at another company.

Should they be warned not to buy Academy's policies? Absolutely not, Weaver said, explaining that would raise costs to everyone. "No life insurance company discourages people who believe they are in good health from buying life insurance," he said.

If Academy's policies are so much more expensive than other companies', how can Academy call its prices "group rates" that are lower than rates for individual insurance? According to Weaver, no comparisons can be made with group coverage. "Even if there were a 'standard' group policy . . . there are so many differences between the Academy policies and most group policies that a meaningful comparison is not possible," he said.

If a meaningful comparison is not possible, why does Academy make that comparison on the front cover of its brochure? The answer, of course, is that a comparison is possible, but it shows Academy's policies are far more expensive than the "group rates" it seeks to identify with. Rather than substantiating its claim to offering group rates, Academy brushes aside the question by claiming the two types of policies are not, in fact, comparable.

Finally, of what real value is a policy that pays death benefits ranging from as little as $23 to as much as $4,240, when that does not begin to replace the average American's annual income— which averages $20,521 for a male and $12,083 for a female? Weaver had no specific answer, but Academy Life appeared to have answered the question in another commercial for a different policy.

This one, featuring actor Merlin Olsen, begins with a conversation between a husband and wife:

WIFE: Tim, when are we going to get more insurance? Our $100,000 life insurance policy wouldn't even replace one year of your income.
HUSBAND: Look, I know we need more insurance, but right now, we just can't afford it.
OLSEN: That's probably not true. Hi! I'm Merlin Olsen. Now there's a way that anyone under the age of sixty-five can get $100,000 of insurance protection for only thirty to forty cents a day: Academy Life's $100,000 Plus Plan pays $100,000 should your death result from any covered accident.

As the wife depicted in the commercial points out, even $100,000 in life insurance may not replace the annual income of many wage earners. Another Academy brochure aimed at veterans makes the same point: it says that even $10,000 to $20,000 in life insurance will make little difference in replacing income lost by the death of a spouse. In view of Academy's own advertising, how does Academy justify selling $4,240 or less in life insurance coverage?

Weaver answered by saying that even a few thousand dollars of life insurance has some value. Perhaps, but not when it costs twice as much as coverage that can be purchased from other companies.

"The guaranteed issue policy is very bad for the public," said Donald D. Cameron, vice-president for product development of Massachusetts Mutual Life Insurance Company of Springfield, Massachusetts, the eleventh-largest in the life insurance business. "People don't read that the death benefit is reduced. The people are just being overcharged."

■

"I am trying to contact you concerning a management position currently available with our company," the buff-colored, handwritten postcard said. "If you are interested in discussing this further, call me at my office." The postcard was signed "Ken Brooks." It had no return address or company name, nor was the type of management job stated.

A call to Brooks produced the information that he works for A. L. Williams. "We are a financial services firm," Brooks explained. "We do a lot of business in tax-deferred annuities and retirement plans. The type of person we are looking for has leadership abilities. Does that describe you?" he asked.

This is one way the Atlanta-based A. L. Williams organization recruits. Another is to leave similarly cryptic notes on windshields in parking lots. If flattery does not work, money does.

A. L. Williams is right up front. "Start MAKING MONEY right now— today," a recent bulletin to agents said. "You do the 'NASTIES' first— show your people how to prospect every day! recruit every day! field train every day! sell every day! Compete: Let's go to BOCA, LONDON, SCOTLAND!!"

The bulletin lists the total commissions paid to A. L. Williams: seventy-five percent of the first year premium payment, ninety-six percent of the second year premium payment, another forty percent of the annual payment if the policy remains in force more than a year, and another one hundred percent of the annual payment over the next ten years.

"Incredible!!!" the bulletin says.

Indeed, A. L. Williams is incredible. In 1967, Art Williams was making $10,700 a year as coach of the Kendrick High School football team in Columbus, Georgia. To supplement his income, he had been selling Christmas trees and refereeing basketball games. Then he tried selling life insurance door-to-door. Finding that he was making more from that than from coaching, he began selling full-time in 1971. With a growing following of agents, he formed the A. L. Williams organization in 1977.

Now a multimillionaire, Williams has some 80,000 agents who carry pictures of their baby-faced leader in their sales literature and listen to rousing pep talks that hold out the possibility they could have six-figure incomes. Recently, the Williams group brought in new annual premiums of more than $150 million. Another one thousand new agent applications are received each week.

In the parlance of the life insurance industry, A. L. Williams is an "agency." That means it is a group of agents who sell the policies of one company. In this case, the company is Massachusetts Indemnity & Life Insurance Company of Boston, Massachusetts, a company founded in 1927. Technically, Williams is but a sales tool of the Massachusetts company. In fact, the Atlanta-based Williams group accounts for more than half of the insurance company's business.

The new business figures of Massachusetts Indemnity tell the story. In 1978, it issued $13.6 million in new term insurance coverage. In 1979, it issued $20 million. In 1980, the figure jumped to $3.6 *billion* in new term insurance coverage. In those same years, the percentage of policies that lapsed—a measure of how efficiently a life insurance company is run—rose from thirteen percent to twenty-six percent.

The secret to low costs, according to Francis E. Ferguson, chairman of Northwestern Mutual Life Insurance Company, is a low lapse rate. "If you have to rewrite your business every four years, the people who remain have to pay a hell of a price for it," said Ferguson, whose company has a lapse rate of under six percent.

Within the life insurance industry, the Williams organization is controversial, if not notorious. Executives of the more established companies mutter about Williams as if he were selling hot stocks. If you really want a story, look into Williams, they suggest.

"As the new guy on the block, we specialize in making mincemeat out of all the big major life companies," said William S. Woodside, chairman of American Can Company, which recently acquired Massachusetts Indemnity by buying its parent, PennCorp Financial, Inc. of Santa Monica, California. "Frankly, I have been amused and a little bit amazed at the life industry's reaction to A. L. Williams," he said in a *National Underwriter* interview. "I experienced the same thing as an old-line producer of cans when new companies, unburdened by old plant and investments and with no unions, competed against us."

The Williams pitch is simple: Drop whole life insurance, buy term insurance, and invest the difference in premiums. The organization provides both the term insurance and the investment vehicle—a choice of mutual funds or other investments. There is no catch—or so Williams's agents tell customers.

"What we try to do is help families, help people," Brooks, who had sent the recruiting postcard, said. "Do you understand whole life? Nobody does. Pretty much it's a rip-off product. Without them spending a penny more, we can give them more coverage and a savings plan or mutual fund investments. We are a marketing company. Our system works. It's an excellent program. The insurance industry is very wealthy as a result of whole life. They own a lot of buildings. We're trying to put that money back in the products," Brooks said.

To learn more about A. L. Williams, Brooks suggested a visit to a seminar the organization holds twice a week. The seminar was held in a cramped, basement room of a suburban office building on a Tuesday evening. People signed in with the name of the agent who recruited them. On the walls were color posters showing a football player presumably about to make a touchdown and a blond family sitting in front of a tree.

DO IT WITH A. L. WILLIAMS, the football poster said. A. L. WILLIAMS CHANGED MY WHOLE LIFE, the other one said.

"It doesn't say if it was for better or worse," one of thirteen people waiting for the seminar commented. "What are they selling?" asked another, wondering if she had heard the A. L. Williams name on the news. The people represented a range of backgrounds: a personable, well-dressed man who works for a savings and loan association; a pudgy young man wearing a yarmulke; an older man who professed to know all about the financial world; and an Indian woman who said nothing.

Promptly at 7:30 P.M., a big man with shaggy, light brown hair began setting up printed posters on a board in front of the room. "I'm Lou Florimbio, and I'm a regional vice-president of A. L. Williams," he said, later noting there are more than twenty-five regional vice-presidents in his area alone.

"Art Williams saw the American consumer is being gouged," he said. "We have a lot of enemies out there. We are controversial. . . . There's no way that they can stop us at this point."

Drawing on the board, Florimbio compared "Company A" and "Company B." Company A gives you a return on your investment of 1.3 percent. It does not give you any interest if you withdraw your money in the first two to three years. If you want to withdraw your money temporarily, it charges you five percent to eight percent as interest for borrowing your own money. If you die, it keeps all your money.

Company B, on the other hand, gives you interest whenever you take out your money. The rate of return is five percent to eight percent. You can withdraw your own money without being charged interest. And it gives back all your money if you die.

What is Company A? Florimbio asked. The answer came back: A company that sells whole life insurance. What is Company B? he asked. A. L. Williams, someone said. No, it's a bank, Florimbio said.

But, he went on, you can put your money in a bank if you buy a Williams term insurance policy.

Florimbio proceeded to explain about the time value of money and how inflation eats away at whole life insurance coverage. He frequently referred to state insurance department prohibitions on making certain statements. "Sometimes, we're not the cheapest," he said.

Drawing on the board, he outlined A. L. Williams's commissions, showing how the agent, his sales leader, his district leader, his division leader, his regional vice-president, and his senior vice-president get to split the money. In addition to sales commissions, agents get $240 in commissions for each person they recruit.

"The average regional vice-president's income is $103,000," he said. "We have two regional vice-presidents for every one hundred people who come to these meetings."

He pointed out that state insurance laws permit applicants to sell for ninety days using a temporary license that requires no examination.

Later, he charged one dollar for a packet of literature and applications to join and to buy a policy. Everyone is expected to buy a policy, he said. The packet includes a glowing cover story about Williams from *The Saturday Evening Post*. The packet also includes a reprint of a 1979 Federal Trade Commission press release claiming whole life policies yield an average return of one to two percent. Instructions to agents inserted in the reprint say no marks should be made on the report before it is given to consumers.

After the meeting, the man from the savings and loan association stopped to talk with the agent who recruited him. Later, he said he thought he'd apply.

"This is what America is all about," he said. "We're entering this new realm of financial services, and we're going to beat everybody."

To find out how the Williams organization actually sells its policies, we will listen to a sales presentation by one of A. L. Williams's more than one thousand regional vice-presidents.

Driving a powder-blue Cadillac, the agent pulled up to a potential customer's home. The agent wore a three-piece, smartly tailored, brown suit with a pin depicting a termite in the lapel. ("Termite" is what agents who sell whole life call sellers of term insurance.)

A Williams agent for three years, he asked to use the dining-room table for his presentation. He pulled out a bound volume of color pictures and charts and began flipping the pages.

"Are you interested in saving money?" he began. After getting the expected response, he added, "We believe people need to build assets. What is your most important asset?" When told it is salary, he said, "You need protection against loss of that income. Once it is protected, we recommend an emergency cash fund." Turning the page, he displayed a picture of Williams surrounded by blue-suited agents. "We show people they have choices," he said.

Explaining how whole life works, he said you cannot have a death benefit *and* a cash payment with whole life. "You can only have one of them at a time," he said.

For the same cost, he explained, A. L. Williams can double the coverage provided by a whole life policy, freeing up additional funds for investing. After fifteen years, the consumer's need for life insurance is probably decreasing, he said. At that time, the policy becomes a decreasing term policy, providing steadily reducing coverage.

Asked how Williams's rates compare, the agent said, "They compare excellently with other term policies."

When comparing with other companies' policies, he did not include the dividends that they frequently pay. He explained that dividends are not guaranteed and therefore should not be considered. Yet he freely cited equally hypothetical returns on Williams's investment funds, which are also not guaranteed.

"We never sell anybody on the first visit," he said. "We would borrow your policies and do a computer analysis. We would do a side-by-side comparison. At that time, we would submit an application."

He ended the presentation with a Williams-approved line: "Would you do business with me if I offer more coverage and more cash accumulation? Would you then recommend me to five of your friends?"

He left copies of articles attacking whole life, along with a copy of the A. L. Williams "constitution." Sounding like the Boy Scout oath, it says, "Sell only term insurance, make no sale on the first call, use no gimmicks or pressure, provide full information. . . . Never mislead or exaggerate, provide prompt service, use only approved sales material, sell quality business. . . ."

One of the brochures showed that Williams's UltimaTerm policy is far cheaper than any other policy, including a term insurance policy from Occidental Life Insurance Company of Los Angeles. But there is one problem: the Williams organization rarely sells an UltimaTerm policy by itself. It sells the coverage as a rider, or attachment, to a far more expensive term policy. That policy, called fifteen-year Modified Term, starts out with a very high first-year premium—$424 for $100,000 in coverage. In contrast, the first-year premium for the same coverage with Occidental is $218. With Metropolitan Life Insurance Company, it is $155.

Indeed, based on the combination of policies as normally sold, Williams sells one of the more expensive term insurance policies. Taking account of the time value of money, the Occidental policy is fifteen percent to twenty percent cheaper than the Williams policy. The Metropolitan term policy is about a third cheaper than the Williams term policy for the same amount of coverage.

When asked later about cost, the agent said Williams policies are expensive but they have to be, to cover the commissions required to sell them. "I don't claim we are the cheapest, but we have to get paid," he said. Because they don't pay high enough commissions, the cheaper policies offered by other companies aren't pushed by their agents, he said. He said Williams's term policies, even if they are more expensive, are still preferable to buying whole life.

He is right about that. But does that excuse giving out incomplete cost comparisons or leading consumers to think that Williams's prices are in any way competitive when they are not?

■

"Where can you get one of the highest tax-deferred—or tax-free—yields on your savings? Try life insurance. Yes, life insurance," said a 1981 *Wall Street Journal* article on universal life insurance. Calling the development "a real breakthrough for consumers," the *Journal* article said, "An entirely new breed of whole life products, currently offering yields of more than ten percent, is finally bringing traditional life insurance that incorporates a savings feature into the 1980s."

"Universal life and variable life are by far the most exciting new instruments ever produced by the industry and seem to have the highest growth potential," gushed *Business Week*. "'For long term savings, I know of nothing that beats it,'" the magazine quoted a life insurance executive as saying.

AT LAST—AN ALMOST IDEAL POLICY, said the headline in *Money* magazine.

If you have been closely watching the moves in the life insurance game, you should be getting suspicious by now. Only one financial writer suggested that universal life may not, in fact, be the greatest thing since sliced bread. When the new policy started to take off in 1981, columnist Jane Bryant Quinn wrote, "You cannot ... take those advertised rates at face value. They are not comparable with the interest rates offered on other savings vehicles."

Citing findings of William C. Scheel, associate professor of finance and insurance at the University of Connecticut, Quinn noted, "That '11 percent interest' that sounds so nifty in the ads is paid only on what's left [after commissions and other expenses are taken out]." She advised, "For the most bang for the buck, it still makes sense to buy a low-cost term insurance policy and keep your savings somewhere else."

E. F. Hutton Life Insurance Company, a subsidiary of the brokerage firm, introduced universal life in 1978. The new design was based on a proposal made in 1975 by James C. H. Anderson, an Atlanta actuary, as a response to criticism of whole life insurance as an inflexible policy that doesn't make sense during inflationary times.

Universal life is identical to whole life except that the consumer can determine the level of death benefits and cash values he wants to develop. With whole life, the ratio between these two variables is fixed. With universal life, the consumer can say he wants a higher death benefit and lower cash values, or just the opposite, based on his needs.

In addition, the cash values of a universal life policy vary based on fluctuating rates that move with market conditions. They usually cannot go below four percent a year, but could go as high as fifteen percent or more. With traditional whole life, the cash values, while guaranteed, cannot go higher than the original stated amount.

Usually sold with an elaborate computer illustration, universal life is usually described as paying high yields that are tax-sheltered—making it sound like a high-flying investment.

Without a computer analysis, there is no way to tell that universal life is, in fact, better than any other whole life policy. What's more, the cash values of a universal life policy are subject to the same tax treatment as whole life. As with an annuity, any gain beyond the premiums paid are taxable when they are received.

Because the advertised rates of return are gross rates of return, only a computer analysis can show what you really get from universal life. In contrast to the advertised claims, this kind of analysis shows that universal life at many comparison points is worse than whole life.

In the early years the policy is in effect, the policyholder, if he dies, has gotten a slightly better deal with the universal life policy. However, by the thirty-eighth year, his beneficiary would have done better with the whole life policy, according to data from Computone Systems, Inc. of Atlanta.

If he turns the policy in for cash, as most policyholders do, he will have done much better with the traditional whole life policy. After seven years, for example, the rate of return, if the policyholder cashes in the policy, is 1.5 percent for the whole life policy, compared with −16.6 percent for the universal life policy. After twenty-two years, the whole life policy returns 7 percent, compared with 0.4 percent for universal life. After thirty-eight years, the whole life policy returns 7 percent, compared with 3.3 percent for the Hutton policy, according to the Computone figures. If the universal life premium is increased to the level of the whole life premium, the cash-in value will look better, but the return on the death benefit will look worse than with whole life.

Whole life will not always look better than universal life, and universal life will not always look worse than term insurance. It depends on the company and the policy. Some companies, for example, may offer an unusually expensive term policy, which may in rare instances come out looking even more costly than universal life.

By and large, however, universal life, as a generic class, offers no monetary advantage over the existing life insurance policies. What it does hold out to consumers is a misleading claim: that it pays "market" rates of interest.

If a federally regulated bank said it pays interest of 11 percent, when it really pays interest of 3.3 percent, it would be in violation of federal banking regulations, according to Robert W. Hefner, director of consumer examinations for the Comptroller of the Currency, which regulates national banks. "If a bank pays a lower rate than it discloses, we ask the bank to make correction," Hefner said, noting that it "hasn't been a real problem." By the same token, he said, if a bank claims it charges 3.3 percent for a mortgage when it really charges 11 percent, the bank regulators would cite the bank for violating the federal Truth-in-Lending law, he said.

In the life insurance business, that is no problem. Congress passed a special law exempting the industry from federal regulation. So E. F. Hutton Life Insurance Company advertises, "Is your life insurance cash value earning at least 11 percent?" And Hartford Life Insurance Co. of Hartford, Connecticut, advertises, "The Solution is the Hartford's revolutionary new Life product. It earns 10.25 percent on Cash Value. That's right, 10.25 percent."

The fact is that the return on these policies, as shown by the Computone figures, is more like four percent or less. If the policies are cashed in within a few years of their purchase, the returns are negative.

By claiming to pay higher market rates, the companies suggest that the abuses of whole life are a thing of the past. Finally, we are told, consumers are getting the competitive returns they deserve. The most reputable publications continue to be fooled.

Reporting that more than one hundred companies now offer universal life, a recent *Wall Street Journal* article said, "The new policies attempt, for the first time, to offer a high market rate of return." Another *Journal* article suggested that whole life's share of new premiums for individual policies dropped from sixty-three percent to fifty-five percent. At the same time, the article said, premiums from new sales of the new "investment-oriented" policies like universal life generated ten percent of new individual life premiums.

Nothing could be further from the truth. The new universal life policies are, in fact, whole life policies. Rather than diminishing its share of the market, whole life's hold has remained about the same for the past several years, according to the Life Insurance Marketing and Research Association, a trade group. Whole life, including universal life, represented eighty-two percent of new premiums in 1982. The previous year, it also represented eighty-two percent of new premiums, according to Helen Noniewicz, a vice-president of the trade group.

Anderson, the Atlanta actuary who designed it, said universal life has advantages over traditional whole life because it is more flexible and can be used to generate more in cash values by increasing the premium. Yet he said it is not the best answer for people who are looking strictly for life insurance. "If you want life insurance coverage only, you're better off with term insurance."

■

The life insurance game provides a special penalty for those who take the claims of many life insurance companies at face value. The "low-cost" policies, the "market rates of return," and the policies sold as antidotes to whole life may, in fact, be the most expensive buys of all, often promoted with the aid of impenetrable computer analyses. In the next chapter, we will take a closer look at computers in the life insurance industry and how they can be used to help or hurt the consumer.

7. THE COMPUTERS

■ The computer printout from Equitable Life Assurance Society of the United States is printed in a distinctive typeface on high-quality paper. It shows, as one example, that the consumer could buy a whole life policy and make a profit of $43,109 by cashing it in at the age of sixty-five.

This is what many agents refer to as the miracle of whole life insurance. You actually get more out of the policy than you put into it, enjoying the security of having life insurance protection all along. The miracle is in no way diminished by an Equitable footnote, which most people will not read and even fewer will understand. It says the cost figures are "not to be considered as policy cost, as interest is not taken into account. . . ."

If the cost figures do not represent the cost, what is the point of presenting them? The point, of course, is that they make it appear you are getting your life insurance free.

However, another printout demonstrates quite the opposite point. This is a printout from Computone Systems, Inc. of Atlanta, provided to more than 7,000 agents and companies who buy the company's computer terminal. This printout shows the actual worth of the cash values, deducting the premiums paid into the policy and taking account of the time value of money.

Assuming an inflation rate of six percent a year, the Computone printout shows, in the case of the Equitable policy, the net payment will be worth −$1,520 by the age of sixty-five, not the $43,109 shown by the Equitable printout. The difference is nearly $45,000, and it shows how, in the life insurance industry, as in any other industry, computers can be used to inform or misinform.

Because of computers, life insurance that was once limited to two basic formats—whole life with level premiums and term insurance with rising premiums—is being offered in a proliferation of variations on those themes. Computers permit the flexibility needed to come up with different approaches. Not incidentally, computers have also cut expenses in the back office, where life insurance policies are issued and claims are paid, contributing to an overall reduction in the cost of life insurance over the years.

In the selling end of the business, computers have assumed an even more important role. For most life insurance agents, the computer has become an indispensable tool. Its seemingly irrefutable illustrations lend weight to the point the agent is trying to make.

In this chapter, we will examine how agents use computers. In one case, New England Mutual Life Insurance Company of Boston uses a computer illustration to demonstrate to customers—erroneously—that whole life insurance is superior to term insurance. In the second illustration, Computone provides agents with information that allows them to determine which policies offer the best rate of return and to compare whole life with term insurance fairly.

■

If there were ever a need for the aid of computers, it is in the life insurance business. If a consumer wants to find out which policy, among the thousands available, offers the best value, there's no way that he can reliably do his own survey, nor is there any existing survey that will tell him what he wants to know. Trying to penetrate what passes for rate books is like trying to find your way out of a pitch black cave with your hands and feet tied. It simply cannot be done, because the necessary information is not there.

Until a few years ago, *Best's Review*, a respected trade publication published by A. M. Best Company of Oldwick, New Jersey, ranked policies according to their interest-adjusted index figures. If a consumer were so inclined, he might have been able to obtain a copy of the annual issue that showed which policies offered the best value for the money. But the publication discontinued the survey. The reasons tell a lot about the life insurance industry in general and, in particular, about the difficulty even experts encounter in determining the cost of a policy.

"We're not going to compare policies because of the bad experience we had," said Andrew D. Gold, manager of the life-health department of A. M. Best Company. Best's asked each company to submit data on their policies as of June 1, 1981, for its 1981 comparison of policy values.

After the article was published, Best's learned that Prudential Insurance Company of America had supplied a new, more favorable schedule of dividends—one that was not yet in effect as of June 1, according to Gold. "Prudential's attitude was, that was the date they wanted publicized," he said. When Best's asked for the correct figures so it could publish a correction, he said, "They wouldn't provide it. We just got it on our own."

In the correction that appeared, Prudential had slipped from first place to twenty-fifth place in a comparison of $100,000 in whole life coverage purchased by a thirty-five-year-old male. On the other hand, Equitable, which did not submit its data the first time, came out lowest in cost.

Since Best's stopped the rankings, it has had no more hassles. "The companies care only if they show up at the top or the bottom of the list," Gold said. "We're waiting to see if the industry cares [that the rankings no longer appear]. They probably wish we didn't do it unless they're number one." More recently, the magazine resumed the comparisons but refrained from showing any numerical rankings.

Best's publishes an even more authoritative tome called The Life-Health Edition of Best's Insurance Reports, a 2,000-page reference book considered the Bible of the industry. The book, available in many public libraries, provides a range of information about each of the 2,100 life insurance companies in the country. It shows assets, officers, types of business, and lapse ratios. It also evaluates the companies' financial soundness and the cost of policies.

Turn to some of the companies with the highest-cost policies and you will be in for a surprise. "Net cost to policyholders is moderate," the reference work said of Academy Life Insurance Company. You would have to read through five pages of explanation of Best's evaluations to find out that "moderate" is the worst possible rating Best's gives. In fact, all of Best's ratings are favorable. They range from "remarkably low," "very low," and "low" to "fairly low" and "moderate." Beginning with the 1981 edition, the book dropped its previous "fairly high" and "high" ratings of policy costs.

"I guess we got a lot of flak from the companies," Gold said, explaining why all the ratings are favorable. "They didn't like it said their cost was higher. They would give us a song and dance about how we hadn't taken representative plans."

■

Against this background, the customer is in no position to determine for himself the price of a policy or to penetrate the companies' computer presentations, as a New England Mutual Life Insurance Company customer found out.

Having just bought a $110,000 term insurance policy, the customer was in a receptive mood. His agent from the Boston-based company had behaved like a gentleman. When it became clear the customer did not want whole life, the agent did not press it. What's more, the agent had fulfilled all his promises. He had scheduled the medical examination at a convenient time in the evening. He had made sure the customer's personal physician returned a medical history on time. Now the agent was here to deliver the term policy just when he said he would deliver it.

After another round of signing forms, the agent brought out a computer illustration for the customer to consider. Titled "Permanent vs. Term and Invest the Difference," the three-page comparison purported to show that whole life insurance is far superior to the term policy the customer had just bought.

The comparison showed that, after keeping the policy twenty years, the consumer in the fifty percent tax bracket would have had to invest the savings in premiums between whole life and term insurance at twenty percent a year to do better with term insurance.

Clearly, no one can hope to sustain a twenty percent return, so whole life must be the way to go, or so the illustration suggested.

In this case, the customer was familiar with life insurance. Nonetheless, it would take several months before the customer fully realized the range of devices that New England Mutual had incorporated in the comparison to load it in favor of whole life.

Perplexed, the customer asked the agent why the death benefit shown in the comparison seemed to increase to as much as $161,720, when he had only purchased term coverage of $110,000. The agent was not sure. The customer tried to read through a half a page of footnotes and disclaimers, but they all blurred before his eyes.

In previous experience with life insurance, the customer had seen many honest comparisons of whole life with term. Invariably, they showed the consumer gets a far better buy with term insurance. The customer mentioned his skepticism to the agent, but the agent had no explanation.

Later that evening, the customer pored over the document still more. Doing his own calculations, he came up with the opposite result. Still, he couldn't fathom what New England Life had done to make whole life look better than term insurance.

The next day, he called a New England Mutual vice-president. It took ten minutes of questioning to get the answer. It seems a portion of the dividends paid by the whole life policy had been used to purchase more term insurance. In other words, the whole life side of the comparison had been beefed up by adding term insurance to it. Whole life looked better in the comparison because it was not whole life. It was a combination of whole life and term insurance.

The vice-president pointed out that one of the footnotes disclosed this fact. Indeed, it did. But the footnote, because of its cryptic language, was close to being unintelligible. Unless one knew what it said before reading it, the enigmatic footnote could not be understood even by a person who is familiar with life insurance.

The customer talked with John A. Fibinger, president of New

England Mutual. Fibinger himself noted two other problems with the comparison: As examples of returns after taxes, it listed a seventy-eight percent tax bracket, which no longer exists. And he pointed out the dividends paid by the whole life policy had been shown one year too soon, again favoring whole life over term insurance.

Somehow, all the discrepancies had been in one direction—making whole life look better. Surely that tells us something about whole life and what it takes to sell it.

But Fibinger, an actuary, maintained the comparison was valid with the exception of the problems he found in the illustration. Adding term insurance to the whole life was necessary in order to equalize all the benefits. After all, he said, a person who dies covered by term insurance leaves his beneficiary with a death benefit plus the extra money saved over buying whole life. In contrast, the person with whole life leaves only the death benefit from his life insurance. He leaves no additional investment funds. "Our people say that to make it a fair illustration, you've got to assume the widow ends up in the same place upon death ..." Fibinger said. "Don't compare apples and oranges."

But term insurance and whole life are apples and oranges. They do not provide the same benefits. Whole life provides one set of benefits, and term insurance provides another set. That is exactly the point. By buying term insurance, the consumer winds up with more benefits, but Fibinger wants to slow the faster horse so the race will be more fair.

"This is the trouble with any cost comparison," Fibinger said. "We have legitimately in the past been criticized for illustrations that were, I will say, phony ... where the death benefits were not equal." To balance the comparison, Fibinger said the death benefits must be equalized by assuming they are equal. But why assume they are equal when they are not? Why assume anything when you can use the real thing?

Bank account interest rates contain no assumptions. Nor does the Computone method. It compares exactly what is being sold.

Although New England Life pays Computone to put its policies on the system, Computone calculates the rate of return. He showed little interest in finding out.

When asked who else would agree with New England Life's method of comparing whole life and term insurance, Fibinger said, "Albert Linton." Linton, unfortunately, is dead, but three other actuaries gave three different opinions.

One, Richard Bayles, a Massachusetts Department of Insurance official, said the New England Mutual illustration is "misleading." A second, James H. Hunt, a former Massachusetts Insurance Department official who acts as a consultant for the National Insurance Consumer Organization—the only group that tries to protect consumers' interests when buying insurance—approved of the illustration because it was similar to Linton's method. (We will learn more about Linton's method later in this chapter.)

A third actuary, E. J. Moorhead, a former president of the Society of Actuaries who once worked for New England Life, pointed out still another device used by New England Life to weight the comparison in favor of whole life. Moorhead said that the illustration had shown the tax consequences of buying term insurance but neglected to show them if the customer had purchased whole life.

"I wish there were a standard [to tell actuaries how to compare whole life with term]," Fibinger lamented. Of course, actuaries are not about to develop standards for making a fair comparison. The overwhelming majority of them work for the companies, and the companies are nearly all selling whole life.

Computer comparisons notwithstanding, the agent carries the most weight with the consumer. It is the agent who has the final say, and the agent who can explain away, or embellish upon, what the comparisons show. For the most part, the agents try to divert attention from cost.

Asked how a consumer can tell the price of a life insurance policy, the manager of a New England Life agency spent two hours over lunch telling amusing anecdotes about customers he has known and his personal experiences in buying television sets. "Our price structure will vary," he said, "but you have to look behind the price. Whole life has all the attributes of a good piece of property." Questioned further, he said, "How do we determine the price? Suppose you are a young man who has a congenital heart problem." He went on to recount how just such a man had been unable to buy life insurance at any price, and when he died, his family was destitute. The point being: forget about price, the customer is lucky to have life insurance at any cost.

Two hours later, the agent was asked again about determining price. He insisted the buyer should follow his agent's advice. "You have to have confidence in the performance of your company [and agent] . . . I have to place my confidence in someone."

When the agent was asked still another time how price can be determined, he suggested using the "traditional" method for comparing price—the method prohibited by thirty-six states as being misleading.

■

Against this tide, Computone tries to tell agents, if not consumers, the truth about life insurance. William Glover, a former IBM employee, started the company in 1965, and two years later, William O. Robeson, another former IBM employee, joined the firm. Originally, the company used computers to help poultry farmers keep track of prices and feed.

In late 1969, Robeson, a big, white-haired man who is now chairman of Computone, decided computers could be used by life insurance agents to analyze their customers' financial needs in their homes. Through people in the industry, he heard of Ray A. Philibert, a former agent and vice-president of a life insurance company, who was then vice-president of an actuarial firm in Atlanta. At that firm, Bowles, Andres & Towne, Philibert had been providing agents with analyses of their customers' life insurance needs on blue index cards.

Robeson met with Philibert in his office and suggested using computers to perform the analyses. At first, Philibert considered the idea a "gimmick," but he woke up at 2:00 A.M. and began planning the system. By 5:00 A.M., he had designed six programs, including several still being used by Computone to analyze customers' needs and compare policy prices and values. When Robeson arrived at his office the next morning at 7:30, Philibert was waiting there for him with a proposal.

Beginning in 1970, Computone and the actuarial firm operated the new service as a joint venture. Rather than using existing computer terminals, the company made and sold its own. Originally, the portable devices used a computerized, female voice to provide answers to questions that were entered into the computer by flipping switches on the terminals.

When the actuarial firm entered bankruptcy proceedings just after starting the new service, Computone acquired the rights to the comparison system and to the firm's staff. Robeson brought Philibert into the company as a vice-president, and Philibert, who now owns one percent of the company's stock, set up Computone's life insurance programs. In 1982, those services accounted for some eighty-five percent of the company's sales of $16.1 million.

Computone occupies the second floor of an unimposing, glass-walled building next to a motel in the outskirts of Atlanta. It has corridors lined with offices of about 200 actuaries and computer programmers. A laboratory in another building makes the terminals that agents and life insurance companies must buy to use Computone's service.

To get a policy comparison, an agent flips switches on a console the size of a briefcase. After the terminal has made contact by telephone with Computone's computers in Atlanta, the agent enters pertinent data about the policyholder—age and sex, for example—along with the code number for the policy to be compared.

The terminal costs between $1,750 and $3,595, and agents are charged for the time they use Computone's computers—typically $5.00 for a printout of one policy.

Agents who want to compare a limited range of policies can rent data disks for their IBM personal computers, which provide comparisons of policies and plans they know they want to sell. Agents who just want to sell universal life may purchase a hand-held Panasonic computer for $700. It analyzes financial needs and produces miniature printouts of universal life policies.

The data stored in Computone computers comes from the life insurance companies, which pay $300 and up to have it stored in the Computone system. Because the values change at each policyholder age, one policy may require entering as many as 100,000 bits—characters or digits—of information.

After the information is fed into the computers, Computone sends the company a printout. Before Computone customers can call up the data on their terminals, the companies first notify Computone that it is accurate.

Depending on how much information is wanted, a printout can run to sixteen pages. Each printout lists the premiums, dividends, and cash values of the policy each year it is held, according to the age and sex of the prospect and the amount of coverage desired. The computer can be asked for smoker or nonsmoker rates, prices based on monthly or quarterly payments instead of annual payments, or rates that include various other options. In portraying rates, the Computone terminal can be asked to use dividends paid by a policy to reduce the premiums, buy more insurance, or accumulate more cash values. In the case of universal life policies, the size of the premiums can be varied each year.

If the customer's tax bracket is entered in the terminal, the Computone printouts will show the net proceeds received by the customer after taxes. According to Philibert, the fact that cash values on whole life and universal life policies are taxable is rarely mentioned in the life insurance industry. "I don't know of a single home office illustration that shows it," he said.

Besides showing the interest-adjusted figures approved by regulators, the printouts list two key price comparison figures for each year the policy is held. The first is the rate of return figure. It shows the annual compounded rate of interest that a consumer would have to earn in a bank account in order to equal the benefits paid by the policy being compared. The rate of return is shown each year the policy is held in two situations—if the policyholder lives and surrenders the policy for cash, or if he dies and his beneficiary receives a death benefit. With those figures, the consumer can compare whole life with term insurance, or the cash value of a whole life policy with the proceeds of a money market fund.

A thirty-two-year-old male interested in buying $100,000 in coverage can see that, if he dies in twenty-two years, his beneficiary would receive a death benefit from John Hancock Mutual Life Insurance Company's whole life policy that would be the equivalent of earning 10.9 percent a year from a bank account. With Massachusetts Mutual Life Insurance Company's whole life policy, the death benefit would be equivalent to earning 13.1 percent a year in a bank account.

By buying term insurance from Metropolitan Life Insurance Company, the same consumer would provide his beneficiary with a death benefit equivalent to earning 24.7 percent in a bank account each year. The term policy will pay nothing if surrendered for cash. But if he surrenders the Massachusetts Mutual whole life policy for cash, he would get a return of 6.7 percent, compared with John Hancock's 4.6 percent.

Computone can also show what is known as the future value of policy benefits, taking account of inflation and how much the consumer has paid into the policy. For example, assuming a six percent inflation rate, the same thirty-two-year-old policyholder with a $100,000 John Hancock policy would provide a death benefit to his beneficiary, less his outlay, of just $15,013. A Phoenix Mutual Life Insurance Company policy would provide a benefit, less outlay, of $17,403. A Northwestern Mutual Life Insurance Company policy would provide $18,051.

If the John Hancock policyholder turned in his policy for cash after twenty-two years, he would get back a net payment worth −$2,553. In other words, he would have plowed more into the policy, after inflation takes its toll, than he got out of it. The Phoenix Mutual policyholder would get back −$1,448. A Northwestern policyholder would receive back $76. However, if the Northwestern policyholder is in the 30 percent tax bracket, he would get back, after taxes, −$1,848, according to the Computone figures.

Since he constantly examines the results of the Computone system, Philibert probably knows more about life insurance rates than anyone in the country. According to Philibert, the rate of return comparisons show term insurance is invariably cheaper than whole life until the age of seventy. "After that, whole life has an advantage," he said.

One of the "games" Philibert said the industry plays is calling a term policy a whole life policy for tax reasons. To make a whole life policy look like a term policy, the companies tack on a $500 cash surrender value only in certain years. Since most comparisons of policy values do not show the values for every year the policy is held, there is often no way for a consumer to see how this particular game is played. But the Computone printouts depict exactly what the consumer gets.

For anyone who wants to rank the values of different policies, the Computone system is invaluable—if the secret access codes can be obtained. While some agents trade the access codes, most never have the opportunity to compare policies sold by some of the largest companies. By and large, it is these larger companies that provide Computone with data on their rates only on condition the information and codes will only be given to their own agents.

Several other companies besides Computone store life insurance rates in computers, but most do not provide the critical rate of return figure. With 6,000 policies from 350 companies in its system, Computone has recorded far more policies than any other computer company. But, like Computone, these other computer firms say many of the life insurance companies provide their rates only on condition their agents will be the only ones to see them.

"The companies don't want to have a price war with each other," said Michael C. Goldberg, president of Financial Data Planning Corporation of Miami, which keeps 1,000 plans of 100 companies in its computer system. "They don't use the internal rate of return. That's not the way the sale is made. It's a matter of trying to solve the client's problems rather than coming out with the cheapest thing on the block."

To see how Computone is actually used by agents, we will visit Edmund W. Forcke, Jr., a Richmond agent who uses Computone printouts to make the sale. He said they allow him to show a client, on the spot, the gross prices of a particular policy. Otherwise, he said, he would have to wait weeks while the home office mails him what is known as a ledger statement listing the premiums. By then, the client might decide he wants a different comparison. "He may have cooled off and bought a refrigerator meanwhile," Forcke said.

But Forcke feels the rate of return figures and prices are not really relevant to the consumer. What is important, he said, is the agent's knowledge. "If they want to get bids, I don't want them [as clients]," he said. "I don't use the rate of return because it will confuse people. People are looking for someone to guide them in making financial decisions."

Still, he said, the rate of return figures are useful for agents. A certified life underwriter and member of the Million Dollar Round Table, Forcke asserted that the interest-adjusted figures approved by regulators are intended to confuse people. "It was a home office cover-up to quiet the public and give them nothing [in the way of price disclosure]," he said. "The real way to do it is the internal rate of return. You don't see insurance companies putting it on policies," Forcke said. "It puts the finger on the companies that don't put out a quality product."

Forcke said even the ledger statements provided by insurance companies don't show what happens to policies after the age of sixty-five; the Computone figures portray policy values to age one hundred, if a policy goes that far. A "lot of policies fall apart" by then, he said.

"As far as I'm concerned, most insurance companies are out to get all they can get. The product Computone delivers is so far ahead of anything any life insurance company delivers, there is no comparison," said the agent.

Over lunch at a private club in Richmond, Forcke outlined how agents sell in the city. "We have a very cohesive group of professional agents," he said. "If I run into a friend [agent] who's doing a good job, I won't replace his policy. We never look at policies," Forcke said. "To me, that's the most insignificant thing we do." After all, he points out, they all pay upon proof of death.

After lunch, Forcke printed out some of the Computone comparisons. Consulting an orange booklet printed by Computone with four-digit access codes next to each policy, Forcke pointed out that many of the companies' policies have blanks where the codes should be. These are the companies that do not want their policies compared. They include five of the ten largest general life insurance companies: Prudential Insurance Company of America, Metropolitan Life Insurance Company, New York Life Insurance Company, John Hancock Mutual Life Insurance Company, and Massachusetts Mutual Life Insurance Company. Connecticut General Life Insurance Company does not participate in the Computone program at all.

Similarly eighty percent of the universal life plans are "private."

Asked why Massachusetts Mutual keeps its rates confidential in the Computone system, Donald D. Cameron, vice-president for product development of Massachusetts Mutual, said, "In Computone, we don't want [the rates] being used in competition by other agents who would put our product in a bad light. Others may try to replace your policy."

However, when Massachusetts Mutual agents encounter competition from another agent, it supplies its own agents with the rate of return figures from Computone so that the competing policy can be compared fairly, Cameron said.

He said the statements that companies give consumers do not tell the real price. "You have to measure the funds flow and take into account the time value of money. When you do the internal rate of return, it does [this] for you automatically," he said.

A certified life underwriter, Cameron said the interest-adjusted figures approved by regulators for comparing price have little meaning. Companies and agents generally use only one of the two sets of figures—the one that measures the cash surrender value. A second figure, called the payments index, measures the cost of the death benefit but is seldom cited. Yet, he pointed out, the death benefit is the reason for buying life insurance.

"It is my personal opinion that the National Association of Insurance Commissioners' interest-adjusted net surrender cost index is not meaningful when comparing the death protection offered by different policies," Cameron said. "In other words, in my experience people buy life insurance for the protection—and not to surrender the policy in ten or twenty years."

Even the Computone figures may not be accurate, since they include the companies' projections of dividends. Dividends, according to an Internal Revenue Service ruling, are merely refunds of premium overcharges. Refunds or not, they can become enormous if a policy is held twenty years or more, eventually exceeding the premiums.

Philibert said companies project their dividends in different ways. Some may take a conservative approach, while others are more liberal. Stockholder-owned companies, since they generally do not pay dividends, cannot show these additional bonuses. However, many of them charge "current" rates along with guaranteed rates, permitting them to engage in the same kind of speculation the mutual companies engage in with dividends.

"You have some companies using current dividend assumptions, and some using new money assumptions. It's a case of who's lying the best," said Philibert.

The actuaries who certify the numbers do not help, Philibert added. Rather than emphasizing consistency, as accountants do, they permit different methods of portraying costs, so long as those methods are footnoted. In any case, Philibert said, most actuaries are more familiar with pension plans than with life insurance.

Many actuaries profess to favor the cost disclosure method

developed by the late M. Albert Linton, who was president of the Provident Mutual Life Insurance Company of Philadelphia and president of a predecessor of the Society of Actuaries in 1936. As the president of a life insurance company and the author of several books extolling whole life, there was good reason for Linton to develop this particular method for comparing prices.

What the Linton Yield does is compute a percentage rate of return if the policyholder turns in his policy for cash. A rate of return percentage is just what is needed to make life insurance prices understandable. But there are two peculiar twists to Linton's method. The first is that it only measures the price or cost of the policy if the consumer turns the policy in for cash.

But what if he dies and a death benefit is paid? That is where the second twist comes in. To account for that possibility, the Linton Yield inflates the rate of return by assigning a hypothetical cost to the value of the life insurance protection purchased by the customer. Proponents of the method argue that the consumer had the value of life insurance protection. Why shouldn't some value be assigned to it?

The problem is the Linton Yield does not tell the actual price if the consumer dies, or if he lives, since it mixes up both possibilities. Nor does it provide any real price. Rather, it presents hypothetical figures.

It is something like inflating the return of a passbook savings account that pays five percent on the grounds the consumer had the value of a government-insured account. It is true that government insurance is of some value and should be considered when deciding whether to put one's money in a bank account or in a money fund, which usually is not insured. But the fact that the bank account is insured does not mean the bank account paid a higher rate of interest than a money fund.

Instead of earning five percent, the actuaries would say the consumer got an eight percent or nine percent return from the bank account. The consumer did not receive an eight percent return. He got a five percent return. The safety of an investment is a consideration separate and apart from its return. By mixing up the two, the actuaries get a meaningless hodgepodge. If banking regulators permitted savings institutions to pad their rates of return in the same way, the banking system would be a shambles.

The truth is the actuaries themselves, in determining prices, do not use the Linton Yield. They exhort people outside the business to use it, but when it comes to comparing prices of different companies, the actuaries use other methods.

"It's [the Linton Yield] of no practical value for the public or the actuaries," said J. Ross Hanson, an actuary who designs life insurance policies.

8. THE INVESTIGATORS

■ "Lynda is a young woman of twenty-eight years of age, and I found her to be extremely attractive." So begins a report in the files of Equifax, Inc. of Atlanta on an investigation into a claim for life insurance benefits. We learn from the report that Lynda is blonde and likes to wear bikinis. That she has a yellow Mustang that she drove down from Toronto to Miami. That she has been living in Miami with a dizzying succession of male friends. And that she smokes marijuana and has tried cocaine and heroin.

We also learn how Lynda met Dr. Kenneth Rawdin, the subject of the Equifax investigation. "She . . . revealed in the interview that she had . . . gone to the doctor to be treated for gonorrhea, a venereal disease that she had gotten from a Hungarian sailor," the report says. Lynda went on to tell the Equifax investigator that she had a brief affair with Dr. Rawdin and found that he was a "poor lover." The report includes Lynda's detailed account of Dr. Rawdin's unsatisfactory bedroom performance.

The details might make good reading in a pornographic novel, except for the fact that the characters involved here are real people. The company that compiled the report is not a supplier to adult book stores, but a $437-million-a-year concern whose stock is traded on the New York Stock Exchange.

The interview with Lynda—to whom we will return later—is included in one of the 200,000 claims investigations Equifax conducts every year. Claims represent only a fraction of the work Equifax does for the life insurance industry. The company also investigates people who apply for life insurance. Each year, Equifax compiles reports on 2 million of these people, or roughly one in eight applicants for life insurance.

While a few other companies perform similar services, Equifax accounts for the overwhelming majority of the business. It is, in effect, the main investigative arm of the life insurance business and another pathway in the life insurance game.

In investigating applicants for insurance, Equifax must comply with the provisions of the Federal Fair Credit Reporting Act, which says consumers must be allowed to review information gathered about them and correct it if it is wrong. However, when investigating insurance claims, there is no equivalent federal statute permitting consumers to review information gathered. It can gather information as it wishes, keep it as long as it wants, and give it to anyone it wants.

Since the companies are exempt from federal regulation, life insurance companies that carry out their own investigations of applicants (as distinguished from investigations done by Equifax) are entirely exempt from the provisions of the Federal Fair Credit Reporting Act.

"Because the industry is regulated by the states and there is no federal regulation, the insurance industry is still wide open on the federal level when it comes to protection of personal information," said David F. Linowes, who was chairman of the federal Privacy Protection Commission, which reported to then President Carter in 1977 on growing threats to individual privacy.

In this chapter, we will examine how Equifax works and what other information is gathered before life insurance companies issue policies or pay claims—and the Byzantine reasons they check into your character, drinking habits, and sex life.

■

In evaluating how well life insurance companies balance their customers' privacy rights against the companies' legitimate need to know their backgrounds, it is important to keep in mind how life insurance rates are determined. The concept of insurance requires sharing of known risks and charging different rates to different classes of risks.

A house built of wood, for example, has a greater chance of burning than a house made of brick. The owner of the wood house should therefore be charged more for fire insurance than the owner of the brick house. By the same token, a driver with a string of accidents and traffic tickets has a greater chance of having another accident. He should be charged more for insurance. Otherwise, costs to everyone are raised unreasonably.

Similarly, a sixty-five-year-old man has a greater chance of dying than a five-year-old child. The older person should be charged more for his life insurance. If people of all ages were charged the same rates, life insurance could no longer exist. A ninety-five-year-old man could then buy a $1 million policy at a nominal rate. As he and other older people die and the companies pay off claims, the industry would go bankrupt.

"Risk sharing brings down the cost to the individual to a manageable level," Richard S. Schweiker, president of the American Council of Life Insurance, wrote in *The New York Times*. "Classifying risks is synonymous to fair pricing," the former secretary of Health and Human Services said.

Along with health and age, sex is an important determinant of longevity. Women, on the average, live almost eight years longer than men. Women therefore should be charged far lower rates than men, or so it would seem. But advocates of equal rights for women do not see it that way. They insist that equity requires females to be charged the same rates as males. This has opened a controversy that has finally put the normally somnolent life insurance industry on the front pages.

The controversy began in 1975 when Nathalie Norris, an employee of the State of Arizona, signed up for an annuity retirement plan offered by the state through Lincoln National Life Insurance Company of Fort Wayne, Indiana. She was paying the same contribution into the plan as her male counterparts. But, because she was expected to live longer, she discovered that she would get $34 a month less upon retirement than would male employees.

Norris sued and won her case in the U.S. Supreme Court. By a 5–4 vote, the justices ruled that federal laws barring sex discrimination in employment also bar plans sponsored by employers from paying better benefits to men than to women. The ruling does not apply to pension plans sold individually by the companies.

Since the ruling, representatives of the National Organization for Women (NOW) have persuaded members of Congress to introduce bills that would take matters one step further. They would require insurance companies to calculate rates on a "sexually neutral" basis, meaning women would pay more for life insurance and auto insurance, even though they live longer and have better driving records.

According to the American Academy of Actuaries, men would pay three percent less for life insurance, while women would pay eleven percent more under the unisexual plan. On the other hand, men would pay six percent more for annuities, while women would pay six percent less. And women's auto insurance rates would jump by 37 percent, while men's would drop by 20 percent, according to the academy.

If those figures are correct, women would get the short end of the stick by a substantial margin. Are women really lobbying to pay more for their life insurance? When pressed on that point, representatives of NOW argue that women don't really live longer than men. It's just that more men smoke than women. In making that claim, they ignore study after study documenting that women nonsmokers live longer than men nonsmokers while women smokers live longer than men smokers. For example, based on its experiences with 100,000 life insurance policies, State Mutual Life Assurance Company of America reported in 1979 that thirty-two-year-old female nonsmokers lived an average of 3.7 years longer than male nonsmokers. Female smokers lived an average of 6.1 years longer.

With full deference to the cause of women's equality, the women in this case have only succeeded in blurring the facts about life insurance rates. The truth is that if there is sex discrimination in life insurance, it is discrimination in reverse. For years, the companies charged the same rates to men and women. Of course, few women had life insurance on themselves. As women assumed a role equal to men in the work force, they had a greater need for life insurance. The companies began offering lower rates to women based on their greater longevity. But even now, most companies reduce women's rates by a factor of three years, instead of giving them the break of nearly eight additional years the latest studies show they deserve to get.

That does not mean, of course, that every woman will live eight years longer. A woman who signs up for a new policy could die the next day in a car accident. In the same vein, a person with cancer diagnosed as terminal could live another twenty years. But the cost of insuring terminal cancer patients at standard rates would be so great that people in good health couldn't afford to buy life insurance. By the same token, charging by sex and age is an attempt to introduce some equity into the pricing system.

Once a company is aware of a health problem or an extra occupational risk, it will usually write a policy anyway but charge more. Some companies make a point of doing just that. An entire mini-industry—brokers who find companies to insure what are known as substandard risks—has grown up around that need.

Who Writes What, an industry guidebook published by the National Underwriter Company of Cincinnati, Ohio, tells agents which companies will consider covering special risks: amputees (Continental Assurance Company), double amputees (Midland Mutual Life Insurance Company), glider pilots (American General Life Insurance Companies), fainters (E. F. Hutton Life Insurance Company), bomb searchers (Prudential Insurance Company of America), people with very high blood pressure (United States Life Insurance Company), or people with transplanted kidneys (Old Line Life Insurance Company of America).

The unfairness in life insurance is not that the companies adhere to mortality tables in determining rates. The problem is that they don't adhere to them enough. Like the auto insurance companies that once charged more in red-lined, ghetto areas, the life insurance companies tend to go with their prejudices rather than with proven facts.

There's little mystery surrounding why people die. Mortality statistics have pinpointed the major, life-threatening illnesses. According to the American Council of Life Insurance, almost three out of four life insurance policyholders die from heart diseases or cancer. The rest die from pneumonia and influenza (three percent), bronchitis and other respiratory diseases (four percent), cirrhosis of the liver (one percent), and other natural causes (13 percent). The balance die in motor vehicle accidents (three percent) or other accidents (two percent), or because they commit suicide (two percent) or are murdered (one percent).

The life insurance companies can and do charge more for people who smoke, are grossly overweight, have illnesses that are documented, or have hazardous jobs. Asbestos workers, building wreckers, and structural iron workers, for example, have higher death rates than others.

In a few cases, these extra charges don't appear to make sense. For example, New England Mutual Life Insurance Company's underwriting booklet shows circus clowns are charged an extra $3.00 per thousand dollars of coverage. So are bartenders. Waiters and waitresses are charged an extra $2.00. But police officers and firefighters are charged standard rates.

Joseph E. Foley, senior vice-president for underwriters at New England Life, said a 1967 study by the Society of Actuaries found that waiters and bartenders really do live shorter lives. On the average, he said, their death rates are about seventy percent above normal. The death rates for firefighters, on the other hand, are just seven percent above normal.

Beyond assessing these extra charges, there is little life insurance companies can reasonably do to predict who will live longer lives. But life insurance companies like to have their bets covered as many ways as possible. So they find out everything they can about an applicant's health and then guess about everything else.

As we shall see in the next chapter, they begin by charging rates that are based on ultraconservative assumptions about death rates and investment returns. Then they have the applicant list his medical history on the application. If it later turns out he concealed a hospitalization or a heart attack, the companies refuse to pay if he dies within two years of buying a policy. The applicant must submit to an examination from the company's own doctor or nurse practitioner if the coverage requested is over certain levels. He also must consent to having his personal physician submit a health history. Finally, the companies check the applicant's files at the Medical Information Bureau, a huge data bank in Westwood, Massachusetts, that keeps track of whether applicants were previously examined for life insurance and rejected.

By the time the companies get through, only God knows more about the applicant's heal'h than they. But that does not satisfy the companies. So they hire Equifax to look into applicants' personal lives.

■

Equifax is employed if the coverage exceeds certain levels, or as a random check on applications. Metropolitan routinely orders Equifax investigations when people apply for $100,000 or more in coverage. In a given year, Metropolitan might order as many as 63,000 Equifax reports in screening 600,000 applicants for life insurance. In a single year, Metropolitan paid $3.4 million for Equifax services.

Equifax offers investigative reports of varying degrees of thoroughness. They have names like Life Validation, Life, Life Personal, and Life Advanced. In general, the information is obtained in a telephone or personal interview with the applicant and one or more neighbors. The applicant, of course, has already answered essentially the same questions when he initially applied for life insurance with his agent. Besides witnessing the answers, the agent often fills in the form himself. The questions relate to employment, income, medical history, and unusual avocations (life insurance companies hate hang gliders). Nevertheless, on the theory that the agent may have an incentive to conceal adverse information, Equifax asks the applicants the same questions.

They are expected to ask: How often does the applicant drink? What does he drink? How many drinks does he consume? Where does he drink? Has the applicant stopped drinking? When did he stop? Why did he stop? Equifax conveniently provides a space on the back of the form where Equifax investigators may list all the alcoholic beverages used by the applicant, along with possible drugs used.

A 1972 Equifax memo distributed to employees gave the flavor of what Equifax was looking for. Beginning "Dear Fellow Worker," it said:

> I don't know you but I see the results of your work. In fact, it is my job to determine how you do your job, so we are in this together. I often wish I could talk to you so we could understand and help each other.
>
> Believe me—it makes the difference. This doesn't tell the story: "Insured drinks to excess on weekends," "Drinks to excess on special occasions," "Drinks to feeling good and drives afterward," "Drinks a few beers daily," "Is criticized for being a heavy drinker," "Used to drink a lot but quit."
>
> We haven't done the job unless we've found out and reported: What he drinks, how often he drinks—daily, weekly, monthly, two to three a year? How much he drinks—if daily, how many, and where, and when? If on weekends, every weekend, or most, or one to two a month? If to excess, feeling good or loud and boisterous or intoxicated? How often—daily, weekly, monthly, one to two a month, two to three a year? Where he drinks—home, tavern, lounge, club, parties, on the job? How long, if he quit, specifically when and why? Does he drive afterwards?
>
> I hope you will keep this and find it of some benefit.

After talking with the applicant, Equifax interviews neighbors, who may know less about the applicant than the checker at the supermarket. The interviewers are often part-time workers who are paid little more than the minimum wage. And the connection between the questions and one's life expectancy is tenuous at best.

The Equifax investigator, among other things, is supposed to inquire into the relationship of any nonfamily member living with the applicant. He is instructed to ask about the applicant's "lifestyle" and associates and about the condition of the applicant's home. Other questions deal with drinking, the applicant's "general reputation" and, depending on the report requested, his "home life."

If the questions sound more like a preemployment check for a job at the Central Intelligence Agency, no matter. If an applicant wants life insurance, he has no choice but to submit to this kind of intrusion.

In the past, Equifax held its employees to quotas designed to insure that they came up with information that could be used to decline applicants or charge them extra. A 1972 memo to managers said: "I have said it before but I'll say it again—'You have done a monumental job, and to place in the upper third grouping in both protective [permitting the companies to charge extra] and declinable is just terrific!'"

Noting that one field representative had uncovered no information that could be used for rejecting an applicant, his manager wrote to him in 1973, "Jim, this is a very poor analysis.... Your protective should be exceeding twenty-one percent, and your declinables should be exceeding five percent."

Equifax has since stopped this practice. It now says it voluntarily allows a consumer to see his report if he has been rejected for coverage. But why should information about applicants' personal lives be gathered in the first place? If any useful information is actually turned up by the reports—which cost the companies $10, $25, and up, depending on the size of the reports—it is difficult to determine.

In the end, virtually all rejections are based, not on information turned up by Equifax, but on medical conditions documented in physical examinations. Four out of five rejections are for heart disease. Some applicants are rejected because they have hazardous jobs. In all, only two percent of all applicants are rejected. Another five percent are charged higher than standard rates.

Medical authorities have yet to uncover any link between the human life span and what neighbors think of a person's reputation or sleeping arrangements. Many life insurance companies, in fact, say they disregard that type of information in Equifax reports. "Living arrangements are not a factor in underwriting. We're not concerned with it," said Robert W. Ninneman, senior vice-president for operations of Northwestern Mutual Life Insurance Company.

Yet the underwriters who decide which people to accept, which to reject, and which to charge extra don't all see it that way. Thomas Magis, an Equifax assistant vice-president, points out Equifax would not ask such questions if life insurance companies did not want them asked. And Glenn W. Noble, associate underwriting officer of Provident Mutual Life Insurance Company of Philadelphia, said lifestyle information could well be of value. "Let's say somebody is criticized for running around with thirteen different women," he said. "There would be an extra hazard on this man's life if one of the parties becomes jealous and did something stupid."

As that suggestion illustrates, any unusual activity can be made to sound life-threatening if one focuses enough on it. Whether it is skipping breakfast, blowing up at colleagues, or traveling frequently on airlines, almost everybody has some character trait or engages in some activity that can be made to appear ominous. Even the marital state can be hazardous: A significant number of people are murdered each year in altercations with their spouses.

Asked if the reports ever uncover a significant fact not disclosed by the applicant, his doctor, or the company's doctor, Noble of Provident Mutual said he would see. He called back the next day, somewhat perplexed. After checking all of the company's 5,700 applications made over the course of a year, he found none had been rejected because of information disclosed in an Equifax report. Ten of the applicants—or 0.2 percent—had been charged higher rates because of Equifax information. None of the information uncovered related to lifestyle.

Equifax can be of help in determining whether to take on a big insurance risk. Foley of New England Mutual Life Insurance Company said the company recently took the application of a cocaine smuggler who wanted more than $500,000 in coverage. Equifax reported that he was under surveillance by the police and regularly flew in cocaine shipments on his private plane. Before New England Mutual had approved the application, the man died in a crash of his plane. Based on the information Equifax turned up, the Boston-based insurance company would not have insured him, Foley said.

But Foley noted that type of information is quite different from lifestyle information, which New England Mutual disregards when it sees it in Equifax reports. "Lifestyle and reputation are not really too life-threatening, unless the lifestyle is a very hazardous one. We're not concerned with things that everyone was [concerned with] twenty years ago," he said. "Things have changed."

It is also true that Equifax or other investigative services can be of help when investigating claims. Even when there is a death certificate, policyholders who are supposedly dead have been known to turn up alive.

Take the case of Phebian Oduwole, a Nigerian living in New York. Her husband said she and her daughter had died in an auto accident in Ghana. Based on police and hospital reports, autopsy reports, and death and burial certificates, Fireman's Fund Insurance Companies paid Christopher Oduwole a death benefit of $100,000. Northwestern Mutual Life Insurance Company paid him $50,000.

He bought a new car with some of the money and sent the rest to a Swiss bank account, providing a nest egg for himself and his wife. The accident, as it turned out, had never happened, and all the documents were phony.

The Nigerian citizen got caught because a Mutual of Omaha Insurance Company claims analyst, looking over the police report submitted with another claim, got suspicious. "There was just a tire blowout, yet everyone was killed. It didn't sit right," he told *The Hartford Times*. The company sent an investigator to Africa, where he discovered that all the documents had been made up.

As a result of a U.S. Postal Inspections Service investigation, Oduwole has since been convicted and sentenced to four years in prison and a $10,000 fine.

As we shall see in this chapter, Equifax is zealous about obtaining facts, raising questions about whether Equifax intrudes upon personal privacy unnecessarily. When questioned on these concerns, Equifax executives grope for answers as if they have never really focused on why they collect the data they do.

Asked, for example, why applicants' lifestyle is relevant to issuing life insurance policies, L. B. Kennedy, Equifax vice-president for life and health reports, maintained questions about lifestyle are important because they can uncover gamblers. "It could get him killed if he gambles beyond his financial means," Kennedy said. Or, he suggested, the financial stress might shorten an applicant's life.

If Equifax were genuinely concerned about people who worry, it could find plenty of worriers by checking its separately maintained consumer credit files. Many people who are behind in paying their rent or electric bills might worry themselves to death. But Equifax is more concerned with worried gamblers.

Like Equifax, the Federal Bureau of Investigation once delighted in knowing who was sleeping with whom. The information gave then Director J. Edgar Hoover a sense of power. After several congressional investigations, the bureau established strict guidelines about what material should be collected in an investigation into violations of federal laws. Gossip about lovers was not among them.

"They are questions that are not relevant to writing [life] insurance," Linowes, the former privacy commission chairman, said of lifestyle questions.

Instead of making decisions about insurance risks, the industry falls into the trap of making moral judgments. Underscoring that point, *The Life and Health Insurance Handbook*, a standard industry reference book, defines what the book refers to as "moral hazard" by saying, "The ethical foundations of insurance have been described as including scrupulous honesty, a belief in work, pride in accomplishment, a desire to preserve what we have, willingness to obey the law, and acceptance of individual accountability for one's own actions." The book goes on to describe those who fail to honor this "code" as presenting a "moral hazard," along with those who "cut corners."

Without condoning cutting corners, one has to wonder if anyone has died of it. The book, in any case, doesn't cite any medical evidence to show a relationship, which is exactly the problem. There is none.

On the other hand, there is evidence that some companies find they can conduct business without snooping into people's personal lives. A study sponsored by the American Council of Life Insurance illustrates the contrasting approaches. It found eleven of eighteen life insurance underwriting manuals examined contained warnings about character or morals.

The study, *Risk Classification in Insurance*, compiled by faculty members of the Wharton School of the University of Pennsylvania, said one company manual cautioned that "lesser sexual deviates (homosexuals and lesbians), persons who are flagrantly promiscuous, and lesser criminals with no organized crime connections may be considered, during the time they are still active, at [an extra forty-five percent charge]." Another company said people sleeping together may be charged normal rates only if they are accepted as man and wife by the community, do not engage in outside immoral activity or promiscuity, have good employment, have had the relationship a long time, and so forth.

Yet six companies assessed no extra charges based on evaluations of character or morals.

"Underwriting is totally irrational," said Herbert S. Denenberg, the former Pennsylvania insurance commissioner. "It's a compilation of all the prejudices of all the underwriting types." Their prejudices, he said, are 40 years behind everyone else's.

As a matter of fact, life insurance companies these days try not to reject applicants for "moral" reasons. When all the investigations are done and the manuals consulted, the companies are faced with the fact that they really do want to write life insurance. Their underwriters, if they reject an applicant, are subjected to increasing pressures from agents who want to earn commissions. If their company does not insure an applicant, another company may.

Still, the companies feel more comfortable knowing Equifax is there, even if that presence does raise the cost of insurance. Pressed to specify what Equifax contributes, underwriters again and again say in interviews that they find they know more about an applicant. More what? That is unclear.

"Moral hazard is a misnomer," said Charles A. Will, a former president of the Institute of Home Office Underwriters. "It's to protect your rear. If you have a go-go dancer [who wants life insurance], she may be all right but you say, 'Why is she buying this?' There are no statistics on it. It's an extra charge for what you don't know."

So Equifax keeps asking the questions and adding tidbits to its files, which now cover (including credit files unrelated to life insurance) some 45 million Americans.

■

The case of Lynda and the ill-fated Dr. Rawdin provides an example of what may go into an Equifax report. His case was a claims investigation, which means the insurance companies questioned whether he had, in fact, died. The question, of course, is a legitimate one when there is no body and no death certificate. Yet, as we shall see, although Dr. Rawdin's body never turned up, Equifax's interest in the doctor and his social activities extended far beyond anything that could possibly shed light on his fate. The massive Equifax file on his private life and the lives of his friends stands as testimony to the life insurance industry's unrestricted ability to invade personal privacy.

When Dr. Rawdin disappeared in an apparent boating mishap off the shores of Miami Beach, six life insurance companies became concerned. Together, they had insured his life for $1.6 million. The companies hired Equifax to determine if the doctor had staged his own disappearance so his beneficiaries could collect on his life insurance.

In making that determination, Equifax interviewed the doctor's former wife, neighbors, and girl friends, including Lynda. Investigators also interviewed the girl friends and neighbors of Dr. Rawdin's business associate and principal beneficiary. They pored over confidential long-distance phone call records. They obtained accident and arrest records, credit reports, and loan records. A janitor was paid $20 for trash from the partner's office. Equifax obtained a security company's logs showing who entered Dr. Rawdin's offices before his disappearance, including a full roster of his patients. They even interviewed a patient in a mental hospital. (The report's conclusion: The patient could be there a long time.)

More disturbingly, Equifax teamed up with the Dade County State Attorney's office in Miami. Working jointly with the prosecutors, Equifax suggested who should be subpoenaed in the government's confidential investigation of the doctor's disappearance. Once witnesses had been compelled to testify, Equifax investigators read the confidential testimony. They then quoted from the testimony in reports distributed to the six life insurance companies. In turn, Equifax investigators shared their information with the prosecutors. Often, the information consisted of hearsay upon hearsay, with some reports containing erroneous facts about Dr. Rawdin's partner.

In at least one instance, an Equifax investigator and a government prosecutor jointly interviewed a witness.

In the end, Equifax compiled 130 pages of single-spaced, typewritten reports. The company turned up little to suggest the doctor had staged his own death. By all accounts, he was close to his sons from his first marriage and saw the three youngest ones on a regular basis. However, on the basis of the reports, the life insurance companies held up payments of claims for five years.

Commenting on Equifax's investigation, Magis, the Equifax assistant vice-president, said such investigations are necessary to explore fully a possible motive for a staged disappearance. "Any situation like this one has a possible romantic motive," he said, noting that the size of the claims called for a more extended investigation.

By any standard, Dr. Rawdin's disappearance was bizarre. Rawdin, a Brooklyn native, had graduated from the Albert Einstein School of Medicine in New York. "The field of preventive medicine is just now opening up," he had told an interviewer the year before the mishap. "Many things can be done now that could not be done twenty-five years ago. No one said that illness that befalls our bodies as we get older must happen."

Since his divorce from his second wife, the forty-one-year-old physician had led an unstable life. Given to whims, he rented a twenty-foot speedboat on Mother's Day, May 11, 1975, telling his oldest son to meet him for a fishing trip. Loading the boat with fishing gear and food, he embarked at 6:00 A.M. By sunrise, his boat had been spotted, speeding in a circle at full throttle. Three fishermen followed the boat and saw it run aground off Bear Cut between Miami Beach and Key Biscayne. No one was inside.

The next day, *The Miami Herald* ran a three-paragraph story. It quoted police authorities as saying Dr. Rawdin's body must have been eaten by sharks. It never has been found.

Police noticed some blood on the windshield, and medical examiners would later differ on whether the pattern indicated the blood had been poured on the windshield or had spurted from a wound. Wedged between a seat and the inner wall of the boat was a plastic packet containing implements for drawing blood.

Equifax entered the case two weeks later when one of the life insurance companies requested a "special disappearance investigation." An investigator from Equifax's Miami office began by visiting National Boat Rentals, the last place Dr. Rawdin had been seen alive.

Quoting the proprietor in his subsequent report, the investigator said the six-foot-tall doctor first came to the rental firm the Thursday before his disappearance. Dr. Rawdin asked about the size of the boats, and the proprietor showed him a twenty-foot model that the doctor said he would rent that Sunday.

"Dr. Rawdin explained that he did not have many opportunities to associate with his oldest son, who was seventeen years of age, and he felt this was a good way of getting to know each other again," the investigator wrote.

When the doctor arrived a few minutes after 5:30 A.M. on Sunday, the proprietor gave him a map of the surrounding waterways and showed him how to proceed to Crandon Park Marina, where Dr. Rawdin said he would be meeting his son and some friends. The trip should have taken about twenty-five minutes. The proprietor also gave the doctor a lecture on the hazards of going out to sea in the rental boats. He said it was his practice to "scare the hell out of people who rent his boats," so they don't try to take them out on the ocean.

"He stated that the subject appeared to be in very good spirits, was quite happy and excited about meeting his son and his friends for a short fishing trip, and seemed to be anticipating an enjoyable day," the report said.

After leaving the rental firm, the investigator drove along Dade Boulevard to the Collins Canal, driving parallel to the route Dr. Rawdin would have taken. "I found a total of six small bridges which crossed this canal. . . . With the exception of one bridge, all the others had a very low clearance limit and, with the water level being close to high tide, would provide very little clearance room for a boat such as the size the subject was using," the Equifax investigator said. "It would require, in my estimation, a boat to move very slowly in order not to hit the underside of the bridges." In addition, the investigator noted that limbs from several trees hung over the canal, requiring boaters to detour around them if they wanted to avoid being hit.

Continuing to an island known as Virginia Key, where Dr. Rawdin's boat had plowed twenty-five feet onto the beach, the investigator interviewed a Dade County marine patrol officer, who told the investigator a search helicopter had arrived at the scene just after the boat ran aground at about 7:00 A.M. The pilot reported seeing hundreds of sharks in the area. The officer said they did not appear frenzied, as they might if they were attacking a body. The officer considered it unlikely that the body had floated out to sea, and he suggested that the accident had been staged.

The investigator next saw the Dade County homicide detective assigned to the case. He told him that Dr. Rawdin and his associate had opened a new business just three months earlier. Called the Institute for Preventive Medicine, it gave patients a series of tests and placed them on an individually tailored regimen of diet, exercise, and therapeutic doses of vitamins and minerals.

Dr. Rawdin's associate had attended medical school but left after an injury temporarily blurred his vision. He acted as executive director of the institute, which was owned by Rawdin. Since Rawdin and his partner had agreed that the latter was spending more time on the business at the Douglas Center in Coral Gables than Rawdin, they decided that the partner would get two-thirds of the profits while Dr. Rawdin would get the rest.

"He [the detective] described the associate as being the talker and the hustler for the business. He was a salesman and would go out and solicit individuals as well as groups in an effort to get them as clients for Dr. Rawdin," the investigator wrote in his report.

The detective said Dr. Rawdin had borrowed heavily to start the institute, which was elegantly furnished with thick carpeting and handmade desks inlaid with Moroccan leather. The loans had come from a bank and from his parents, and some of the life insurance Dr. Rawdin purchased had been required by the bank before it would loan him the money. The detective quoted Dr. Rawdin's accountant as saying the doctor's income was less than $25,000 a year.

The evening before the incident, Dr. Rawdin was up with his partner until 3:00 A.M., talking about the new business, the detective quoted the partner as saying. The detective also told the investigator about minute amounts of blood found on the boat and a plastic packet with a small glass vial and three needles found in the boat. "These were the type of needles and packet which normally contained a syringe and four needles used by the medical profession for drawing blood," the investigator said. A needle might have been missing, according to the police detective.

The detective theorized that Dr. Rawdin might have intended to throw the packet overboard, but the wind caught it and blew it back in the boat. In the opinion of the detective, the pattern of blood on the windshield indicated it had not come from a wound because it ran down the glass in a thin line.

Rawdin's parents later said their son often took medical items with him if he thought drug addicts might steal them from his car.

Stirring dozens of unanswered questions, rumors, and hunches, the Equifax investigator recommended an "exhaustive" investigation into the circumstances behind Dr. Rawdin's disappearance. Based on his recommendation, all six companies—Transamerica Life Insurance & Annuity Company, North American Companies, University Life Insurance Company of America, American Home Assurance Company, Reliance Life Insurance Company, and Sentry Insurance Company—eventually joined in the investigation.

After getting approval from the companies to continue, the investigator conducted a search of public records, including civil suits, land records, and divorce cases. He also looked up credit bureau reports on Dr. Rawdin and his partner, which are not public.

Next, the investigator interviewed Lynda, Dr. Rawdin's last girl friend. Devoting nine single-spaced pages of his reports to the interview, the investigator enumerated her experiences with sex and drugs, her opinions of Dr. Rawdin and his friends, and her physical assets. A separate, one-page report from Equifax's Toronto office listed addresses and auto registration numbers of Lynda, her stepfather, her boyfriend, and a girl friend.

Visiting Lynda in her apartment one Wednesday evening, the investigator began by taking note of Lynda's physical appeal, then related Lynda's story of how she happened to be living in her present apartment. According to Lynda, she had last been employed as a receptionist and switchboard operator in Miami. More recently, she and a girl friend had been living there rent-free in the Miami apartment with the approval of the manager. However, the manager had recently suffered a heart attack, and his wife found out about the arrangement. She had given the women until the next morning to move out.

Turning to the question of how Lynda met Dr. Rawdin, the Equifax report said, "It was around October 1, 1974, that she noticed that she had a urinary infection, and because she did not have a local doctor, she asked a girl friend for the name of a physician she could consult." The doctor was not in, but the receptionist referred Lynda to Dr. Rawdin.

Lynda was his last patient that day, and they sat and talked for an hour. Lynda first said she went to see the doctor to obtain a prescription for antibiotics. "She later revealed in the interview that she had actually gone to the doctor to be treated for gonorrhea, a venereal disease which she had gotten from a Hungarian sailor whom she had stayed with approximately four days, a short time previous to this," the report stated.

Dr. Rawdin asked her out to dinner, but she declined. The next week, she began experiencing severe pains in the abdomen. Dr. Rawdin had Lynda admitted to a hospital, where a surgeon removed her appendix. Dr. Rawdin visited her in the hospital every day and seemed quite interested in her. After she was discharged from the hospital a week later, he made a date with her for the following Sunday.

After going out to dinner, they attended a party given by a friend of Dr. Rawdin's, according to the report. The friend was a "hippie type" who used hard drugs. After smoking several joints at the party, they went back to Dr. Rawdin's apartment. She spent the night and ended up moving in with him. After a week, ". . . she became very aware of what was going on, as he was making very heavy sexual demands on her," according to the report. "He would continuously want to fondle her and was always chasing her around the apartment.

"I would like to point out at this time," the investigator wrote, "that I pursued a line of questioning into the sexual habits of Dr. Rawdin in an effort to determine if he possibly was a homosexual.

She did describe him as being a 'poor lover' and [said that he] preferred oral and anal sex rather than the normal sex act. She stated that she did not believe that he was homosexual and did not give her any indication of this."

Lynda said the twice-married doctor would have an occasional glass of wine or drink a "side car" when they went out for dinner. He smoked pot on occasion, but did not indulge heavily. "She stated that she herself enjoyed smoking pot, and would occasionally 'pop some pills'. . . . She had never used heroin or cocaine on a regular basis, although she had experimented with both of these drugs in the past."

In the last few days before moving out of Dr. Rawdin's apartment, the report said, he had wanted only anal sex, which disgusted and hurt her. "Because of this, she made the decision to move out away from him and not have anything further to do with him."

Leaving Dr. Rawdin's garden apartment complex near Dadeland Shopping Center, she moved in with a male friend on North Kendall Drive in Miami. After a few days with him, she moved into her own apartment, since her boyfriend from Canada was about to visit her. When the boyfriend arrived, she lived with him at the spacious Four Ambassadors Hotel for six weeks. However, they broke up after they both went back to Toronto for a month.

When she returned to Miami, Lynda decided she was tired of the life she had been living. She wanted to be alone and get herself "straightened out." However, she soon became lonely and called Dr. Rawdin, who urged her to meet him for dinner, according to the report. Although she did not want to resume the type of sexual relationship they had had, she met him for dinner at the Captain's Table. They went back to his apartment and went to bed for a short time. He got up to work on his income tax returns.

After several more nights with Dr. Rawdin, she moved out a second time. "She stated that, although he was not as sexually demanding as before, she did not like the type of sex acts that he was demanding from her, and it was because of this that she felt she could no longer stay with him."

Lynda stayed with another male friend for a week. While she

was sunning herself at his pool, another man she had known showed her a newspaper clipping reporting Dr. Rawdin's disappearance.

"She stated that she was quite shocked, and she then decided to go on a 'big high.' She did this by taking several pills as well as smoking pot," the Equifax report said. "She stated that she actually remembered very little of what transpired Monday night." During the evening, she moved out of the boyfriend's apartment and registered at a Holiday Inn with a girl friend. The next night, they stayed with another male friend. The following evening, they stayed with a friend of his.

"They went to a party Thursday night that was heavy with drugs," the investigator wrote. "On Friday, she and [the girl friend] drove off for Canada in her Mustang."

Lynda told the investigator Dr. Rawdin had never suggested going fishing but had mentioned the possibility of renting a boat, going out in the ocean, and smoking pot while watching the lights of Miami. She said he called several boat rental firms, but they had no boats that could be taken out on the ocean.

"She stated that she could not believe that Ken would just disappear, as he was not the type of individual who would cause his family any grief," the report said. "He loved his children very much, as well as his parents."

Noting that he felt Lynda had been honest with him, the Equifax investigator said he learned from the homicide detective that Lynda had given him a similar account of her dealings with Dr. Rawdin.

The investigator next interviewed Dr. Rawdin's accountant and close friend, who had been waiting to meet him for the fishing trip planned for the day the doctor disappeared. The accountant said he had not gone fishing in fifteen years, and he did not think Dr. Rawdin had gone fishing in at least that long. However, he said the doctor was an excellent swimmer and scuba diver. Dr. Rawdin took the same vitamins he prescribed for patients at his institute and normally subsisted on three or four hours of sleep a night. Because of problems related to his two failed marriages, Dr. Rawdin was seeing a psychiatrist, the accountant told the investigator.

The accountant described Dr. Rawdin's second wife, an airline stewardess, as a "very free-spirit type of woman" from California. She had known Dr. Rawdin for a year before they got married, and they were divorced just two months later, the accountant said in the report. "He stated the reason for the divorce was that they were just not compatible and [the ex-wife] was rather loose and spirited and wanted to go her own way." The report continued, "He explained that Dr. Rawdin loved his children very much and was very close to them. He was very concerned about their welfare and kept in constant touch with them."

According to the accountant, it was Dr. Rawdin's idea to buy large amounts of life insurance. Both the accountant and the partner had tried to talk him out of purchasing so much. Since he was in good spirits before his disappearance, the accountant said he believes Dr. Rawdin had an accident.

Dr. Rawdin's second wife, the airline stewardess, told the Equifax investigator that she had talked with Dr. Rawdin by telephone a week before his disappearance. "She stated he was somewhat inadequate as a sexual partner when they were living together; however, she believed this was due to the hard and long hours he put into the business," the report said.

The Equifax investigator next learned about a man who had tried to commit suicide by jumping into Biscayne Bay. Failing to end his life, he climbed an electrical transformer. When apprehended, he had a sheet of Dr. Rawdin's printed memo pads in his wallet. "From the office of Dr. Kenneth S. Rawdin," it said.

Interviewing the man at the mental hospital where he had been committed, the investigator noted that the man's right arm had been amputated because of the electrical burns he received in his suicide attempt. "He indicated he has a hard time remembering anything since his mishap," the investigator noted in his report. "When the name of the partner was brought up, the subject was holding a glass of water, and his hand began to shake and he dropped a packet of tea onto the floor." The man then stared into space. "Due to the actions of the subject and his general mannerisms, it appears he might be in the psychiatric unit for quite some time."

Reporting back to the insurance companies, the investigator said he had provided the homicide detective with the details of his investigation and had shared what he had found with the prosecutors as well. In one meeting with the State Attorney's office, he said, he had spent three hours discussing the case. During that meeting, ". . . information that I had developed during the course of my investigation was passed on to them," he said.

Near the end of the meeting, "I was told that I would have the complete cooperation from both departments [police and State Attorney's office] in any developments that might occur pertaining to this case, as well as their working together with me in this investigation," he told the companies. "I would like to point out," the investigator continued, "that with the State Attorney's office being involved in this investigation, we now have subpoena power." The investigator went on to describe subpoenas that were about to be issued, including one for Dr. Rawdin's partner.

In July, the investigator informed the insurance companies that long-distance phone call records had been subpoenaed and "we are in the process of checking these various numbers out. . . . I am working very closely with the State Attorney's office and have suggested to them that they subpoena [the partner's secretary]."

The partner himself had rebuffed the investigator's efforts to interview him, referring him to his lawyer, who never set up an appointment. However, the State Attorney's office gave the investigator something better—access to the associate's confidential deposition, given in response to a subpoena. After reviewing the document, the investigator forwarded to the insurance companies seven single-spaced, typewritten pages of notes summarizing the depositions of the associate and of his girl friend.

In the deposition, the partner traced in minute detail his where-abouts in the days leading up to Dr. Rawdin's disappearance. He later gave a 450-page deposition in the legal proceedings conducted to determine the disposition of the life insurance proceeds.

By the end of the year, Dr. Rawdin's associate had moved from Miami without leaving a forwarding address, and Equifax tried to find him because the insurance companies wanted him to appear in legal proceedings brought against them by the associate. Although the investigator noted the State Attorney's office had not charged him with any crime, the prosecutors worked together with Equifax to try to locate the associate, the reports show.

One of the insurance companies notified Equifax that it had received an affidavit from Dr. Rawdin's partner stating he was trav-eling in the United States, Canada, and Europe. So Equifax inter-viewed the Minneapolis notary who had notarized the document. But the notary knew nothing more than what appeared on the document.

When Equifax learned that the associate might have been treated at the Mayo Clinic, the Equifax Minneapolis office reported it had the Mayo Clinic's records checked but could find no sign of him.

Interviewing the associate's former neighbors, the investigator found one who "appeared to know more than she was relating," so the prosecutors subpoenaed her. But she knew nothing about her ex-neighbor's location. Equifax interviewed the moving company that had transferred the partner's belongings to a warehouse, and the investigator talked with his mailman and the former supervisor of the partner's mother at the school where she had taught. Repeat-edly, Equifax checked credit bureau files on the elusive associate, his girl friend, and others who came under scrutiny.

One evening, the investigator met with a prosecutor and an inves-tigative reporter from *The Miami Herald*. "We began matching up our notes on various aspects of this case . . ." the report said. "Subsequent to our meeting . . . a newspaper article appeared in *The Miami Herald* on November 30, 1975, which we will attach to this report," the investigator said.

Headlined PHYSICIAN STILL ALIVE, SOME FEEL, the story quoted Dade County Medical Examiner Joseph H. Davis as saying the blood on the boat's windshield, based on a photograph he saw, had been "poured gently" by a deliberate hand. Meanwhile, the article said, "[the partner] has vanished."

Based on an examination of the same photograph, another medical examiner, Dr. John Feegel of Atlanta, was prepared to give the opposite testimony in the civil litigation. According to Dr. Feegel, the blood pattern could have come from a wound "in very close proximity to the boat and/or windshield." What's more, Dennis Mayer, an official of the National Oceanic and Atmospheric Administration in Miami, was prepared to testify that Dr. Rawdin's body could well have been caught by the Gulf Stream and would never have washed ashore, according to a summary of the expected expert testimony in the case given to lawyers for Equifax.

At this point, the lengthy legal process took over. In 1980, a probate judge declared Dr. Rawdin legally dead, prompting the companies to raise other grounds for denying the claim. However, they have since paid Dr. Rawdin's associate $657,500 as settlement for the $1 million in death benefits owed to him. He, in turn, filed suit against Equifax and others, claiming he was forced to close the practice and was hounded out of Miami because of the company's tactics. Equifax settled the invasion of privacy lawsuit by agreeing to pay the associate $70,000 and writing him a letter of apology.

"We acknowledge that various activities alleged in your complaint did occur," the letter said in part. "Although we reiterate that we intended no injury, we recognize that these activities may have caused you considerable anxiety and harm, and that they therefore should not have occurred," the November 24, 1982, letter said. In addition to the Equifax settlement, the State of Florida, on behalf of the State Attorney's office, agreed to pay the former partner $15,000.

"I've never contended the insurance companies didn't have a

right to conduct a thorough investigation," said Dr. Rawdin's associate. "But there have to be tighter controls when writing reports that can be defamatory."

■

Clearly, the investigations themselves need to be more rigorously controlled. The industry pays little attention to the cost effectiveness of hiring Equifax to gather information that is of questionable value. And practically no thought is given to the implications of storing such nonsense in files on the personal lives of millions of life insurance applicants.

In their insensitivity to privacy concerns, it is as if the investigators, along with the rest of the life insurance industry, are living in another age. Operating in a regulatory vacuum, there is no reason why the industry should feel compelled to enter the current era. So practices outlawed years ago in most other businesses continue unabated.

The industry's effort at developing a "model" state privacy bill is but one example. Designed to thwart passage of a federal privacy statute governing insurance companies, the new state law was recommended by an industry-dominated committee that included W. Lee Burge, chairman of Equifax, and Robert S. Seiler, general counsel of Allstate Life Insurance company, who describes himself as the industry's chief opponent of federal privacy legislation covering the companies.

One of the effects of the new law is that it erodes the rights that consumers already had to sue companies that falsely disseminate information about their personal lives. As Dr. Rawdin's partner's experience indicates, that right is crucial. He now believes that if it were not for the perseverance of his Miami attorney, he would have been helpless against Equifax. Because of his experiences, he is attending law school.

9. THE INVESTMENTS

■ A drunk, seeking spare change, wanders through the burnished revolving doors of the Newark headquarters of Prudential Insurance Company of America. He has come to the right place: Prudential, the largest life insurance company in the world, has $67 billion in assets.

Each week, Prudential invests another $200 million in real estate, bonds, stocks, and mortgages. Every day, a chain-smoking man in Prudential's white marble headquarters buys bank certificates of deposit to temporarily invest what amounts to Prudential's spare change—typically $40 million in a single day.

"It's a kind of universal power plant, vast of maw and spout, breathing in and breathing out," *Fortune* magazine said of Prudential in 1964. "Its function is the collection and redistribution of the people's savings. As the giant mechanism pumps away, there are few U.S. businesses—or even U.S. citizens, in fact—that escape the effect of either its updraft or its downdraft."

As the largest company in the business, Prudential and its investment operations illustrate what happens to your life insurance dollar once it is paid to an agent for a policy. After it goes to pay commissions and other expenses, that dollar winds up being invested in bowling alleys, wineries, and skyscrapers. The income from those investments—$46 billion a year—goes to reduce the total premiums charged for life and health insurance and annuities.

For the most part, the companies invest wisely, and in this chapter, we will see how they do it, taking a look at several investments that did well and one that did poorly. The problem is not an abundance of poor investments but rather an abundance of riches well beyond what is needed to cover policyholders' claims. As we shall see, the companies use ingenious accounting to hide the extent of their vast treasures, allowing them to retain the money tax-free and magnify their power.

When people think of money, they think of Wall Street and banks. Yet Prudential's assets are exceeded by only three financial institutions, Citibank, BankAmerica, and Chase Manhattan Bank. Prudential has more money than either Exxon or General Motors. Within the financial world, only the banking industry has more money than the life insurance industry, which accounts for one in eight dollars invested by Americans and U.S. institutions.

Unlike banks, life insurance companies are long-term lenders, which gives them more muscle than banks. In financing real estate development, banks make construction loans, which endure only while construction is in progress. Before a bank will agree to make such a loan, it must know that a developer has obtained a "permanent" lender. The permanent lender agrees to loan money to pay off the construction loan. Repayment is usually required over a period of twenty or thirty years.

Life insurance companies are the major source of this long-term financing, giving them veto power over entire construction projects. Life insurance companies are able to make such long-term commitments because the nature of their business is long-term—often an entire life span.

The amount put away in investments or reserves is prescribed by state insurance laws. The types and mix of investments are also limited. For example, no more than ten percent of total assets can be invested in common stocks. Some twenty-four pages of the insurance laws describe the other restrictions.

In determining how much money the life insurance companies should retain for future obligations, the regulators and the companies play a fascinating game. Until recently, the regulators required the companies to pretend that people will die at the same rate they did in the 1950s, although the death rate is about forty percent lower now. The regulators updated the required mortality table, but it still depicts a death rate considerably higher than the actual death rate. What's more, the companies, for the most part, continue to adhere to the old table in determining prices.

The companies play the same game with the rate they assume they will earn on their investments. That rate is crucial. Since so much of life insurance companies' income flows from its investments, the amount of investment income can have a substantial impact on the premiums they charge.

What the companies do is pretend they will earn very little on their investments—as little as three or four percent—when they are really making better than double that rate. They then raise their premiums on the grounds their future investment earnings will not be sufficient to offset their costs. When it turns out they do have substantial investment earnings, the companies stash that extra money away as reserves.

In the less-than-competitive world of life insurance, that frolic only makes sense. If the companies raised their expectations of future investment income, they would only have to lower their premiums. Or they would have to declare the excess money as profits, which are taxable. Why reduce premiums unduly, when people cannot discern the prices anyway? This way, the companies can hoard the excess tax-free.

The regulators play along with the charade, passing laws that require unrealistic investment assumptions at the request of the companies. Until recently, the laws required the companies to assume they will earn no more than four percent on their investments. More recently, the regulators revised the law to permit a floating investment assumption that now hovers around six percent. However, most of the companies continue to use the old four percent rate or even a rate of three percent.

Life insurance executives claim that they start with outdated death rates and investment returns when determining prices, but then lower them because they know the assumptions are too conservative. This tactic usually disarms meddlesome questioners. It is true that, under the insurance laws, prices may be reduced below the minimum assumptions established by law if the money to pay for the lowered prices comes out of a different financial pot called surplus.

But this stratagem lasts only so long. Somebody paid for the money in the surplus accounts. They are not inexhaustible. Eventually, the money required to keep the assumptions conservative comes out of the consumers' pockets.

If these unrealistic assumptions are not enough to hide the companies' profits, the regulators require still another stratagem that does. An accounting system unique to insurance companies downplays the companies' income and assets. This gambol makes the job of the regulators easier. If they can make the companies pretend they have less money than they do, the companies will be forced to keep on hand more funds than they need to cover expenses and death benefits. That means the regulators can regulate less. It also means that life insurance companies are pots of gold.

The accounting system they require is called statutory accounting. It differs from Generally Accepted Accounting Principles (GAAP)—the method used by most other companies and accountants—in that it undervalues almost everything. A significant portion of a company's assets may be in the form of office furniture, office machines, cars, and other fixed assets. Yet statutory accounting does not recognize them as assets at all.

The biggest difference is that statutory accounting requires the companies to deduct from their income all the expenses of acquiring new business in the first year, instead of spreading it out over the life of the policy, according to George E. Bouchie, a manager of Coopers & Lybrand in Boston who specializes in auditing insurance companies.

We can see the effect of this sleight-of-hand by looking at companies that are required to report their financial results both ways. Aetna Life & Casualty Company, being regulated by state insurance departments, reports its figures to them using statutory accounting. On the other hand, as a publicly owned company, Aetna is required by the Securities and Exchange Commission to use GAAP accounting when reporting to stockholders. According to GAAP accounting, Aetna's life insurance division in one year had total premiums and investment income of $9.2 billion. According to statutory accounting, it had only $8.0 billion in total income. It is something like the emperor's new clothes in reverse. If the regulators say a company has received $1.2 billion less than it did, then for all intents and purposes it did.

We can see the same vanishing act by looking at Aetna's life insurance assets. According to GAAP accounting, they came to $31.7 billion. According to statutory accounting, they amounted to only $31.3 billion—a difference of $434 million.

The different ways of accounting for the money may seem of little consequence, but they actually hide billions of dollars in excess funds. In the actuarial profession, there is a rule of thumb: For every percentage point reduction in investment returns, reserves have to be increased ten percent. As a result, said William A. White, chief actuary of the New Jersey State Insurance Department, "Presently, the excess in life insurance reserves would be on the order of a third." If that is true, the excess amounts to some $70 billion.

Asked about this, Richard V. Minck, executive vice-president of the American Council of Life Insurance, said, "I think the companies believe they could survive and remain solvent if they reduced the reserves by a third." But he added, "I don't know if the regulators would want to because they worry about the long-term nature of the companies' obligations."

The differences have not gone unnoticed among investors looking to buy life insurance companies. "The reserves are so redundant that there are plenty of willing buyers," said Frederick S. Townsend of Conning & Company, a Hartford, Connecticut, stock brokerage firm. "The companies are reserving too much; probably a third or more of the reserves are not necessary in life insurance companies," he said.

Clearly, no one wants the companies to fail to honor their commitments. But hoarding extra billions of dollars does not serve the consumer. The practice goes on because the companies don't mind.

Indeed, the laws requiring unrealistic investment and mortality assumptions are introduced at their request. Once the laws go into effect, the companies use even more conservative assumptions than they are required to use.

"The more reserves the company gets, the more money they control," explained James P. Gibbons, Jr., president of the holding company that owns Consumers United Life Insurance Company. "A lot is tax-free, they get interest, and they don't have to give it back to the policyholders," he said. "The name of the game is using the money. They use your money and invest it. They take that cash and they buy buildings. . . . It's a small coterie of people making decisions about enormous amounts of money."

■

For the most part, the people who make those decisions are unimposing white males who rarely receive attention from the press or public. Yet their decisions can make or break a city, turn an industry into a thriving metropolis or a mortuary, or run a stock through the ceiling or down to the basement.

In investing in real estate, the smaller companies tend to rely on realtors and mortgage bankers, who receive a fee or commission for originating an investment deal. The larger companies have staffs fully equipped to originate projects and even build them.

By any standard, the company that has won at this game is Prudential. It owns all or part of the Empire State Building in New York City, the New York Hilton, the Hyatt Regency in Chicago, First International Plaza in Houston, Alcoa Twin Towers in Los Angeles, Embarcadero Center in San Francisco, and Poydras Plaza in New Orleans. The company's Prudential Center in Boston and Prudential Plaza in Chicago dominate the skylines of those cities.

Prudential accounts for one in ten of the dollars invested by the life insurance industry. It insures roughly one in four Americans over the age of eighteen. There is nothing else like Prudential in the world.

Prudential's billions started with pennies paid by poor factory workers to obtain industrial life insurance. Prudential's founder, the lean, bearded John F. Dryden, was a Yale University dropout who became a life insurance agent and then decided to set up his own company selling insurance patterned after the industrial insurance sold in England.

Apparently because the charter Dryden drafted gave him too much discretion in the handling of funds, New York State declined to let him do business there. Moving across the Hudson River to Newark, he found financial backers, despite the depression following the Panic of 1873.

With $6,000 in cash and another $24,000 in pledged capital, Dryden's company opened its doors in 1875. The office was a below-street-level store front on Broad Street, just a few blocks from where Prudential's gleaming marble corporate headquarters stands today. It was called the Prudential Friendly Society, named after the British company that had started selling industrial insurance some twenty-five years earlier.

By the end of 1875, Prudential had 284 policies in force. "One of the most gratifying facts connected with this society is its strength and security," the *Newark Register* noted at the time, adding that Prudential "may be said to be founded upon a rock." Despite the seeming connection with its advertising slogan, Prudential did not begin using the motto "Prudential Has the Strength of Gibraltar" until 1896. It was devised by Mortimer Remington, an advertising executive with the J. Walter Thompson Company, as he peered from the window of the train he was taking between Newark and New York at a sheath of rocks jutting into the sky. By the turn of the century, the British government was regularly sending Prudential a piece of the rock of Gibraltar whenever the company needed it to display in a newly opened office.

Today, the man who presides over Prudential's wealth is Frank J. Hoenemeyer, a soft-spoken, up-through-the-ranks investment officer who rides through Newark's trash-strewn streets every day to decide how the largest builder and long-term lender in the world will allocate its wealth. As vice-chairman of the board, Hoenemeyer makes $499,947, a tad under the salary of Prudential's president, David J. Sherwood, who makes $514,818 a year.

Hoenemeyer does not personally become involved unless an investment amounts to $100 million or more. Rather, his role is to decide how much of Prudential's available funds will be invested in stocks, bonds, real estate, or mortgages. In making those decisions, Hoenemeyer commands an army of more than 3,500 investment officers, economists, lawyers, accountants, stock analysts, and clerical personnel. Once a month, he holds a meeting in his high-ceilinged, blue-carpeted office to forecast economic trends and plot strategy. Those forecasts, in turn, influence how much money will go into the various forms of investments.

Describing what Hoenemeyer does, Raymond A. Charles, until recently Prudential's senior vice-president for bond investments, quoted Hoenemeyer as saying "'Knab [Donald R. Knab, senior vice-president for real estate investments], you take so much [billions of dollars], and Charles, you take so much, and I'll keep so much as a reserve.'"

Present and former colleagues describe Hoenemeyer as objective in evaluating investment opportunities, demanding as a boss, and personally inscrutable.

"I never really knew what he was thinking," said Edgar F. Bunce, Jr., who reported to Hoenemeyer as senior vice-president for common stock investments. Burton G. Malkiel, a Prudential director who is dean of the Yale University School of Management, said of him, "He is one of the smartest investment people I've run into."

A modest sailor who collects French impressionist paintings, Hoenemeyer likes to travel and to putter in the garden of his Madison, New Jersey, home. Unlike Prudential Chairman Beck, Hoenemeyer is not a gregarious type. When senior officers meet at a resort, Hoenemeyer is likely to call a meeting while Beck is out on the golf course. When Hoenemeyer travels on Prudential's fleet of helicopters and jets, he brings along a briefcase stuffed with papers.

Born in Cincinnati, Hoenemeyer is the son of a securities salesman who suggested when his son was in high school that he pick some stocks and see how they fly. The younger Hoenemeyer picked the Curtiss-Wright aircraft company and a parachute maker. Both did well.

After receiving a master's degree from the University of Pennsylvania's Wharton School, Hoenemeyer, in 1947, became a trainee in Prudential's bond department in Cincinnati. He moved up to become a vice-president, senior vice-president, and then executive vice-president in charge of investments.

"What I look for is intelligence and ability to work with other people," said Hoenemeyer. Bunce, the former senior vice-president for common stock investments, said Hoenemeyer's management style sets people up to compete against each other. "Frank likes to have two guys snarling at each other," he said.

"Hoenemeyer is stubborn," said Donald S. MacNaughton, who preceded Beck as chief executive officer of Prudential. A lawyer who started at Prudential in 1955 at a salary of $12,500 a year, MacNaughton now heads Hospital Corporation of America. "I suggested to him one time we should buy common stocks," MacNaughton said of Hoenemeyer. "The market [Dow Jones industrial average] was 620, 640. He gave me reasons why their current policy not to buy was right. I said I think you're wrong. He did what he wanted because he's stubborn.

"Of course, he was vindicated," MacNaughton said, adding that he chose not to second-guess Hoenemeyer out of respect for his financial acumen.

American presidents come and go; short of blowing up the planet, their power to change things is limited by laws and the need to get congressional approval. Hoenemeyer has been in charge of Prudential's billions since 1965. No one outside investment circles has heard of him, but he is indisputably one of the most powerful people in the country. "It is a lot of money," Hoenemeyer conceded. But he said the decisions are not made by one person.

In deciding where and how to invest, Hoenemeyer and his staff try to gauge whether a city will grow or stagnate. That the Phillies happened to have won the World Series when Hoenemeyer visited Philadelphia did nothing to harm the city's chances of getting more from Prudential's coffers. "It's going to do something for the town," Hoenemeyer said. "You get a feeling about a city from the people you see on the street. . . . What's their attitude? Do they seem to be walking purposefully?"

Right now, Hoenemeyer is big on Houston, Dallas, San Francisco, and Denver. These are cities "where you get a sense of excitement," he said. Predictably, Prudential has been plowing money into real estate in each of these cities.

Funds are not automatically allocated to particular parts of the country. "We look for attractive possibilities. . . . We look at the risk-reward situation," Hoenemeyer said.

Hoenemeyer takes the long view. Like the captain of an ocean liner preparing for a voyage, he wants to make sure the ship starts on the right course so it will eventually end up in the right place. "If we don't have some losses," said Hoenemeyer, "we take the position we've been too stringent."

In the eyes of its competitors, Prudential is more aggressive and innovative than most other insurance companies. Prudential was one of the first insurers to develop its own real estate projects. Previously, the companies had been content to lend money and let developers do the building.

Prudential stubbed its toe several times, spending $108 million to build a complex of three forty-two-story apartment and condominium buildings in Guttenberg, New Jersey, overlooking the Hudson River between the Lincoln Tunnel and the George Washington Bridge, only to see it lose money because of cost overruns and a dearth of tenants.

Knab, the senior vice-president for real estate investments, sees developing as a way to make a greater contribution than by merely lending. "We become part of the creative process as producers of the financing and as developers and owners," said Knab, a swashbuckling, $296,287-a-year executive who directs the efforts of 1,300 people. "When you build a new project or property, it stimulates the creative process, requires courage, testing your theories, and you say 'yes' or 'no' or 'maybe.'"

"Very few insurance companies are qualified to do development," said Jay A. Pritzker, chairman and president of Hyatt International Corporation. "Prudential is trying to do it. Even they have trouble," he said. "You need a guy who will stay up until midnight."

In deciding where to invest, Hoenemeyer keeps his personal predilections to himself. He abhors airport motels, but when they came into vogue he realized that they could be commercially successful, and he approved financing to build them. "One of the things I learned a long time ago is you shouldn't judge real estate or clothes by what you like. You realize there is a market out there that might like it," Hoenemeyer said.

Under his management, Prudential rarely does anything in a small way. When the company decided to broaden its range of financial services, it gobbled up Bache Group, Inc., one of the largest securities firms on Wall Street, for a cool $385 million in cash in 1981. Prudential expects to use Bache's customer base of more than 600,000 to sell a range of financial products.

In typical Prudential fashion, Prudential President Sherwood called Beck on a Thursday in Ocean Reef, Florida, where the Prudential chairman was vacationing, to let him know that Bache was up for sale. Beck gave the go-ahead to work up a proposal, and by the time he returned on Monday, Prudential was ready to make an offer. Canceling previously scheduled appointments without explanation, Beck worked out the details with officers and directors. Four days later, he announced Prudential's offer to buy one of the oldest securities firms on Wall Street, giving Prudential a foothold on an entire new market.

Even before Hoenemeyer's accession Prudential moved with giant steps. When the company saw a need for more office space in Boston in the 1950s, it boldly mapped out the Prudential Center in the neglected Back Bay area. More than double the size of Rockefeller Center in New York, it included a gleaming white fifty-two-story tower that was then the tallest building in Boston. Encouraged by Prudential's presence, other developers—including the Christian Science Church—began building, renovating, or expanding in the area. Today, the Back Bay area is an attractive and bustling shopping and cultural center.

If only because of its sheer size, Prudential is able to guarantee that a project will be successful. Even if the project is risky, Prudential has the resources to stick with it over time. A good example is an office park Prudential built on land owned by Princeton University.

For years, Princeton officials had pondered what to do with 1,600 acres of wooded land the university owned adjacent to its New Jersey campus. The land had been purchased in 1952 for possible campus expansion, but only a portion of it was actually being used by the university, as a center for scientific research. As education costs continued to climb and grants from government agencies dropped off, university officials decided in the early 1970s that the land should earn a return that would supplement Princeton's endowment.

The university hired a consultant in 1972 to draw up a plan for an office park and research complex. The idea was to emulate office parks at the Massachusetts Institute of Technology and Stanford University.

Aside from its proximity to the university, the James Forrestal Center, as it is called, had little to recommend it. The heavily wooded ground was not near a major city, and the surrounding area was nothing more than a pleasant suburban community. In addition, the real estate market at the time was tight.

"As far as I know, Princeton was hitting everyone they could to build at the center," said John F. Moran, who was vice-president for facilities at Princeton. "We talked to hundreds of companies. . . . It was a difficult real estate market. We had a bare piece of land."

In April 1974, William T. Cahill, the former New Jersey governor who was a lawyer for Princeton, set up a meeting at Prudential between Princeton officials and top Prudential officers, including MacNaughton, then chairman and chief executive officer of Prudential. At that meeting, Princeton presented a plan for developing the land jointly with Prudential. Prudential showed little interest.

More meetings were held the next year, and Princeton changed the game plan. Now, the university was not insisting that it share in the ownership of the project, as long as it continued to own the land underlying it. In a separate transaction, the headquarters of the

Robert Wood Johnson Foundation were being constructed on the site, and zoning regulations had been changed.

Still, Prudential would be taking a chance in going ahead, said Jeffrey A. Decker, then Prudential's real estate manager for New Jersey. "It was an unproven area. It was speculative."

Under Prudential's method of operating, ideas for projects usually percolate up from regional offices. The regional offices compete to get their projects approved by higher-level, more experienced executives, who decide how to apportion the available funds.

Because of the changes in the way the project was being presented, said Arnold G. Rebholz, who was chief of Prudential's New Jersey real estate office, "Over five or six months, I came to the conclusion there was a reasonable chance of success." However, a higher-level investment committee still had doubts, and the original project was scaled back so Prudential could pull out after the first 54,000-square-foot building was constructed.

The doubts proved to be unfounded. So far, Prudential has poured more than $40 million into the project, building ten white, low-slung office buildings. As tenants, Princeton's Forrestal Center counts IBM, Xerox, and Mobil Corporation. Since the park opened, the price of the land has increased fourfold according to Robert J. Wolfe, the manager of the center.

A drawback is that Prudential does not share in those increases. Under the arrangement worked out with Princeton, Prudential leases the land for up to seventy years. At the end of that time, the buildings revert to Princeton. However, Prudential can raise its rents in line with the appreciation in the value of the land.

Currently, some of the buildings are earning Prudential a return of as much as fifteen percent on Prudential's initial investment, while others are earning less. Prudential views the Forrestal Center as "very successful." Other developers have begun to build nearby, and the center is an attractive adjunct to the university, which receives well over $400,000 a year in income from it.

Before Prudential goes ahead with a project such as the Forrestal Center, the investment must be approved by the finance committee of Prudential's directors. Once a month, the committee meets in Prudential's spacious board room. Dominated by an oval, mahogany table that measures forty feet across, the beige-carpeted room has red upholstered chairs and nameplates designating where each director sits.

Directors receive a synopsis of each proposed transaction before the meeting. They are also told what stocks Prudential plans to buy, so they will not trade in them for their personal accounts. At one chop, the finance committee may approve $500 million in investments. "It's the only place besides the federal government where you omit the 'zeros' automatically," said Malkiel, the Yale dean who is a Prudential director. "One of the things I enjoy about Prudential is that while we often disagree, one has a feeling of a management that is very responsive to the directors and will often change its mind after discussions with the directors," he said.

With so many billions of dollars entrusted to them, Prudential directors and officers are popular on the cocktail circuit. According to Hoenemeyer, many of the directors occasionally refer potential investments to him or to other investment officers for possible consideration. The requests are considered on an *ad hoc* basis.

"I wouldn't hear about a suggestion all the time if a director suggests an investment of a bond or real estate," Hoenemeyer said. "I would guess in a given year we get fifteen to twenty referrals from directors. Except in very rare circumstances, it would be a director saying, 'Joe, the developer, is looking for a mortgage. Would you call him, or he'll call you.'" In a few instances, Hoenemeyer said, the director making the suggestion is more closely involved. For example, the director might have represented the developer as his lawyer. The director would then abstain from voting on the matter when it comes up for approval by the board, according to Hoenemeyer.

"Beck [Robert A. Beck, chairman of Prudential] has his friends, too," Hoenemeyer said. "They say they're looking for financing, can you introduce us ... Beck recommends investments, and sometimes it's someone he knows well or he met at a cocktail party and passes it along to the head of the department. If Bob said you can believe this guy, you can trust him, that's one thing," Hoenemeyer said. "Otherwise, you follow it up more."

Said Beck, "A guy in my club will say, 'I have a nice piece of property that you might be interested in.'" After he has referred a possible investment to Prudential officers, Beck said he usually does not know if it goes through.

According to Knab, perhaps six investments referred by directors each year actually wind up in Prudential's real estate portfolio. Most often, they are located in New Jersey. "When an individual uses a good connection, he has probably exhausted other possibilities," Knab said. "We tend to view them with a jaundiced eye."

Sometimes, Prudential directors find themselves subjected to political pressures. David L. Yunich, a Prudential director who was formerly vice-chairman of R. H. Macy & Co., said then New York Governor Nelson Rockefeller asked him to torpedo Prudential's plans to buy a major share of bonds to build a sports complex in the New Jersey Meadowlands.

The complex was to be the home of the New York Giants, and Rockefeller wanted the football team to remain in New York. Rockefeller "pressured me to scuttle the Meadowlands," said the Scarsdale, New York, resident, who is a member of Prudential's finance committee. "They were going to put the Giants out of business. There was a real power play." In the end, said Yunich, he voted to approve the financing, and the investment paid off.

In the board rooms and legislature of New Jersey, Prudential's power is unquestioned. "If the president or chairman of Prudential makes ten calls, it can get the sports complex built," said Jon F. Hanson, a Hackensack, New Jersey, developer.

Given its power and wealth, Prudential's physical location often takes visitors by surprise. Catty-corner to a Gino's hamburger stand and across the street from a wig store in the economically depressed city of Newark, Prudential corporate headquarters is practically the last vestige of what was once a booming city. If Hoenemeyer favors cities where people walk with a spring to their gait, Newark does not make it. Few cities in America have so many unsmiling people.

At night, the streets are practically empty, as if war had been declared and the curfew had passed. Around Prudential's quitting time of 4:10 P.M., there is a mass exodus to the train station so people are not caught going home in the dark. Even Federal Bureau of Investigation agents have been mugged there on their way from their offices to the train station.

The decision to stay in the crime-ridden city has turned a number of talented Prudential executives away. Financial reporters are sometimes taken aback when told Prudential has no executive offices in New York, although Prudential does maintain a suite at the Waldorf in New York so investment officers can meet with Wall Street movers. Because of a decentralization program begun in 1946, the majority of Prudential's 75,000 employees and agents work in other parts of the country. But Prudential's continued presence in Newark has prevented the collapse of a city that some say will enjoy a comeback because of its proximity to New York City.

Still, the people who run the company work in Newark, and they were shaken when a riot took twenty-three lives, laid waste to dozens of blocks, and caused $8 million in damage in July 1967. After touring the burned-out areas, then Prudential President Orville E. Beal presented a plan to an industry group already considering ways of investing in so-called socially desirable projects in the inner cities.

Under the capitalist system, any investment that is legal and turns a profit is theoretically socially desirable. But life insurance companies, in investing funds on behalf of widows and orphans, must be mindful of the fine line between conserving policyholders' money and helping to further socially desirable ends.

In a matter of months, Prudential could turn Newark into a gold mine, with lovely, tree-shaded boulevards and businesses thriving on subsidized rents. But there is little question that such a move would result in lower returns to Prudential policyholders.

"Everybody [in the industry] said it ought to be done, but we won't have as good a rate of return," recalled the mild-mannered Beal, who started with Prudential in 1926 just out of high school.

Beal suggested sharing the risk. "I went to the meeting and said, 'Why don't we start off with the idea that we can pledge it and pro-rate it,'" he said.

By September, then President Johnson announced that the life insurance industry would allocate $1 billion towards the effort. In the end, some 161 companies representing ninety percent of the assets of the industry contributed to the program according to their size. Prudential, being the biggest, allocated the most to the program.

Over the next five years, the commitment grew to $2 billion. According to the Center for Corporate Public Involvement, an industry group that coordinated the efforts, the money produced 116,000 housing units, sixty day-care centers, two industrial parks, and forty nursing homes.

In evaluating the program later, the companies figured that, because of a higher rate of foreclosures and loan delinquencies, they had lost about a percentage point in yield when compared with their other investments.

In carrying out its commitment to the cities, Prudential financed Gateway Center in Newark, a complex of offices and a hotel attached by an overhead bridge to the railway station that shuttles commuters to New York City. For a number of years after ground was broken in 1968, the project ran in the red, with the hotel less than half occupied and the office building not yet completed. In 1976, Prudential had to take it over from the developer, Food Fair Properties, Inc. After spending money on remodeling the hotel and finishing the office building, Gateway began to report a profit, and Prudential is now planning a second office building in the Gateway complex. For Prudential, the deal had a side benefit: Prudential can get anyone a room at the hotel, a five-minute walk from corporate headquarters.

Currently, life insurance companies plow some $2 billion a year into socially desirable projects. The focus has broadened to include projects that benefit the middle-class—smoking cessation programs, treadmill stress tests, and jogging and exercise courses. But the majority of the programs still focus on urban ills.

Aetna, for instance, allocates $63 million a year for such projects as rehabilitating neighborhoods at the request of community leaders. Through its foundation, Aetna also contributes to the public schools in Hartford, where the company is the largest landowner and employer.

■

The amounts earmarked for such projects represent a pittance compared with the more than $111 billion the companies plow each year into long-term investments. Yet it's better than nothing, and many of the companies' other investments in companies or office buildings may help the poor by providing jobs. Indeed, by pouring life insurance premiums back into the economy, the companies aid a broad range of economic classes.

The bread-and-butter of these investments has always been corporate bonds, which represent $213 billion, or more than a third, of the industry's assets. This segment of the investment business is fraught with technical jargon: bonds, debentures, sinking funds, debt instruments, and notes.

There is really no mystery here. All the words describe ways of lending money. A bond or a note is simply a loan; the loans may be made just as banks make them. In that case, they are called direct or private placements. Or they can be made through a public offering. In that case, they are called public offerings. The terms and conditions are disclosed to the public in statements cleared by the SEC, and anyone can plunk down money and participate in the offering through securities dealers.

Before these public offerings are made, underwriters such as Morgan Stanley & Company or Salomon Brothers check out the finances of the companies, advise the companies on what rates to charge, and provide assurance that the bonds will be purchased by buying the entire offering. They resell the notes or bonds to the public, less a percentage that they keep for their efforts. Rating services like Moody's Investors Service or Standard & Poor's Corporation rank the loans according to their prospects for repayment. Moody's, for example, uses nine ratings ranging from "Aaa" for "gilt edged" bonds that are judged to be of the best quality, down to "C" for bonds judged to have extremely poor prospects. If the loans are not being offered publicly, the life insurance companies usually rate them internally.

The greatest proportion of the industry's bonds—$49 billion worth—are invested in public utilities, permitting electric, telephone, and water companies to expand their services to customers. A company like Aetna may hold as many as eighteen bonds of Alabama Power Company in its portfolio, with maturity dates—when the principal will be repaid—as far off as the year 2007.

Prudential's bond portfolio reads like storefront signs on Main Street, U.S.A. That is because Prudential has long had a policy of allocating some of its bond investment funds to smaller companies. Because these companies may not have the track record of a blue-chip company, Prudential can charge them higher rates, since Prudential takes more of a risk in lending to them.

After bonds, the greatest percentage of the industry's assets is invested in mortgages that usually secure loans on buildings and shopping centers. Mortgages account for more than a quarter of the total assets, or some $142 billion. Another $21 billion is invested in real estate, and $56 billion is invested in common stocks.

Another category of assets, loans to policyholders, accounts for $53 billion, or nine percent of the industry's assets. Since the interest rates charged for these loans is usually lower than the market rate, life insurance companies would rather people not borrow on their policies.

State insurance laws require Prudential and the other companies to file a listing of their investments with the insurance departments of each state where they do business. Since that usually means all fifty states, the companies print the hefty listings and bind them. In Prudential's case, the listing consists of a book the size of a world atlas. It is half an inch thick, eighteen inches long, and twelve inches wide. It takes nearly half a minute to thumb through the pages just listing Prudential's bonds. Each page lists one hundred or so.

About one in five of the bonds is for $50 million or more, and many exceed $100 million in principal amount: International Minerals & Chemical Corporation, $185 million; Indian Head, Inc., $100 million; International Harvester Credit Corporation, $95 million; Gulf & Western Industries, Inc., $125 million.

Within those pages, there are many success stories. Take Scan-Optics, Inc., which was started in 1968 by an engineer and four other founders who thought they could compete with International Business Machines Corporation in the design, manufacture, and sale of optical character readers. OCR's, as they are called, "read" printed or typewritten pages and transform the information into data that a computer can understand and store. In the case of Scan-Optics, based in Hartford, Connecticut, the OCR's could also read handwritten printing.

After attracting an initial investment of $500,000 from neighboring Travelers Insurance Company, Scan-Optics found itself unable to raise substantial additional capital through the then lagging avenue of public offerings. Suggesting Prudential as a source of last resort, a loan broker arranged a $2.5 million investment from the life insurance company in 1971. Subsequently, Prudential plowed another $3.9 million into the company.

The investment has paid off for Prudential. Scan-Optics' revenues more than doubled between 1979 and 1982. Its stock increased in price from $1.00 to $2.00 to as much as $17.00 in 1983. Now, Prudential is selling a portion of its 28 percent stake in the company for $12.5 million at $13.00 a share. At that price, it still has another $7 million in common stock remaining in the company.

"Without Prudential, the company would not have had the money to pursue the opportunities we saw," Richard J. Coburn, the original president of Scan-Optics and now a director of the company, said. "Because of their willingness to hang tough, [the company] has been the only independent in the industry [not associated with a computer firm] making a substantial profit."

Other life insurance companies have made investments as diverse as America. Northwestern Mutual Life Insurance Company of Milwaukee has invested more than $300 million in oil and gas investments. The company owns a quarter of a Mobil Corporation under-sea oil and gas discovery in the Gulf of Mexico. In California and Oregon, Northwestern has a half interest in 170,000 acres of timber. It has another half interest in the surface rights to 1.1 billion tons of coal in Gillette, Wyoming.

At any given moment, life insurance companies may be among the largest stockholders of major national corporations. Prudential, for example, recently owned $109 million of the stock of Citibank, the largest bank in the country, according to a quarterly compilation of institutional holdings by Computer Directions Advisers, Inc. of Silver Spring, Maryland, Aetna owned $192 million in stock of International Business Machines Corp., while Equitable Life Assurance Society of the United States, the third largest in the country, owned $245 million of IBM stock.

Equitable owns or has financed hotels, shopping centers, and office buildings in every major city. In New York, it jointly owns with the Trump Organization the sixty-eight-story, $180 million Trump Tower on Fifth Avenue. It gave a $25 million loan to build the Grand Hyatt Hotel on Forty-second Street over Grand Central Terminal. In Dallas, it provided a $57 million loan to build the glass-sheathed Dallas Hyatt Regency. In St. Louis, it financed Busch Stadium. In Boston, Equitable made a $30 million mortgage loan to build a new Jordan Marsh store in the downtown area. In the Washington, D.C., area, Equitable provided financing for construction of the glittering White Flint Mall in Maryland's Montgomery County.

Metropolitan paid $400 million for one of the industry's more visible investments, New York's Pan Am Building, a fifty-nine-story aluminum and stainless-steel-sheathed skyscraper that leads directly to Grand Central Terminal and is in the middle of some of the choicest property in the world. When the normally ultraconservative Metropolitan made the purchase in 1980, the price was the highest ever paid for a single building. But while the price appeared high at the time, real estate experts felt the investment in the octagonal building would pay off over the long haul.

■

Life insurance executives like to point to the seemingly endless body of laws that govern their investments to show how well-regulated the industry is. In most states, for example, the laws say life insurance companies may invest only in companies that have a record of earnings over five years. But most of the laws have loopholes, and this requirement is one of them.

Claiming the investment laws were too rigid, the companies got the insurance departments to let them use four percent of their assets to invest in stocks, bonds, and other investments that fall short of meeting these and other standards laid down by the regulators. This bundle of unaccountable money is invested under what is known as the "basket clause."

In return for the chance to use this play money, the companies agreed that only a portion of the value of these investments would be considered or "admitted" when determining if they have enough assets to back up policies. Since the companies already have an overabundance of wealth, the restriction is of little consequence, and the companies get to use the money largely as they please. "The feeling is it's sort of mad money," said William A. White, chief actuary of the New Jersey State Insurance Department.

In most states, there is no way to determine how the companies use this clause, since most states do not require the companies to designate in public filings which investments fall within the "basket" exception. New York State does have such a requirement, and we can get an idea of how the clause works by examining a "basket" investment of New York-based Equitable.

In a special report to the New York State Insurance Department, Equitable listed nearly one hundred "basket" investments. There is nothing on the three-page, typewritten listing to show why any of the investments qualify for "basket" treatment. One of the investments consisted of a total of $5.7 million in loans made in the mid-1970s to L&M Oil and Gas Company, a Kentucky gas drilling company.

As we shall see, L&M was indeed a basket case. Not only did L&M have no record of earnings for five years, it was losing money at the time the loan was made. What's more, it informed Equitable before most of the money was disbursed that it could not meet key requirements of the loan agreement. After making just two payments of interest on the loans, L&M defaulted. After Equitable took back L&M's assets, it lost $607,895 in a single year on the investment.

If these circumstances seem bizarre, the fact that a top-selling Equitable agent in Florida received a $50,000 finder's fee from L&M for getting Equitable to make the first loan does not necessarily explain it. The agent said he talked with Coy G. Eklund, then Equitable's president and chief executive officer, about having the loan approved. Eklund said he applied no pressure on Equitable investment officers to go ahead with the loan. And Edward C. White, Jr., who headed Equitable's bond department when the first L&M loan was made, said he felt no pressure. "Coy said [the agent] is coming in, and to listen to him," the retired Equitable officer said.

"I felt it was a good loan," said the agent, who described his role as that of a mortgage broker entitled to a fee for his services. He said the $50,000 represented one percent of the initial loan amount of $5 million.

Equitable says it sees nothing wrong with the investment. State insurance laws prohibit officers or directors of life insurance companies from receiving anything of value for negotiating, procuring, or recommending a loan or purchase or sale of property; however, the laws say nothing about agents.

An Equitable spokesman maintained the company expects to do well with the L&M investment. "The initial problems with the investment have been corrected, and the property is operating at a profit," he said. Noting that the loan was secured with a lien or mortgage on L&M's property, the Equitable spokesman said, "We make many loans like that to companies that don't meet the earnings test."

According to records filed with state insurance departments, Equitable's return on the investment in a recent year amounted to one percent—hardly a sign of a successful investment.

How often agents or other insiders of life insurance companies benefit by recommending an investment is hard to say. As we shall see in a later chapter, the regulators pay little heed to the problem, considering it beyond their purview or too difficult to probe. Without investigating each transaction, it is impossible to know how widespread the practice may be.

The story of L&M and Equitable's involvement with the company, if not a model of how policyholders' funds should be invested, makes a fascinating tale: It includes a murder in a rural area of Kentucky over the impending foreclosure of the Equitable loan; the dealings of a raspy-voiced, eighty-year-old Texas promoter who professes to be worth billions of dollars; and the involvement of a soldier of fortune who rescued an American from a Mexican prison and was later played by Charles Bronson in the 1975 movie *Breakout*.

It was the Texas promoter, Dewitt T. Langford, who started L&M in the early 1970s. The idea was to develop commercially the Shrewsberry Gas Field, a hodgepodge of gas wells drilled in back-yards, dairy farms, and tobacco fields in Leitchfield, Kentucky. About sixty miles southwest of Louisville, Leitchfield consists of two streets, two restaurants, four traffic lights, and 5,000 people.

The rolling terrain is not well suited to farming, and the residents eke out a meager living. Everyone knows each other's business in the town. Still, Leitchfield has some of the friendliest people you would ever want to meet.

Equitable made the loans to L&M primarily so it could build a twenty-three-mile pipeline to transmit gas from the wells to an interstate collection line operated by Midwestern Pipeline Company. Many townspeople already knew that the gas field operated by L&M had long been known to have low-pressure wells that were not capable even of heating the homes of the people of Leitchfield, let alone those of outsiders.

"As a kid, I remember that the town relied on the Shrewsberry Gas Field for gas in winter, and the town would run out of gas every winter," said James Allen, the thirty-eight-year old publisher of the biweekly *Grayson County News-Gazette* in Leitchfield. "There's gas out there, but there's not enough pressure," he said.

At first, Langford wanted to build the pipeline through Leitchfield. In return for a right-of-way, he offered to sell the city as much gas as it wanted. The byplay between Langford and the city over his proposal caused much snickering at city council meetings, Allen recalled. "Langford would come to the city council meetings . . . and the council would ask, 'Can you prove you have this much gas?' He would say, 'I have geological surveys showing there's plenty of gas in the ground.' He would never produce the proof, so the city never entered into an agreement with him," Allen said.

Robert D. Meredith, the former city attorney for Leitchfield, explained that the gas wells are undependable because they generate little pressure. "You can't depend on a well to sustain itself. I don't know why anyone would loan $5 million to build a gas line where there are not proven reserves. You open the wells and let them run and see how the pressure drops," he said. Later, Equitable would admit in court proceedings that it never did get an expert evaluation of the wells before lending $5.7 million to L&M.

When Equitable agreed to lend millions to Langford and his partners, it produced a ripple in the tiny community. "It amazed me that the mayor and city council of Leitchfield never succumbed to Mr. Langford's representations, and a company like Equitable did," said Meredith, who later acted as an officer of the court in valuing the property during the foreclosure proceedings.

"I remember feeling if I had had an Equitable policy, I'd have been real scared," said Jerry W. Guffey, who has represented Langford in legal proceedings and is now the county attorney. "The name [Equitable] connotes stability and very careful investment. I was surprised they got into it."

Langford formed L&M with William Moser, an Indiana investor who represented the "M" in the company's name, while "L" stood for Langford. When Moser sold his interest in L&M, he was replaced by William G. Reynolds, who has since died. Reynolds's father,

Richard S. Reynolds, Sr., founded Reynolds Metals Company, the giant producer of aluminum products, in 1919.

Langford's origins, and the exact nature of his business dealings, are difficult to determine. James F. Dinwiddie, a local lawyer, once asked the big, powerfully built Langford for his name and address during a deposition in a civil suit. "Dewitt Talbot Langford," he said, "and my address, I have several of them." Asked how many he had, he said, "Well, that is something else. . . . My main base is in Texas, one out here in Leitchfield, and one in Bowling Green [Kentucky]. I'm here most of the time in Bowling Green. I have one in California. Texas is my main address. I had better give them my Texas address, hadn't I?"

Asked about his finances, Langford said in the 1978 deposition, "I've got all the finances I need. I've got billions." The incredulous Dinwiddie asked Langford if he was claiming to be a billionaire. "You might say that. I would say that," he replied.

"That you are worth a billion dollars?" the lawyer asked. "I would say probably two and a half billion. I'm like du Pont. I keep my money because I keep it working. I ain't got no cash. Show me a man who knows his business, and he ain't got no cash."

Gary S. Logsdon, a lawyer for Reynolds and later for Langford, recalled that Langford met the Reynolds aluminum heir through William ("Wild Bill") Cheeley, an executive with Reynolds's international division who later moved to the Kentucky area. In proposing the L&M venture to Reynolds, Logsdon said Langford proffered a study done by his son. The study purported to show the gas field had vast reserves. It was based on a method developed by his son to tell where oil and gas reserves lay by merely flying over the territory waving a black box, according to Logsdon.

Many recall that Langford could make it all sound real. "Langford has a way of wooing people and almost makes you believe the gas is there," said Dinwiddie. "He would paint the pipes red and fly people over it."

It was Reynolds who knew an Equitable agent and enlisted his help in getting a loan from the life insurance company. Besides the $50,000 finder's fee, disclosed in a deposition of an Equitable vice-president, the agent got to write a $2 million life insurance policy on the lives of Langford and two other partners in the venture.

Just after receiving the first portion of its loans from Equitable, L&M sent the life insurance company a six-page letter that said L&M had already failed to meet a number of the conditions to getting the loan. In fact, the letter said L&M had not met the standards even before it ever got any money from Equitable.

Among other things, the letter said L&M did not have the capital required by Equitable. It did not have books that were good enough to produce a certified financial statement. It had lost $40,080 on total income of $28,000 in the previous six months. It did not have clear ownership rights to much of the land Equitable mortgaged to secure payment of its loan. Finally, it did not even know if it had the insurance coverage required by Equitable as a condition to getting the loan.

What's more, L&M admitted in the letter that, after receiving some of the money from Equitable, it had violated the loan agreement by paying off certain loans and obtaining a new loan from a bank. After listing the violations, L&M asked Equitable to waive all the requirements, and it did.

Equitable's attorney, John H. Helmers, acknowledged in a court document filed in the ensuing litigation that, after receiving the letter, Equitable disbursed another $3 million in new loans to L&M. A year later, Equitable blithely gave L&M another, additional loan of $750,000.

By the time Equitable foreclosed on L&M three years later, the company owed $7.4 million in principal and interest, according to a deposition of an Equitable officer in the foreclosure proceeding. L&M's assets were sold on the steps of Grayson County Circuit Court at 1:00 P.M. on December 17, 1979. At the time, L&M had ten producing gas wells and a steel pipeline ten inches in diameter, according to a report of the sale filed with the court.

Two days before the sale, Langford had a meeting in his red brick house in Shrewsberry, Kentucky, with a partner, Victor E. Stadter, and Stadter's friend, James "Burt" Tregoning. Stadter was the soldier of fortune who was played by Charles Bronson in the movie *Breakout*, an account of the 1971 escape of Joel David Kaplan from a Mexican prison.

For nine years, Kaplan had languished in the Santa Maria Acatitla Penitentiary near Mexico City for murdering Luis Melchior Vidal, a Puerto Rican from New York, while the two were visiting in Mexico City. Over the years, Kaplan had consistently asserted his innocence, and his family, which has sugar and molasses interests and once owned the Welch Grape Juice Company, feared that he might die if forced to serve out his twenty-eight-year term.

It was Stadter who masterminded Kaplan's escape. While prison guards watched a movie, a helicopter dropped inside the prison walls on August 18. It picked up the bearded Kaplan and a cellmate, then disappeared. Stadter, a Californian, was at the controls of a small airplane that took Kaplan out of Mexico shortly before midnight. Mexican newspapers would describe the escapade as the "jail break of the century."

Stadter and his wife stayed with Langford for a month while looking for a home in the Leitchfield area. It is not clear how Stadter and Langford originally became friends. By the time Stadter and Tregoning, accompanied by their wives, went to Langford's red brick home on the night of December 15, 1979, the relationship had soured.

According to Langford, the two visitors demanded he sign over his gas leases. The conversation soon became heated, according to Stadter, and Langford suggested they leave. Stadter testified in the later murder trial that Langford got up from his seat as if to escort him to the door. Instead, he flipped over a sofa cushion where a gun was hidden. Aiming the gun at Stadter, Langford shot him in the stomach, Stadter testified. Stadter's wife testified she saw Tregoning lying dead on the floor. Langford was found clenching a gun and a switchblade.

After deliberating three hours and forty-five minutes, a Leitchfield jury convicted Langford of manslaughter in the second degree.

"I had a gunfight," Langford explained recently. "A friend

[Stadter] tried to make a deal on the pipeline." In an interview, he admitted shooting both of them. In the trial, Langford said he fired in self-defense.

By the time the foreclosure proceeding was completed, L&M owed Equitable $8.2 million in principal and interest, according to a determination by Grayson Circuit Court Judge Kenneth H. Goff. Equitable bought back the assets by canceling the debts. Equitable had already written off the investment as a loss. Nevertheless, Equitable decided to try to get gas out of the fields on its own.

Currently, the pipeline built to transmit 20 million cubic feet of gas a day is carrying 3 million cubic feet, according to Travis Kerr, the compressor operator. The coupling to the interstate line is one and a half inches in diameter, while the L&M pipeline itself is ten inches in diameter, he said, adding, "We ain't got the gas."

■

The bottom line in evaluating how well the companies do their job is the overall investment return. Here, as in the rest of the life insurance game, the companies have succeeded in blurring the standards of comparison so successfully that it is impossible to say which company does the best job of investing. The reason is related to the accounting methods used by the companies and the fact that they don't realistically reflect the value of their assets. If the accounting system does not fairly value common stocks, as an example, and Prudential happened to have made a killing in common stocks one year, how can one compare Prudential fairly with other companies that did not do well in common stocks?

So the fact that Prudential, in a recent year, earned 8.02 percent on its investments after expenses, while Equitable earned 8.94 percent, is a meaningless statistic. Without consistent standards, there is no way of knowing how well the companies performed. They continue to accumulate their billions without having to account to anyone for their rates of return, and the consumer cannot tell if his dollar is being invested wisely.

10. THE REGULATORS

■ The popular songs at the time were "Wait 'Till the Sun Shines, Nellie," "In the Shade of the Old Apple Tree," and "My Gal Sal." Albert Einstein propounded his special theory of relativity in a paper published in Bern, Switzerland. Palmolive soap was introduced, the Royal Typewriter Company was founded in New York, and Vicks VapoRub was first marketed under the name Vicks Magic Croup Salve.

In that same year, Upton Sinclair exposed U.S. meat packing conditions in *The Jungle*, a novel that delved into such matters as red-dyed minced tripe sold as deviled ham, sausage containing poisoned rats, and lard that included the remains of employees who had fallen into the boiling grease.

Just a few years earlier, *McClure's* magazine had begun publishing articles by crusaders such as Ida Minerva Tarbell, who revealed in "History of the Standard Oil Company" that John D. Rockefeller controlled ninety percent of U.S. oil-refining capacity. J. Lincoln Steffens exposed the squalor in America's urban centers in *The Shame of the Cities*.

Against this turbulent background, James Hazen Hyde, first vice-president of Equitable Life Assurance Society of the United States, threw a French costume party. The date was January 31, 1905, and the ballroom of Louis Sherry's Restaurant on Fifth Avenue in New York had been decorated to resemble the court of Louis XIV.

"After leaving their wraps and coats in the dressing rooms, the guests found themselves in a Versailles garden," *The New York Times* reported the next day. "All through the corridors and halls there were lemon and orange trees, and in rustic tubs there were bushes covered with pink flowers." The Astors, Rockefellers, and Vanderbilts were among those attending the ball.

Said to cost $100,000, the party symbolized what many felt was the imperiousness of the life insurance business in general and of Hyde in particular. It led, surprisingly, to most of the laws that govern the life insurance industry to this day.

As a twenty-six-year-old vice-president of Equitable, Hyde was already making $100,000 a year and running the company. His father, who had been chairman, had left him a controlling share of the company's stock through a trust fund arrangement. The younger Hyde affected French clothes, took frequent trips to Europe, and gave fabulous parties at his "chateau," called "The Oaks," in Long Island, New York. Commenting on the display, *The Evening Post* scolded, "There are unwritten guarantees in finance, and this is one of them. Large responsibility ill becomes a social butterfly."

Already, some Equitable directors had been expressing displeasure among themselves at Hyde's profligate activities. The costume ball was but one more example. Meeting in February at Equitable's home office at 120 Broadway, a nine-story building that was considered one of New York's first skyscrapers, a faction led by President James W. Alexander tried to oust Hyde from the company and turn it into a mutual. The attempted coup was given more impetus by the fact that Hyde, under the terms of his father's will, would soon have absolute control of his father's Equitable stock, worth some $400 million. The rump group declared that Hyde's acts as vice-president had provoked criticism of the company and raised questions about its soundness.

In April, *Everybody's* magazine focused attention on life insurance machinations with an article dealing with manipulation of insurance company investment funds through subsidiary trust companies. The same month, Hyde publicly admitted membership in a syndicate that had underwritten a number of banking securities issues purchased by Equitable.

As the controversy mounted, the warring factions at Equitable leaked choice tidbits about the opposition to New York's highly competitive newspapers. The spectacle of financial czars battling for control did little to enhance trust in the financial institutions involved. By June, Hyde had agreed to sell his stock and give up control of the company. The move did not appease the critics. The new management was soon found wanting, and now there were hard facts to support the suspicions that had been aired all along.

Jumping rather tardily into the fray, the New York State insurance superintendent, Francis Hendricks, revealed in a report that several Equitable officers and directors had been abusing the public trust. The report said Equitable had purchased bonds and stocks of companies owned by those same officers and directors; that Equitable had leased a building to a safe-deposit company owned in part by Equitable directors, who had realized handsome profits from the arrangement; and that substantial sums were being kept at low interest in a Philadelphia bank. The superintendent's report took the breath out of any of Equitable's remaining defenders, while its timing inevitably raised questions about the adequacy of insurance regulation.

"Why did the New York department, in its various examinations, never find these things which Mr. Hendricks has discovered within the past two or three months?" wondered *The New York Times*. Citing questionable expenses being footed by Equitable policyholders, *The New York World* began a series of a hundred editorials under the heading, "Equitable Corruption."

With criticism rising, the New York State legislature on July 20 decided to appoint an investigating committee. It would be headed by New York State Senator William M. Armstrong. In casting about for an investigator to head the study, Armstrong asked a newspaper editor to recommend a lawyer who would be incorruptible.

In August, Charles Evans Hughes, later to become chief justice of the U.S. Supreme Court, was vacationing with his family in Switzerland. A messenger delivered a cablegram to him. Based on the editor's suggestion, Armstrong wanted the red-bearded Hughes to direct the investigation.

Hughes immediately sensed the importance of the undertaking. Rousing his family at 4:00 A.M., he began a thirty-mile trip down from the Alps to the nearest railroad station. After being reassured that his previous representation of some of the Equitable board members did not present a conflict, Hughes accepted Armstrong's offer.

The investigation that followed, known as the Armstrong investigation, sent tremors through the industry. It resulted in the resignations of the New York State insurance superintendent and a number of life insurance executives. More importantly, it resulted in the body of laws that largely governs the way the industry operates and is regulated even now. Never before—and never since—had any one event so altered the way the life insurance industry does business.

Today, state regulators in New York and elsewhere refer to the Armstrong investigation as if it had happened yesterday. In many respects, it might have. While the investment transactions that benefited officers and directors have largely faded in memory, many of the same abuses disclosed in Hughes's exhaustive report exist today—usually with the express approval of the regulators. In this chapter, we will see the reasons many of those abuses are allowed to continue.

■

The concept of life insurance has been evolving since Greek and Roman times. The first known use of insurance—by the Babylonians and Phoenicians—covered goods, not lives. The Greeks and Romans created a type of life insurance by forming societies that paid for the burial of their members. Upon joining, the members contributed fees that were invested and later used for burial costs. In the Middle Ages, guilds that insured the cargoes of ships logically extended the coverage to the captains' lives.

The earliest life insurance companies were formed by indepen-

dent underwriters who agreed to share risks. It was these underwriters who wrote the first known life insurance contract, which
insured the life of William Gybbon in 1583. The policy described
Gybbon as a citizen of London and a salter, or one who salts meat
or fish. The beneficiary was listed as Richard Martin, whose relationship to Gybbon is not known.

The policy insured Gybbon for just one year, and, as it happened, he died within the year. The underwriters refused to honor
Martin's claim for benefits, contending the term of the policy was
based on a lunar calendar rather than a solar one. Judge Valentine
Dale of the British Court of Admiralty ruled otherwise, and the
claim was paid, according to the court record, which is preserved
at the British Library in London.

These awkward beginnings were to be expected. Insurance is a
sophisticated concept. It requires putting aside immediate, selfish
concerns and sharing costs so that all can benefit in the long run.
Peasants eking out a living were in no position to buy insurance.
The wealthier classes tended to look upon insurance more as a
gambling opportunity than a vehicle to provide security.

Life insurance became more popular when Lorenzo Tonti, an
Italian physician and banker, devised a life insurance plan in the
1660s similar to a lottery. Called a tontine, the policy called for par-
ticipants to place their money in a pool of funds that was eventually
distributed only to the last survivors. Naturally, most of the partic-
ipants never got to share in the distribution, and they received no
benefits when they died.

While the idea popularized the life insurance concept, the spectacle of pyramiding returns and betting on people's lives created a
stigma that was hard to shake. France and England, among other
countries, passed laws outlawing life insurance. In part, the legislators feared that people would kill each other if they bet on each
other's lives. The exception—embodied in life insurance contracts
today—was when the policyholder had an insurable interest,
meaning a reasonable expectation of loss as a result of the death of
the insured. Through that provision, insurance companies hope to

prevent people from buying a policy on a stranger, then murdering him to get the life insurance benefit.

Still, the line between gambling and life insurance is a fine one, if it exists at all. Life insurance is a gamble that the policy will someday be needed to cover a loss. That doesn't mean we buy life insurance hoping it will pay off, or that buying life insurance is foolhardy. It means we want to have the secure feeling of knowing that a loss, if it occurs, will not be devastating. For that reason, life insurance is a prudent gamble. A tontine, on the other hand, is a gamble without the prudence. The difference is one of degree.

From the tontine concept, life insurance steadily progressed. In 1699, the first life insurance company set up separately from other organizations was established in England. Called the Society of Assurance for Widows and Orphans, it limited its membership to 2,000 people who had to be no more than fifty years old and could not hail from the "marshy and unhealthy parts." Upon joining, they paid five shillings. When a member died, they paid another five shillings. In return, the company promised to pay 500 pounds upon a member's death.

The colonists tended to buy life insurance from English companies. However, in 1759, the first life insurance company, called the Corporation for the Relief of Poor and Distressed Presbyterian Ministers and of the Poor and Distressed Widows and Children of Presbyterian Ministers, was chartered in America. Beginning with annuities for ministers' wives, it later offered life insurance as well. The company, known as the Presbyterian Ministers' Fund, still exists, offering a range of policies to clergy of any faith.

Although the idea of mutual companies dates to the 1700s, the first mutual company chartered in this country to sell policies to the general public was New England Mutual Life Insurance Company, started in Boston in 1835.

Up until this point, the companies had only rudimentary death statistics that they could refer to when determining rates, and no way of relating the death statistics to the amount of reserves that should be put aside. In 1852, with the help of his older children and a previous English table that had been used there, Elizur Wright, known as the father of life insurance, completed 203 pages of tables that showed how much in reserves should be kept at the end of each year. Each page had required 800 to 1,000 computations. The prodigious work provided a basis for insuring that life insurance companies would be sound.

When some life insurance companies failed, the need for regulation became apparent. In 1858, Wright, a Yale University graduate who had been a mathematics professor and newspaper publisher, became the first insurance commissioner of Massachusetts. A year after Wright became commissioner, New York State was the first state to establish a separate department for regulating insurance.

The chief reason for regulating insurance is that it requires payment for future services. If you hire a painter to paint your house, and he fails to perform, you simply do not pay him. If a life insurance company fails to perform, it is too late to do anything. The money has already been paid, and the customer is dead.

The industry greeted the idea of regulation with something less than enthusiasm. A prominent insurance journal ridiculed the idea as an "absurdity" that implicitly called into question the character of company officers. Nevertheless, Wright, in 1861, persuaded the Massachusetts legislature to strengthen his powers by passing laws permitting him to examine the affairs of any life insurance company in the state. In addition, the companies had to make periodic reports to the insurance department.

Troubled by the companies' failure to refund any money to policyholders if they do not die, Wright also persuaded the legislature to pass a "non-forfeiture" law that required the companies to pay a death benefit if sufficient premiums had been paid, even if the policyholders had stopped making payments. Convinced that some companies were spending too much on expenses, Wright lifted the charters of fourteen companies and publicized the names of the companies he believed were not solvent.

This did not endear Wright to the insurance companies. In an early example of how state regulation works, the industry got

Wright removed as commissioner, although the companies later hired him to perform actuarial work.

The companies, meanwhile, became more aggressive in their sales tactics, and the commissions of agents gradually soared from five percent or ten percent to as much as forty percent of the first year's premium. By 1865, there were sixty-one life insurance companies doing business in the United States. They had at least $622 million of coverage in force.

One of the more prominent companies was Equitable. The company had been started thirty-one years earlier by Henry B. Hyde, the father of the notorious James Hazen Hyde. The elder Hyde, a cashier at another life insurance company, decided to start his own company after getting into an argument with his boss at the Mutual Life Insurance Company of New York. According to one of the elder Hyde's early agents, "There was an indescribable something about him, too winning to be resisted." By the end of its first year, Equitable had $1 million in life insurance in force.

In 1867, Equitable hit upon the tontine idea to boost sales. Sounding like the advocates of whole life today, the younger Hyde announced that the tontine plan—called a modified tontine— would help the living. Unlike the earlier form, the policies paid death benefits in every case. However, dividends and, in some forms, cash surrender values were paid only if a policyholder lived through ten-, fifteen-, or twenty-year periods. Those who survived the cutoff points shared in the reserves forfeited by the others who had dropped out or died.

In describing the virtues of the policy to others in the business, Hyde pointed out that two out of three policyholders would stop paying before the payoff period, so they got few benefits. In any case, the investment return was not guaranteed. From Equitable's standpoint, Hyde told colleagues, the policy was foolproof.

While Wright condemned the tontine as "life insurance cannibalism," the New York State insurance superintendent, William Barnes, said, "The tontine system seems so natural and applicable to certain classes of policyholders, that like many discoveries in science and art, the wonder is how it could have remained so long dormant and undiscovered."

In fact, Hyde's policy was not that different from today's whole life policies. Current policies pay dividends only after one to three years. Hyde's did not pay them until the tenth year.

Hyde's aggressive sales tactics provoked what were known as "tontine wars." In published letters and pamphlets, companies and agents lined up on either side of the question of whether tontines should be sold. The unseemly display only contributed to the air of public mistrust that led to the Armstrong investigation.

For all the attacks on its soundness, Equitable was the third largest life insurance company in the country when the Armstrong Committee began its investigation. It had $80 million in surplus funds. On the other hand, the Armstrong committee had only a $50,000 appropriation. What Equitable did not have was Charles Evans Hughes.

The son of a Baptist minister, Hughes had graduated from Brown University and, in 1884, from Columbia University School of Law. While a partner in a private law firm in New York, he had been asked to act as counsel to a state legislative committee investigating the cost of natural gas in New York City; the probe would drastically reduce the price of gas in the city.

Referring to his previous work, *The World* stated editorially, "The committee could do no better" than to choose "the patient and persistent prober of the gas trust abuses. . . . Mr. Hughes would get the facts."

The hearings began September 6, 1905, in a chamber of New York's City Hall. Forty-five company officials, some under subpoena, occupied front-row seats. The forty-three-year-old Hughes quickly won acclaim for his questioning: incisive and persistent, but polite and patient. If he didn't know why he was asking for a particular fact, he would say so. When subjected to abuse by some of the life insurance executives, he responded calmly.

Repeatedly, the executives claimed their transactions were private. "Those relations are confidential, sir," one said.

"There is nothing confidential about the insurance business now," Hughes replied.

When Hughes pressed Richard A. McCurdy, president of Mutual Life Insurance Company of New York, for his salary, the elegantly dressed chief executive expounded on the virtues of life insurance and of his mutually owned company, which he called "a great beneficent missionary institution."

"Well," Hughes replied, "you have made a very full explanation. . . . The question comes back to the salaries of the missionaries." As it turned out, McCurdy was making $150,000 a year.

Aided by accountants and actuaries, and access to the companies' books, Hughes would draw out facts on one issue, switch to another, and then come back to the first. By the time his questioning was complete, the witness often had given away more than he intended. The effect, along with the front-page attention the investigation was receiving, was devastating.

Focusing in particular on the three largest companies in the business—New York Life Insurance Company, Mutual Life, and Equitable—Hughes documented that officers and directors of the companies had been enriching themselves by investing in stocks while directing their companies to invest in those same stocks; charging their relatives low rents in buildings owned by the companies; and keeping large interest-free balances of the companies with banks where they had ownership interests.

. Hughes revealed that some of the companies were paying agents what were then considered exorbitant commissions—forty percent to fifty percent of the first year's premium. He showed how much of this new business quickly lapsed, losing money for consumers and the companies. He excoriated the companies for charging poor people even higher rates through industrial life insurance policies. And he found the companies, even though many were mutuals owned by policyholders, accumulating vast sums beyond what they needed to meet their obligations to policyholders.

In a masterfully written report prepared in just six weeks, Hughes concluded in February 1906 that much of the blame could be laid on the shoulders of the state regulators. Repeatedly, Hughes compared his findings with their examination reports, which had earlier given the companies a clean bill of health. The regulators, he had found, were concerned almost exclusively with the solvency of the companies and had little regard for the question of whether they were operating in the public interest.

In explaining that phenomenon, Hughes noted the closeness of the industry to the state government. He revealed that companies had been paying lobbyists under the rubric "legal fees," and at least one such lobbyist operated what the press dubbed the "House of Mirth," after the Edith Wharton novel that was then a best-seller. It was an Albany house where state legislators, including two from the Senate Insurance Committee, were entertained.

Infrequent as the examinations of the companies had been, Hughes wrote, they still would have uncovered the abuses if "they had been rigorously conducted with the purpose of exposing whatever abuses existed." However, he noted, the New York State Insurance Department had a long tradition of focusing on the question of whether the companies were solvent while ignoring other issues.

"Most of the evils which have been disclosed by the investigation would have been impossible had there been a vigorous performance of the duties already laid upon the department, a vigilant watchfulness in the interest of policyholders, and a courageous exercise of the powers which the [state insurance] statute confers," Hughes said.

The investigation won praise from conservatives and liberals, and Hughes, a Republican, went on in 1906 to become governor of New York. He subsequently was named an associate justice of the U.S. Supreme Court and, eventually, chief justice.

The resulting insurance reforms passed first by New York State and then most other states, guide the industry to this day. These laws, for the first time, placed limits on the size of agents' commissions, restricted the amount companies could accumulate as surplus funds, prohibited officers or directors from having a financial interest in investment transactions, and required extensive disclosure to insurance departments of commissions, legal fees, collateral loans, bank balances, and investment dealings.

■

Today, as in 1905, the assets of the companies are ample and sound. In a recent five-year period, only 12 of the 2,100 life insurance companies in the country became insolvent. In 1982, one life insurance company became insolvent, compared with 42 banks insured by the Federal Deposit Insurance Corporation. Taking into account the number of banks and life insurance companies, the rate of bank failures was five times greater than the rate of life insurance company failures.

According to Beck, the chairman of Prudential, "Regulation by the states is vastly superior to what it would be if it were regulated by the federal government. No policyholder to my knowledge has lost his funds in a life insurance contract. I don't know of any other business where that's true."

But while the regulators have successfully kept life insurance companies solvent, as in 1905, they have virtually ignored the selling side of the business. The practices on that end most nearly resemble the way securities were peddled before the Securities and Exchange Commission was established in 1933.

Unlike the securities and banking industries, the insurance business never made the transition from state to federal regulation. Successive courts, including the U.S. Supreme Court in 1868, had ruled that insurance could not be federally regulated because "issuing a policy of insurance is not a transaction of commerce." But in 1944, the Supreme Court, ruling on a criminal antitrust case brought by the Justice Department against fire insurance companies, reversed itself. Momentarily unprotected from the standards governing all other businesses, the industry immediately began lobbying Congress for an exemption.

In 1945, Congress passed the McCarran-Ferguson Act, a law drafted by the industry to exempt insurance from federal regulation and the provisions of the antitrust laws. The catch was the federal laws dealing with antitrust violations would apply unless the states themselves regulated those areas. So the industry got the states to pass antitrust laws, insuring that the industry would keep its exempt status intact.

"It was a practical thing. The way the bill was drawn, the federal government would intervene if the states don't regulate," recalled Robert E. Dineen, then president of Northwestern Mutual Life Insurance Company, who said he helped draft the bill that was passed.

Under the system that has developed, each state has an insurance commissioner who is generally appointed by the governor or another state official. In eight states, the commissioner is elected. Besides regulating life insurance, the commissioners have responsibility for property casualty insurance, including auto insurance; title insurance, which insures against defects in legal ownership to property; health insurance; and workmen's compensation insurance, among others.

As part of their duties in regulating life insurance, the commissioners examine and license agents. With the exception of credit life insurance, which insures lenders against the possibility that a borrower may die, the commissioners have elected not to set life insurance rates.

A large portion of the commissioners' time is devoted to simple filing: keeping agents' licenses in order, making sure that the companies provide voluminous reports on their financial condition on time, and keeping track of new policies sold by the companies.

The commissioners have ample powers. They can, for example, suspend or revoke the authority of a company to do business in their states. Yet in practice, those powers are rarely used. Revoking authority to do business could harm the rights of existing policyholders in the state. Also the prospect of telling a billion-dollar company that it is no longer welcome to do business is politically infeasible.

It makes as much sense to threaten a life insurance company with suspension of its right to do business as it would for the Securities and Exchange Commission, faced with a violation by, say,

American Telephone & Telegraph Company, to threaten to suspend its right to operate. The SEC, armed with laws passed by Congress, has a number of less severe penalties that it can mete out, from monetary penalties to jail sentences after conviction by a court.

The state insurance departments either do not have these powers or do not use them. They are simply not equipped to deal with the issue of punishment. State governments, in general, are more comfortable renewing auto registrations than regulating the affairs of multibillion-dollar corporations, and lack of funds is a chief reason.

"I have twenty-five employees [including secretaries] and regulate nine hundred and fifty companies and twenty-three-thousand agents. It just can't be done," said James R. Montgomery, III, deputy insurance commissioner in Washington, D.C., who often takes complaints from consumers about auto insurance companies while trying to analyze the books of companies worth hundreds of millions of dollars.

A 1979 report by the General Accounting Office found that the budgets and staffs of state insurance departments vary widely and appear to bear no relation to the number or size of the companies they regulate. For example, for each company regulated, Iowa had a budget of $7,722, while Nevada had a budget of $289,504. New York had a budget of $60,453 per company, while Wisconsin had a budget of $7,764 and Hawaii had a budget of $143,815. The number of employees per regulated company ranged from 689 in New York to fifteen in Vermont.

The GAO found that only about seventeen percent of the employees had training and accreditation in the professions most needed in insurance regulations: law, economics, accounting, and—most important—actuarial science, since to properly regulate, the insurance departments need actuaries who can speak the language of the industry.

Anyone who has taken mathematics courses can call himself an actuary. However, only fellows of the Society of Actuaries, which administers a series of qualifying tests, are recognized as being fully professionally qualified, and the industry employs nearly all of them. There are 4,776 fellows of the society. Of that number, 12 are employed by the New York State Insurance Department, two by California, two by Massachusetts, and one each by New Jersey, Pennsylvania, Maine, and Iowa. With the exception of a few academics, all the rest work for insurance companies or trade associations.

■

By all accounts, the best example of the quality of state regulation is the way credit life insurance is regulated. The first credit life policy was issued in 1917 by the Morris Plan Insurance Society. At first, premiums were based on the age of the applicant. Now, credit life rates are usually the same, regardless of the age of the policyholder.

When you borrow to buy a car or a house, the car dealer or lender will often require you to buy a credit life insurance policy. In addition to all the other safeguards built into your loan agreement, the credit life policy will guarantee that the loan will be paid off in the event of your death. The death benefit will go to the lender, not to you.

In most cases, the credit life policy suggested is issued either by a life insurance company owned by the lender or one that pays commissions to the lender. For example, if you want a loan from First Virginia Bank of Virginia, you have to buy a credit life policy. And First Virginia has just the credit life insurance company for you: First Virginia Life Insurance Co.

In a recent year, this particular life insurance company, which is owned by the holding company that owns the bank, paid out less than a third of its premiums in the form of benefits. It paid $1.4 million in fees to the bank. It kept $2.3 million—or forty percent of its investment funds—in interest-free checking accounts at the bank. And it still managed to pay to the bank holding company dividends accumulated over several years of $1.3 million. Such fabulous profits are not uncommon in the credit life business, a subset of the life insurance industry that accounts for $1.6 billion in premiums a year.

The problem is that the consumer is essentially a captive of the credit life companies. He fears that rejecting the life insurance company suggested by the lender will harm his chances of getting a loan. In any case, the premiums do not seem very high—perhaps $33 on a $5,000 loan—and it is too much trouble to look elsewhere.

To get business, the credit life companies offer commissions to banks or car dealers. The higher the commissions, the more business the credit life companies get. From the consumer's standpoint, it is not really all that different from sales of ordinary insurance, which is purchased blindly on the word of agents. The companies in both instances pay higher commissions to make more sales, and the extra cost is passed along to the consumer.

What makes credit life different from ordinary life insurance is that more of the premiums wind up in the pockets of the owners of the companies instead of going for expenses, including commissions. As a result, this particular abuse is acknowledged by many industry leaders to be an embarrassing problem. Prudential, for one, has thrown its weight behind reducing the rates in some states on the grounds the unseemly profits make the entire industry look bad.

Not content with commissions of sixty percent or more of the premiums, many auto dealers set up their own credit life companies. Often, the details are handled by syndicates, so the auto dealer does not have to know the difference between a premium and a dividend. The arrangements go by various names and have their own lingo: "exotics," front companies, reinsurance, and captive companies. Taking advantage of the patchwork nature of state regulation, the dealers usually set up the companies in Arizona, where requirements for starting a company are minimal. At last inquiry, all that was needed was $75,000.

Often, the offices of these companies consist of a sign amidst hundreds on the wall of an actuary's or lawyer's office. One of the most popular addresses is Suite 646, 234 N. Central Ave., Phoenix. Suite 646 turns out to be in an older office building in downtown Phoenix, where an actuary has his office. Asked why a particular credit life company listed at his address does not have its own office, the actuary, a big, florid man, waved his hands toward the bookshelves. "They do have an office," he said.

Because of what the industry calls the "reverse competition" in the credit life business, the regulators set maximum rates for this type of insurance. However, they set them so high that the profits continue to cascade into the companies. In some states, like South Carolina, Louisiana, Mississippi, and Alabama, the rates are double what they are in other states, like Pennsylvania, Rhode Island, Wyoming, or New Hampshire.

William F. Burfeind, executive vice-president of the Consumer Credit Insurance Association, the credit life insurance company trade association, acknowledged that credit life insurance is more expensive than ordinary insurance, but he said ordinary insurance cannot be purchased in the small quantities offered by credit life companies.

While that is true, most people already have life insurance. If they need additional coverage, they can increase the amounts they presently own at far less cost. Because of the lack of adequate price disclosure, they have no way of knowing what the price differences are. Nor are they told about the profits generated by credit life insurance.

Referring to the companies that flock to his state to sell credit life insurance, Arizona Insurance Commissioner J. Michael Low said, "Other commissioners say, 'Why don't you do something about it?' The answer is not to ban them in Arizona," Low said. "What they ought to do is reduce the rates, then you'll squeeze the profits."

But reducing the rates often takes more courage than most commissioners are willing to muster, and their reluctance may have a basis in fact. Wesley J. Kinder, a former California insurance commissioner, blames his removal as commissioner in part on a bruising fight he had with the credit life industry when he sought to lower the rates. "I think my position on credit life well may have had some influence on the decision not to reappoint me," he said. "Their political muscle seems disproportionate."

H. Peter Hudson, Indiana's former commissioner, said, "I think my departure [as commissioner] was because I had offended people close to the governor [Robert Orr] who were in credit life insurance."

What is important here is not whether these two former regulators were removed by the industry but rather their perception that the industry has the power to remove them. That perception is not dispelled by the comment of the Consumer Credit Insurance Association's Burfeind: "Most everybody when they fail at attempting something likes to place the blame on somebody. It may be that they [the commissioners removed from their jobs] were attempting to do something that was not reasonable."

Kinder's removal is particularly poignant. He was replaced as California insurance commissioner by Bruce Bunner, an accountant who was quoted in the August 27, 1983, *National Underwriter* as saying, "The industry approached me [to take the job]."

■

Under the system of state regulation, each state enforces the laws to varying degrees—or not at all. For example, if a life insurance company decides it does not like the regulation in its state for some reason, it can elect to be regulated by the department of another state—never moving its executive offices in the process. Academy Life Insurance Company of Valley Forge, Pennsylvania, for example, is regulated by the Colorado Insurance Department.

If that seems bizarre, consider this: besides complying with the laws of their own state, the companies are expected to comply with some, but not all, of the laws of the other states where they do business when selling in those states. In some instances, the regulatory hodgepodge allows such companies to engage in prohibited transactions in states where they do business so long as the results of the transactions are not included in the assets counted, or admitted, for purposes of determining if the company is sound.

"Each state has different regulations for reserves and policy forms. Some states require provisions in policies that contiguous states prohibit," said Robert M. Best, chairman and chief executive officer of Security Mutual Life Insurance Company of Binghamton, New York. "In Pennsylvania, we filed language that they required but New York State prohibited. . . . In some states, there is regulation that doesn't exist very much. Some states are severe."

Customers of Washington Gas Light Company received an example of that with their gas bills. Like many utilities throughout the country, the gas company offered life insurance at a "low group rate." However, the "low group rate" offered through Continental American Life Insurance Company of Wilmington, Delaware, is actually higher than the same company's rates for individual policies.

In a classic illustration of how splintered state regulation works, the Washington, D.C., insurance department had raised no objection to the "low group rate" claim. Washington takes the position that it will not question a policy if it has been approved by another state. In this case, the policy had been approved by Rhode Island, known as having lenient insurance regulation, so the District washed its hands of the matter. But the Maryland Insurance Department did object. So Maryland customers of Washington Gas received with their bills the same offer received by Washington customers, except the claim that it was a group policy had been deleted.

Wayne A. Mills, a Washington Gas executive, brushed aside Maryland's ruling, saying the policy cannot be compared with individual policies, since it takes all applicants regardless of health. However, the brochure for the policy says the extra cost of taking all risks is covered by reducing the death benefits in the first three years.

"When they say it's 'group,' it gives the impression they're selling at a lower rate. . . . [It's] a ruse to get around consumer laws," said Edward J. Birrane, Jr., who was Maryland insurance commissioner at the time.

A key function of the regulators is conducting examinations of the companies' finances. Depending on the state, examinations may be conducted every three, four, or five years. It is not unusual for an examination report to be issued years after the effective date of an examination. The 1980 examination of Equitable, for example, showed its condition as of 1975.

"A company may be insolvent by the time we get the reports," said Montgomery, the deputy insurance superintendent for the District of Columbia.

Because of that, the commissioners in 1974 started an "early warning" system that lets them know if companies operating within their states have sagging finances based on their last financial reports to the commissioners. The reports still rely entirely on the accuracy of the companies' own claims.

As corporate finances become more sophisticated, it is easier to conceal a shortage in assets. These days, dozens of life insurance companies may be owned by one holding company. The subsidiaries and the holding companies may engage in complicated transactions among themselves, creating the impression that their assets are more abundant than they really are.

Equity Funding Corporation, which became insolvent in 1973, demonstrated how that can be accomplished. Creating the biggest insurance scandal in the history of the industry, the company's life insurance subsidiary listed 99,052 life insurance policies on its books when 56,000 of them—representing $2 billion in coverage—never existed. What's more, some $62 million of the $117 million in loans the company claimed to have made were phony.

The scandal came out when a former employee tipped Raymond Dirks, a Wall Street securities analyst, who related the story to *Wall Street Journal* reporter William E. Blundell in Los Angeles. The first agency to take any action in the case was the SEC, which charged that the company and its officers had engaged in a massive scheme to manipulate the price of the company's stock.

In part, the Los Angeles-based Equity Funding Life Insurance Company had hidden its activities from insurance examiners by engaging in sham loan transactions with its parent company. A similar problem—while more openly disclosed—occurred when the Arkansas Insurance Department ordered Baldwin-United Corporation's insurance subsidiaries to replenish their anemic assets in late

1982. The companies did so with securities of other Baldwin-United affiliates, doing little to forestall the subsequent bankruptcy of the entire conglomerate.

Nevertheless, the state insurance departments, as a rule, continue to examine each life insurance subsidiary as if it were a separate entity, unrelated to its parent company or to other subsidiaries owned by the same parent.

Once an insolvency occurs, policyholders may or may not get their claims covered, depending solely on where they live. Twenty-eight states have guaranty laws aimed at reimbursing policyholders for losses from insolvencies, but they usually cover only the first $50,000 in coverage. Moreover, they are funded by contributions from companies *after* an insolvency occurs, raising the very real possibility that companies could object to paying. After all, some have argued, why should healthy companies have to pay for the mistakes of the ones that go bust? In the rest of the states that have not passed such a guaranty law, policyholders are totally unprotected.

Still, their claims are often covered anyway because other companies purchase the policies of companies that go under. Life insurance companies are not like banks, which are besieged by depositors looking for their money as soon as there is a sign of trouble. Most of their obligations are to people who have to die before their families can collect. As a result, only $18 million has been paid by the insolvency funds since 1970.

Yet many in the industry worry that a large failure might not be covered by other companies. If there were a major insolvency today, the present system for covering such losses would be totally inadequate, according to Armor H. Hank, associate general counsel of Nationwide Life Insurance Company of Columbus, Ohio.

In their examinations, the regulators have found that the chief cause of life insurance insolvencies is insider deals—loans or other investment transactions undertaken by officers or directors with their own company. Yet the laws that restrict such loans to officers or directors tend to be as watertight as strainers.

Many states that prohibit loans to officers or directors allow them if the loans are made by another life insurance subsidiary within the same holding company. Still other states have no prohibition on loans to officers or directors.

By the same token, payment of commissions to officers or directors may or may not be illegal, depending on the state. Some states prohibit them entirely. Florida, on the other hand, permits them as long as they are paid in accordance with the terms of a contract. Illinois specifically permits them so long as they are not "excess" commissions—a vague term that could mean almost anything. Most of the laws are so out of date that they neglect to mention newer forms of investments that may have come into existence since 1905.

As in 1905, the state regulators tend to take on faith the word of the companies that the transactions of officers and directors are proper. "We wouldn't go on a witch hunt. We wouldn't deal with conflicts of interest unless we heard that something is wrong," said John A. Conover, chief insurance examiner of New Jersey. Among other companies, Conover is in charge of examining Prudential, with its $67 billion in assets, and Mutual Benefit Life Insurance Company, with some $7.3 billion in assets.

To aid the examiners in checking on directors' transactions, directors are supposed to file conflict-of-interest statements listing their personal holdings. The examiners can use the statements to check to see if the life insurance company invested in those same stocks or companies. However, said Conover, the examiners do not spend much time on the statements. "The conflict-of-interest statements are too voluminous to copy. We don't have the staff to handle it all. We're not really looking for that kind of stuff. We don't have the time or the staff to go into depth to check on conflict-of-interest statements and the details of transactions. The CPAs [certified public accountants] don't get paid enough to do it, either. It's up to the companies to do," he said.

According to Conover, "The directors have the responsibility [for policing themselves]. The magnitude of the animal probably means a lot gets by."

On the average, the New Jersey Insurance Department assigns

the equivalent of ten people each working a year to examine Prudential's $67 billion in assets. "If you have one hundred people there full-time, you'll probably find something. The bank examiners have four times more people.... We really are just doing the major things. We count securities. We wouldn't look for a director in [connection with] mortgage loans. It would take someone who would tip us off. It's not likely we would catch an improper loan to a director. We would have to fall upon it," said Conover.

The examinations usually consist of bulky recitations of information that can be obtained at most libraries from A. M. Best Company's *Best's Insurance Reports*. Unlike bank examination reports, insurance examinations are publicly filed in state insurance department offices. However, they rarely contain anything of any interest. "The examination reports vary from dreadful to occasionally good," said Richard V. Minck, executive vice-president of the American Council of Life Insurance.

If the regulators stumble across an irregularity, their response is often muted and slow. That is true even in New York, known as the toughest regulatory state, as illustrated by the following case history.

■

In 1972, two officers of Teachers Insurance & Annuity Association of America invested in the stock of Decision Data Corporation. Just weeks later, those same officers had an affiliate of Teachers purchase $5.5 million in stock of the same company. At the time, the officers were in charge of investment decisions for the affiliate College Retirement Equities Fund (CREF), which provides pensions to university employees. Teachers itself is the ninth largest life insurance company in the country; it sells only to university employees.

Normally, such a large purchase would send the price of a stock upward. However, the computer firm's stock eventually fell, and the affiliate ended up selling the stock at a loss of $5 million. The insurance company executives also took a loss on their personal purchases, which had amounted to $48,400.

The timing of the officers' personal purchases came to light during a 1974 SEC investigation of fluctuations in the price of Decision Data's stock. The commission's New York office called in the two insurance company officers to testify about their investment transactions. In testifying about the purchases by Teachers, they also revealed that they had personally invested in the computer firm.

The word got back to Teachers, which took swift disciplinary action: The officers could never again make investment decisions involving Decision Data. And they got only half their usual annual raise. Both officers still retained their executive positions, and one was later promoted to senior vice-president.

The New York State insurance examiners only learned about the officers' personal purchases because they noticed a discussion of the SEC investigation in the minutes of Teachers' directors' meetings. When the examiners completed their report of the condition of the company as of 1974, they included a reference to anonymous officers of Teachers under the heading "conflict of interest." As described in the report, the officers had taken advantage of their knowledge that the affiliate would invest in the computer firm by investing in the firm themselves.

While noting that the insurance company had taken "disciplinary measures" against the officers, the examiner said in the report that he did not consider them adequate. The officers' actions, he said, raise a question of whether they had violated the bylaws of the insurance company. Those bylaws, in turn, mirror prohibitions in the insurance code against officers having a financial interest in a transaction, the report said.

Teachers hired a law firm to challenge the findings, and the report was held up while Morton Greenspan, then general counsel of the insurance department, reviewed it. In a 1978 internal memorandum, he concluded the Teachers' officers' actions had "come within the prohibitions" of the insurance law.

Still, no action was taken, while more meetings were held. The department finally decided against taking any action against the officers, for reasons that are still unclear. The report wasn't issued until 1980, eight years after the stock purchases had been made and six years after the insurance department found out about the violations. One of the officers went on to manage a pension fund. The other officer—who said he did not understand the company's policies on conflicts of interest—retired.

Teachers attributed the promotion of one of the officers to his subsequent contributions to the company. It said it took action against both officers by cutting their raises and censuring them. While the officers had violated company rules, Teachers does not believe they violated the law, a company lawyer said.

The man in charge of regulating Teachers at the time was Alvin H. Alpert, then chief of the New York State Insurance Department's life insurance bureau. Repeatedly, the white-haired Alpert had gone up against the big companies. When insurance commissioners, spurred on by Prudential and other companies, tried to cut the amount of disclosure required in statements filed with insurance departments on the grounds it was too costly to compile, Alpert, looking more like a down-at-the-heels college professor than a regulator of billion-dollar companies, stood up at a meeting in New York and said flatly the proposed measure would make regulation almost impossible.

Yet Alpert said he finds nothing wrong with issuing a report in 1980 based on the condition of a company in 1974. "Normally, there are objections before a release of a report," said Alpert, who has since retired from the department after ten years as chief of the life insurance bureau. "Our concern is for due process." If companies do not take appropriate action against officers, the department cannot "second-guess management," he said.

What was unusual about the Teachers case was not that the regulators took so long, or even that they did nothing, but rather that they found out about the violations at all.

■

In regulating agents, as in regulating the companies, the state insurance departments tend to be passive. Most of the states have a law broadly prohibiting agents or companies from making misrepresentations. To find out whether regulators ever charge agents under that law, a *Washington Post* research assistant, Andrea Kingsley, called all fifty insurance departments. Officials of sixteen states had no recollection of any cases of misrepresentation ever being brought. Officials of most of the remaining departments said they thought three to fifteen such cases were brought each year, but they said they had no hard figures to back that up.

"Quite often, after a fairly extensive conversation which went around in circles, [I] found there was no recollection of any action taken due specifically to misrepresentation," Kingsley said. The regulators said misrepresentation is either extremely rare or hard to prove. Usually, they said, an agent would have to admit his guilt for the regulators to be able to bring a case.

As a rule, the cases that have been brought against agents stemmed from complaints of competing companies when their policies were replaced, she reported. The penalty, in any case, was a fine of a few hundred dollars or probation.

Yet, as the first chapters of this book demonstrate, there is no dearth of examples of misrepresentation by agents. "Misrepresentation by agents is chronic. The regulators will do nothing unless they get a complaint from the public. The public is helpless because it takes weeks to understand what life insurance is all about," said Donald Malik, the former Connecticut General agent.

Underscoring that point, Minck of the American Council of Life Insurance pointed out that the regulators are hampered in regulating the sales process because they get few complaints from the public. That, in turn, is often because consumers don't know enough to complain, he said. "Unless somebody has experience in [life insurance], he has no way of knowing there was a misrepresentation," Minck said.

The Federal Bureau of Investigation, if it wants to find out something, sends an agent wired for sound. Because pitches by securities salespeople are easier to understand than presentations made by life insurance agents, there is no need for the SEC to resort to such methods. The SEC disciplines hundreds of salesmen a year for misrepresentation. But the insurance departments do not think of themselves as enforcers. "The complaints all boil down to lack of communication," said Seymour Shapiro, assistant chief of the New York State Insurance Department's consumer bureau.

■

At the heart of the system of state regulation of insurance is the National Association of Insurance Commissioners (NAIC), composed of the commissioners of the fifty states and the District of Columbia. Founded in 1871 to help coordinate the system of state regulation, the NAIC has a small staff based in Kansas City, Missouri, and a budget of less than $1 million. The organization's chief function is developing what it calls "model laws." The NAIC is, in effect, a mini-Congress devoted exclusively to drafting insurance laws.

Once proposed by the NAIC, the model laws are passed by most of the states. There is a model law governing insider trading, insolvencies, and accounting procedures. There is even a model regulation telling the companies how to compile biographical data about their officers and directors.

The theory behind this procedure is that no one state has the expertise to draft an adequate bill, but all fifty can combine forces to come up with technically sound measures. By introducing the same bill in fifty states, the NAIC hopes to achieve some uniformity as well. Otherwise, life insurance companies operating in all fifty states would have to change their policy forms and ways of doing business in each state.

On paper, the idea sounds reasonable. What could be wrong with a "Life Insurance Solicitation Model Regulation"? When drafting the model laws, however, the commissioners appoint technical committees that are dominated by the industry. As a rule, the technical committees draft the laws, which are then recommended to state legislatures by the insurance commissioners. In the end, the model laws ratify what the companies want to do in the first place.

"Ostensibly, [the committee] is to advise on technical matters, but nine times out of ten it drafts the model regulation," said William A. White, chief actuary of the New Jersey State Insurance Department. "[The technical committee] opposes anything that would be intolerable to the industry."

The industry, in this case, usually means the American Council of Life Insurance, which represents 591 life insurance companies. These companies account for ninety-five percent of the life insurance in force in this country. The American Council happens to be one of the most professional trade and lobbying associations in the country. Its 281 employees knows more about the life insurance business than any twenty state insurance agencies.

When regulators are asked about life insurance, they often display no hesitancy in referring the questions to the council, which is happy to accommodate. Likewise, when the NAIC is asked how many states have passed its model laws, it suggests a call to the American Council.

With a budget of $23 million a year, the council's resources dwarf those of the NAIC or any state insurance department. The amount contributed by Prudential—$1.7 million—alone exceeds the budgets of most of the departments.

White, who once worked for the American Council as an associate actuary, said the council usually appoints a committee to follow the work of the NAIC technical committees. The job of the council's committee, said White, is to "channel, control, and counter" the NAIC committee's recommendations.

Because of the companies it represents, the council's word is usually gospel. As a member of a 1975 NAIC committee on improving cost disclosure, White said, he wanted to require disclosure of agents' commissions. In that way, he felt, consumers would be forewarned that agents have a financial incentive to sell whole life over term insurance. "The [American Council] concluded there was no point in most of the points raised. The industry advised there was nothing worth doing. The task force essentially accepted their recommendation. At that point, there was no one on the task force who could challenge the industry," said White.

A case in point is the NAIC's model law dealing with industrial life insurance. Within the life insurance industry, there is probably no greater abuse than the way industrial life insurance is sold to the poor. In part because of criticisms of industrial insurance, the NAIC in 1979 established a committee to look into the allegations and recommend a model law for adoption by the states. The committee first met in October 1980. The insurance departments of twelve, mostly southern, states participated.

The commissioners began with the conclusion that industrial insurance serves a "useful social function," then set up a series of technical committees and subcommittees to study its sale.

One subcommittee was to determine if industrial insurance really is more expensive than ordinary insurance. Computers are not required to determine the answer. The disparity is so great that all one has to do is compare the premiums between industrial and ordinary policies to see the twofold to fourfold difference.

The subcommittee appointed for this task consisted of two members: William H. Davies, Jr., who recently retired as chairman and chief executive officer of Commonwealth Life Insurance Company of Louisville, and Ira L. Burleson, vice-chairman and general counsel of Liberty National Life Insurance Company of Birmingham, Alabama. Both of these companies continue to collect on large blocks of existing industrial insurance; they also sell ordinary policies that are collected by agents in people's homes.

Focusing on the way the insurance is sold rather than the actual prices, the subcommittee concluded, "There is not sufficient evidence based upon reliable statistical studies to reflect that the home service method of marketing insurance products is or is not more expensive, as a general rule, than other systems of marketing. . . ."

Another group headed by Burleson of Liberty National gathered information about how agents sell industrial insurance. The source of the information was the home service industry, rather than consumers. Calling the Life Insurers Conference, which represents the industry, a "fine organization," the report thanked the home service trade organization for printing and distributing the surveys.

The group blandly reported that supervision of agents "did not appear to be a big problem." In fact, its report said, "The home service system offers more control of agents than the general agency system [used by most companies selling ordinary policies]."

Another group consisted of a mix of regulators and company representatives chaired by Eugene W. Bates, executive vice-president of Western and Southern Life Insurance Company of Cincinnati. While conceding that expenses per $1,000 in industrial coverage are "high," the group attributed that to the small size of the policies and the expense of collecting at home. It recommended bringing some ancillary aspects of industrial insurance more in line with ordinary insurance. For example, instead of allowing a grace period of twenty-eight days before a policy is canceled because of nonpayment, the committee suggested extending the grace period to bring it into line with the provisions of ordinary life insurance policies. The difference was all of three days.

At the same time, the group recommended keeping the $1,000 cap on the size of an industrial policy. It is this lid that encourages agents to load up customers with thirty policies to give them sufficient coverage. The committee also recommended that the companies offer discounts to people who pay their premiums ahead of time. In doing so, the committee, in effect, ratified the practice of collecting in advance, a practice that leads to agents pocketing premiums or using them to pay for other people's insurance.

The committee made no mention of the out-of-date mortality table that contributes to keeping industrial rates high. Based on the committee's recommendation, that table would still be required by regulators.

In December 1982, the regulators reported back to the full NAIC. They recommended almost exactly what the committees had suggested. "There is not sufficient evidence to reflect that the home service method of marketing insurance products is or is not more expensive than other systems of marketing," the regulators told the NAIC. In coming to that conclusion, the regulators had lifted word-for-word the previous determination of Davies and Burleson, the two life insurance executives, except that they left out the qualifiers.

One of the committees included a consumer representative, Jimmie Lynn Ramsaur, then with Legal Services of Middle Tennessee. Although she went to two meetings, she said she had little or no effect on the outcome. For reasons she does not understand, she said she was never asked to vote on the committee's recommendations and still has not been given a copy of the report.

When told of the report's findings, Ramsaur said, "[The report] misses the point. . . . The question is how much does it cost." She added, "The reason they put me on there was so they could say they had a consumer on it. They were receptive to very few things I had to say. . . . I felt like my being there was a joke."

"That thing [the NAIC committee] was just a farce," said Montgomery, who was a member of the committee as the District of Columbia's acting insurance superintendent. "They appointed people who sold industrial insurance, and the report was taken as it was presented by them." Montgomery said he did not oppose the group's recommendations because he felt he would not be able to garner support to come up with different conclusions. In any case, he said, he did not have the time to devote to the task.

But Bates of Western and Southern Life Insurance Company applauded the report and the regulators' decision to appoint industry officials to the committees. "It prevents them from doing dumb things because they don't have all the facts," he said.

By placing their stamp of approval on industrial insurance, the regulators had guaranteed that it will continue to make money for the life insurance companies and soak the poor.

Most often, the NAIC committees are notable for what they don't do rather than what they do. In 1978, the NAIC appointed a committee to come up with a solution to a problem that had vexed the regulators for years. It has to do with the way the prices of policies are disclosed using the interest-adjusted method approved by the regulators. Using this method, the price comparisons are usually made after a policy has been in effect for ten years or twenty years. Many companies structure their policies so the amount of dividends or cash values they pay each year swells just before the tenth and twentieth years. The result, of course, is that the disclosure figures, being based on the tenth and twentieth years, give a misleading impression of the price of the policy.

Prudential's whole life policy provides an excellent example. Figures of Computone Systems, Inc., show that the cash values of a Prudential whole life policy rise from the seventeenth year to the twentieth year the policy is held in this progression: $2,031, $2,088, $2,144, $2,204. But after the twentieth year—the one used by the regulators for comparing costs—the increases in cash values suddenly diminish: $1,750, $1,758, $1,764, $1,768.

The actuaries call this "manipulation," an unfortunate word-choice because it implies deceit. It is unimportant what the motive is for making a policy look better at the comparison points. The important thing to keep in mind is that it serves to defeat the purpose of the cost disclosure system.

In appointing a committee to resolve the problem, the NAIC declared it would test the use of "broad-based" study groups. It turned out "broad-based" meant the technical committee did not consist entirely of life insurance executives. Instead, eight of the twelve members were life insurance executives. One of the members, who initially served as chairman, was Julius Vogel, then senior vice-president and chief actuary of Prudential.

Since the NAIC gets its funds from the states, and the states barely provide enough money to pay the salaries of the insurance commissioners, the NAIC has no money to speak of. So the committee members met at Prudential's Newark headquarters; at the Hartford, Connecticut, offices of Aetna Life & Casualty Company; and at the offices of the American Council of Life Insurance in Washington, D.C., among other places. The traveling expenses of the non-industry members—and the hotel bills when the committee met at hotels—were paid for by a collection taken by some of the companies.

A crucial task of the committee was to define manipulation. If the definition did not include policies that looked better around the tenth and twentieth years, the work of the committee would be pointless.

One of the committee members was Joseph M. Belth, a professor of insurance at Indiana University. Belth has been knocking his head against the wall for years, trying to get the companies to say what their prices are. While some of his methods can be intricate, he is the unsung hero of the effort to make life insurance more understandable.

Belth suggested the committee define a manipulated policy as any one that looks better at the tenth and twentieth years than at other comparison points. "When manipulation is said to be present, there is no intent to suggest that the manipulation is necessarily deliberate on the part of the company," he said in his suggested definition.

But the confidential minutes of the October 16, 1979, meeting held at the American Council's offices in Washington show the definition that was accepted came almost word-for-word from Prudential's Vogel. According to that definition, "Manipulation is present if a policy's progression of premiums, dividends, and benefits makes the policy appear unrealistically attractive, and such progression is determined to have no acceptable rationale." Vogel's suggested definition had been: "For purposes of this report, manipulation is said to be present if a policy's progression of premiums, dividends, or benefits has no plausible rationale other than to make the policy appear deceptively attractive in competition."

By Vogel's definition, only those policies purposely designed to thwart the intent of the cost disclosure law would be considered manipulated. Under that standard, of course, Prudential's policies are perfectly acceptable. No one knows why the flow of benefits from Prudential's policies happens to improve around the tenth and twentieth years. Vogel, who supervised the design of the policies, said what he calls the "bulges" in benefits appear for "benign" reasons. He said the values have to change at some point. "They [the bulges] are perfectly innocent," said the soft-spoken Vogel. "You will find them on every policy sold in the U.S."

Which, of course, is exactly the point. The insurance regulators are not about to ban policies sold by the major life insurance companies. According to Belth, the Vogel definition would make any antimanipulation regulation impossible to enforce.

"You would have to get into a guy's mind [to show manipulation under the committee's definition]," said Belth. What happened was simple enough, he said. "The industry people outnumbered the non-industry people."

After filing a report in 1981 with the new definition of manipulation, the committee went out of existence. No action has been taken on its recommendations, which include, among other things, more study.

As in the case of the committee appointed to study industrial insurance, the manipulation committee succeeded in ratifying the existing industry practice. By appointing industry people to the committee, the regulators had, of course, guaranteed that result.

"It raises a fundamental public policy question that they [state insurance departments] have to resort to using the industry to regulate the industry," said Harold D. Skipper, Jr., an associate professor of insurance at Georgia State University in Atlanta.

It is important to distinguish between what happens at the NAIC and what happens in Congress. As we all know, members of Congress pass laws that permit themselves to accept millions of dollars in campaign contributions from political action committees (PACs) that are thinly disguised corporate contributors. They accept tens of thousands of dollars in fees for appearing at one or two corporate luncheons. And some go on hunting and fishing trips paid for by lobbyists of various industries.

But they also appoint highly trained professional staff members who are given free reign to draft legislation that benefits the members' constituents. The professionals are not outnumbered by members of the industry, as they are on the NAIC committees. They do not draft legislation in the offices of the companies they are trying to regulate, nor do they look for handouts from industry associations to finance their meetings.

The companies argue that having fifty state departments strengthens regulation by providing more resources and by allowing more flexibility. With fifty departments, each one can experiment with new approaches, according to the industry position. Said Prudential Chairman Beck, "As long as you're regulated by at least five states, the combined weight and strength of all five has an effect. . . . Each may have their strengths. When you do that for companies operating in all fifty states, you get a very effective system."

In practice, the arrangement has the opposite effect. If one state takes a tough position, the companies can isolate it by pointing out that none of the other states agree with its position, and that the company will be at a competitive disadvantage. An attempt to depart from the NAIC model laws meets with the same refrain, with the added argument that laws that vary from state to state only add to the cost of doing business. Having fifty regulators is like having fifty parents; it means the companies can play one off against the other.

Former Maryland Insurance Commissioner Birrane saw that happen when he objected to the NAIC model bill that required disclosure of interest-adjusted price figures *after* the sale had already taken place. If consumers are to be given the figures, they should get them before they receive the policies, he decided. As it is, he said, "Every company is going to make its policy as dissimilar as possible so it can't be compared." But Birrane said the industry opposed such a measure, citing the increased cost of complying with a different version of the bill in Maryland.

"I wanted disclosure before the sale, and the industry yelled it would be a disservice to the public because of the amount of time required," he said. "[The industry wears] you down. They have the organization, the resources, the people," Birrane said when he was still insurance commissioner. Birrane, a lawyer, now represents insurance companies before state insurance departments.

In reviewing the recommendations of the industry-dominated committees, the regulators and their staffs meet twice a year in places like San Juan, Mexico City, Miami Beach, Las Vegas, and New York. The principal expenses of the meetings—the meeting rooms, printing, and transportation of NAIC staff—are picked up by the industry through registration fees.

When meeting in New York, the commissioners took over the opulent Waldorf-Astoria. On any given day during the one-week event, as many as thirty suites or banquet rooms were being used by companies and trade associations to entertain the regulators. Just as the "House of Mirth" gave the companies a chance to get closer to Albany legislators in 1905, the functions gave the industry a chance to lobby and develop contacts.

On a Monday evening, the American Council of Life Insurance, in a large, mirrored room, provided regulators and their staffs with a well-stocked bar and hors d'oeuvres. The National Council on Compensation Insurance, in another room, was serving an equally elegant spread.

For breakfast, regulators could dine on sausage, bacon, eggs, cereal, and freshly squeezed orange juice served from a buffet in the Empire Room. The tab was picked up by National Home Life Assurance Company of Valley Forge, Pennsylvania.

In keeping with usual practice, a number of smaller companies operated around-the-clock refreshment bars in suites on upper floors. "It's contact work," said Leonard H. Rosenberg, chairman of Chesapeake Life Insurance Company of Baltimore, Maryland, describing the continental breakfasts, Bloody Marys, and coffee he serves at the functions. "We keep the suite because these are people we deal with—commissioners and their staffs—who approve our forms," he said.

On a Tuesday night, the regulators attended a party for 3,000 people in the Waldorf's three-story-high, turquoise-carpeted ball-room. The clams casino and quiche served under gold streamers cost $18 per person. Liquor was served from fifteen bars at $40 per bottle. The tab was picked up by the New York life insurance companies, agents, and trade groups. The invitation said the party was held through the "good offices" of the New York State Insurance Department.

During the week-long meeting, life insurance companies took commissioners and their staffs to expensive restaurants and plays. The then Virginia insurance commissioner, James W. Newman, Jr., went to the Four Seasons with an attorney from Equitable. "We didn't talk about business," Newman said.

"I had any number of invitations to plays and private dinners," said Kinder, then California insurance commissioner and president of the NAIC. "If I wanted to see any play, I would be given tickets for it. It was, 'What would you like to see?'"

At the meeting, Arizona Insurance Commissioner Low proposed closing one of the two annual meetings to the industry. The idea was beaten down. "There are a lot of younger commissioners who feel the receptions and lunches are nonsense," Low said. But he said the commissioners do not receive enough from their per diem travel allowance to pay their expenses at the meetings. "If you want to feed yourself, you have to go to one of the industry lunches or dinners," he said.

"The NAIC meetings are a laugh," said John R. Ingram, North Carolina's insurance commissioner. "A lot of commissioners are timid about taking on the industry.... The commissioners vote with the industry. The record is there."

In a 1979 report on the adequacy of state regulation of insurance, the General Accounting Office, the audit arm of Congress, said, "GAO found that insurance regulation is not characterized by an arms-length relationship between the regulators and the regulated. While the extent of the 'revolving door' problem may be overstated by critics of state regulation, about half of the state insurance commissioners were previously employed by the insurance industry and roughly the same proportion joined the industry after leaving office. The meetings of the [NAIC] are numerically dominated by insurance industry representatives. Its model laws were drafted with advisory committees composed entirely of insurance industry representatives."

A more recent survey by the author found about a third of the commissioners who left their jobs within the past four years had joined the industry.

"The industry has a strangle hold on the insurance departments. The industry appoints the commissioners, who are straight out of the industry and as dedicated to the industry as [former Pennsylvania Insurance Commissioner Herbert S.] Denenberg was dedicated to the consumer cause," said White, the chief actuary of the New Jersey State Insurance Department. He said flatly, "The industry calls the shots."

■

Denenberg had no interest in joining the industry. After winning the November 1970 gubernatorial election on a platform promising greater consumer protection, Milton J. Shapp appointed him insurance commissioner at the suggestion of consumer advocate Ralph Nader.

Denenberg could afford to lose his job. The feisty lawyer took a cut in income from $60,000 a year to $25,000 a year to become commissioner in 1971.

Over the next four years, the unabashedly publicity-hungry Denenberg introduced the industry to a new way of regulating: trial by press release. If he did not change the industry's ways, it was not for lack of trying.

Denenberg came to the job with all the right credentials. A Harvard Law School graduate, he has a doctoral degree in economics and insurance from the University of Pennsylvania's Wharton School, and he is a Chartered Life Underwriter. Before being named commissioner, he was Loman Professor of Insurance at the University of Pennsylvania.

Denenberg speaks the language of the industry, and he speaks the language of the man on the street. "*Populus Iamdudum Defututusest*," or, roughly translated, "The consumer has been screwed long enough" is the slogan he keeps on his desk. Denenberg saw an industry mired in traditional ways of doing things that made no sense. He used publicity to try to introduce change.

In June 1972, Denenberg issued his first *Shopper's Guide to Life Insurance*, a small booklet that used the newly developed, interest-adjusted figures to show which companies offered the cheapest and most expensive policies. He followed that up with press releases listing the best and worst companies. When some of the more expensive companies reacted by lowering their rates, he issued new releases fingering the new offenders. The guides showed that rates for the same coverage varied by as much as 170 percent.

Denenberg was everybody's enemy—the lawyers, doctors, health insurers, hospitals. The Pennsylvania Medical Society demanded that he be fired. The Pennsylvania Trial Lawyers Association demanded that he be fired. Sometimes, the calls for his resignation piled up on the same day, he recalled gleefully. By taking on all the established interests, he appeared to be less of a threat to any one interest. And his open, energetic manner defused many critics.

Best's Review, the insurance trade publication, published a range of anonymous comments about Denenberg from industry executives. They showed that Denenberg had their attention: "He's stubborn and unwilling to accept criticism." "He could be a positive force for reform, and I hope he will be." "His indictment of the insurance industry is destructive." "He has no malice. He'd never take advantage of you in a personal situation." "He's arrogant." "He likes people, and people like him."

Denenberg is the third of eight children of Russian immigrant parents. His father died of a heart attack when Denenberg was ten, leaving no life insurance or savings. Nevertheless, Denenberg's mother, Fannie, saw three of her sons attend law school and three become doctors. A social critic, Denenberg's mother gave him some of his best ideas.

The Omaha native told an interviewer in 1970 that he was attracted to insurance because of his "basically pessimistic view of things and a yearning for establishing just a little certainty and security." While a professor at Wharton, he began his attacks on the insurance industry, raising eyebrows among the more conservative faculty members.

Later, he would say, "When I gave speeches, I would judge the impact by how long it took the Wharton School to complain." "I've been writing for eight years how bad the system is," he told *The*

Philadelphia Daily News a month after taking office. "Now I'm finding out I'm right."

Denenberg immediately recruited volunteers, many of them
law students, who helped him gather information for his crusade.
Dubbed "Denenberg's Demons," on one occasion they followed him
to the offices of an insurance company, where they took an unan-
nounced look at the company's books while startled officers looked
on.

"You remember me," Governor Shapp introduced himself to
600 journalists, politicians, and executives at a Gridiron Dinner in
Bellevue, Pennsylvania, just after Denenberg became commissioner
in 1971. "I'm the guy who brought Herb Denenberg to Harrisburg."

Finding life insurance policies impossible to understand,
Denenberg told the insurers, ". . . make it readable or I won't
approve it." Now, he said, the companies boast in advertisements
that their policies are readable.

Denenberg does not really understand why he created so much
controversy. "The criticism was unbelievably strong," said Denenberg, now a consumer reporter for a Philadelphia television station.
In attacking his cost comparison guides, "They would say cost was
only one thing."

He said, "I feel that this is what a government official is supposed to do. And people are always so surprised. It's as if they do
not understand—they must never have read their high school civ-
ics books."

Looking back, Denenberg mused, "In many ways, it [the
industry] tends to be honest. They will screw the public but will
not steal." In that respect, he said, things have not changed much
since the early 1970s.

"It's like the life insurance companies and the regulators are living in another age," he said. "People are putting billions in the
wrong policies and getting low returns and little coverage. It's massive fraud and deception and nobody bats an eye because there's
no fire where fifty people are killed," he said.

■

For all the concern about Denenberg, there is a saying in the life insurance industry, repeated with only a trace of a smile, that fifty monkeys are preferable to one gorilla. The federal government, of course, is the gorilla, and the industry carefully guards against coming into its clutches. The most recent example is the industry's response to a 1979 Federal Trade Commission report that criticized the virtual impossibility of determining the price of a policy.

Noting that price competition in the industry is so ineffective that companies paying returns of two percent on their whole life policies compete successfully against companies paying four percent to six percent, the one-inch-thick report said the average rate of return on a whole life policy was between one and two percent.

"Our study discloses that American consumers are losing billions of dollars yearly as a result of ill-informed and inappropriate life insurance purchase decisions," a July 10, 1979, FTC press release said.

The fact is, the rate of return on a whole life policy cashed in after six years is usually negative, but averages can be tricky. As the FTC's report stated, the averages cited by the FTC were not averages but estimates of averages.

The FTC's staff had fallen victim to actuaries who had urged the commission to use the Linton Yield approach to determining returns. That method, as we have seen, is nothing more than a mixture of hypothetical assumptions. Adding them up is an interesting academic exercise but is as reliable as a weather forecast. When reporting on the value of the chief product of an industry with more than $600 billion in assets, guesses are not good enough.

The FTC study did not receive much attention in the press, but the industry feared that agents selling term insurance would cite the FTC's conclusions in their sales pitches. The companies, agents, and trade associations began a barrage of criticism that resulted a year later in a law that made it highly unlikely the FTC would ever again tell American consumers what is wrong with life insurance.

According to the law, the FTC may not study the industry without the consent of the House or Senate commerce committees. In 1979, as in 1945, Congress had used its powers to retain for the industry a privileged status not enjoyed by any other financial industry. Even the banking industry, with all its clout, would not dream of trying to persuade Congress that it should not be studied by a federal agency.

For an industry regulated by the states, the power of the life insurance industry on the federal level is formidable indeed. "What do House Speaker Tip O'Neill, Senate Banking Committee Chairman Jake Garn, and Lloyd Bentsen, a member of the Senate Finance Committee, have in common?" a review of political activities by the American Council of Life Insurance asked. "Answer: They were each in the life insurance business in some capacity prior to their current political careers. Democrat O'Neill, for example, was a successful agent in Massachusetts. Republican Garn sold insurance in Salt Lake City. And Democrat Bentsen was president of an insurance company in Texas after he had served as a congressman from that state," the council said. The newsletter to the industry went on to list sixteen members of Congress with insurance backgrounds.

While an insurance background doesn't guarantee that a member will be favorably disposed to the industry, it can be helpful. Money is more helpful still. The political action committee (PAC) of the National Association of Life Underwriters, the chief agents' group, was the fourth biggest spender among trade association PACs in 1982 and 1983, according to Federal Election Commission figures compiled by PACs & Lobbies, an independent group. The underwriters contributed $1.1 million to federal candidates in that election cycle. Other agent groups contributed another $690,000, according to the figures, or a total of nearly $1.8 million.

"No one can really stand up against them," said Stephen F. Beck, a Senate Banking, Housing, and Urban Affairs Committee economist who played a role on another committee in the subsequent legislative effort to gut the FTC's authority. "They're everybody's bread-and-butter constituents. They're motherhood and apple pie. They're small business and they're very well organized and give a lot of money in the campaigns."

In the case of the FTC report, the industry did indeed marshal its forces and talk up its side with friendly White House aides. However, the FTC had not helped its own cause.

The FTC's basic conclusion—that consumers are losing money because they cannot tell the price of life insurance—cannot be seriously disputed. The FTC staff did a thorough job of highlighting the shortcomings of price disclosure in the industry. But the FTC, from the inception of the study in 1976, had overlooked the fact that Congress had already made known its views on federal jurisdiction over insurance. Whether one agrees with it or not, the McCarran-Ferguson Act specifically said the FTC Act shall apply to the insurance business only to the extent it is not regulated by state law. The subject of the FTC study—cost disclosure—is regulated by state law.

While lawyers can argue the fine points, the FTC had given the industry all the opening it needed. In a Senate hearing requested by John H. Filer, chairman and chief executive officer of Aetna Life & Casualty Company, the fourth largest in the business, the insurance executive told the Commerce Committee three months after the FTC report came out that the FTC staff had engaged in "reckless misrepresentation of the business." "To put our case directly," he said, "the FTC staff, in order to justify the intervention of the federal government, set out to make it appear that this industry was hiding its costs and misleading its customers into making poor purchase decisions."

Two weeks later, Filer and Prudential Chairman Beck met with Senator Howard W. Cannon (D–Nev.), then chairman of the Commerce Committee, to ask for a bill clarifying the FTC's jurisdiction. Cannon himself had spent only a few minutes with Beck and Filer, excusing himself to attend to other business while they discussed the FTC report with aides. He later asked his staff assistant, Michael J. Mullen, what he thought.

Mullen had been harboring doubts about the FTC's authority to study life insurance for a year. On January 25, 1979, he wrote a memo to Cannon letting him know he planned to meet with FTC staff members "to get an in-depth briefing from the FTC on their insurance proposals and, in particular, the FTC's view of its jurisdiction over the insurance industry." Subsequently, he asked the Library of Congress's Congressional Research Service to look into the legislative history of the McCarran-Ferguson Act. A week before the FTC study was released, Mullen got an answer. The service had concluded that there was "no hard evidence" to support the FTC's claim that it had authority to study life insurance costs.

A lawyer who was offended by what he considered a breach of congressional intent, Mullen presented his views to Cannon. Based on Mullen's recommendation, Cannon introduced a measure that would restrict the FTC's authority.

At the time, the FTC was already under attack from businesses ranging from funeral homes to used-car dealers for proposing consumer-protection requirements that they saw as burdensome. The move to restrict the FTC's authority in still another area fit right in with the prevailing mood.

The American Council of Life Insurance, which had been hanging back while Filer and Beck spoke for the industry, began presenting the industry case to members of the committee. Cannon circulated a memo to committee members outlining why he felt the FTC's position was "without any legal foundation."

The committee approved his measure unanimously. Attached as an amendment to the FTC Act, it passed it the next year as part of the Federal Trade Commission Improvements Act of 1980.

FTC Commissioner Michael Pertschuk, who was FTC chairman when the study was initiated, said Congress knew about the FTC's study while it was proceeding and never raised an objection. "The study was in our budget appropriation for five years," he said. "No one in the Commerce Committee raised an objection until after the attack by the industry."

Ironically, it was Filer's Aetna that showed up the worst in the FTC's confidential rankings of the costs of 200 policies. Because of the successful campaign by Filer and the industry, the FTC never released these figures to the public. Now the commission is so shy of the industry that it will not release the figures even when they are requested under the provisions of the Freedom of Information Act.

11. WINNING THE GAME

■ In his job at the National Institutes of Health, Dr. James A. Magner analyzes the molecular structure of a hormone that stimulates the thyroid gland. One recent evening at home, he tried to figure out the life insurance policy he purchased two years ago.

Glancing at the rows of figures, Magner said he cannot understand just what the coverage is or what benefits it provides. Before buying the policy, Magner said he tried to compare the numbers with at least one other company's—New York Life Insurance Company. But when he got back a complicated set of figures, he found there was no way to reconcile them.

"I try to be an intelligent consumer," he said. "It was inscrutable."

So, like about half the people who buy life insurance policies, Magner wound up buying from someone he knows—his sister-in-law, an agent with Equitable Life Assurance Society of the United States. He said he still doesn't know if he got a good buy.

Dr. Magner is one of the millions of victims of the life insurance game. Well-educated, intelligent, and relatively well-off, the physician nonetheless wound up buying a variable life policy, a variant of whole life that costs $1,424 a year and gives him coverage of $100,000. For about a fifth of that premium, he could have gotten the same coverage with term insurance and invested the rest in his money fund or his tax-free municipal bond fund.

The two agents never showed him that option, and Dr. Magner has neither the time nor the inclination to learn the intricacies of the life insurance game. Even if he did, he would have no reasonable way of penetrating the morass that passes for cost disclosure in the industry.

"I've been around [life insurance] all my life, and I still can't understand it," said James R. Montgomery, III, the deputy insurance superintendent of the District of Columbia, who is also an actuary. "I, as a professional regulator, cannot make a comparison [of two policies' costs]."

The losers in the life insurance game cut across American society. They include members of the great middle class like Dr. Magner, the disadvantaged who buy industrial policies, the new-car buyers who buy credit life insurance to cover their loan payments, and even—as we shall see—federal workers covered by group insurance.

In the end, it is widows or widowers who suffer. They find out too late that the life insurance policies tucked away for them in drawers or safe-deposit boxes do not begin to cover the loss of income sustained upon the death of a family breadwinner.

Usually, the insurance companies pay the claims without dispute. This isn't the problem. But if the industry sold life insurance the way it should be sold—meeting the buyer's needs first, before the company's needs—people would have enough protection when they die.

We will examine three examples in point: a widow whose husband had too little insurance; one whose spouse had none at all; and a man who, dying young, couldn't have foreseen the enormous burden he bequeathed his wife.

Then we'll explore how it could have been different: what the ultimate solutions are, how the industry has blocked them all, why the companies are able to write their own rules, and what *can* be done today to beat the life insurance game.

■

Few widows actually find themselves forced out on the street because of inadequate life insurance coverage. But they usually find they face a drastic drop in their standard of living. Trying to manage their grief, they also find they have to cope with a panicky feeling whenever the dishwasher breaks down, the garbage disposal goes on the blink, or their children tear their clothes while playing.

"I wish I had had more life insurance," said one forty-four-year-old widow. "It's been traumatic. You're trying to get rid of your grief and trying to be two parents, and then you have all the financial problems dropped on you."

The widow's husband, a securities salesman, died of a heart attack. He made $32,000 a year. She was left with a second mortgage on their home and about $6,000 in consumer loans they had obtained to pay off hospital bills for one of their three sons after he was injured in a motorcycle accident.

The Social Security payments she receives as a surviving spouse just cover the $750 in total monthly mortgage payments. Her husband's group term life insurance policy paid her just under $100,000. After using $5,000 of the benefit to cover funeral expenses, she placed the rest in a money fund. At one point, she was earning $16,000 a year from the fund, but now the proceeds are considerably less. She has to pay taxes on the earnings as well. She feels she has no choice but to keep the money intact.

"You can't spend the principal," she said.

She once worked as a telephone operator but feels now she would have difficulty finding a job. With two sons who are seven and twelve, she believes she should be home most of the time. Testing her worth in the job market frightens her, and she has been trying to avoid thinking about applying for jobs.

"I live very carefully," she said. "I don't have any social expenses anymore. Friends take me out to dinner. To have children is to owe your life to Sears."

Instead of buying a new car, she had the family's 1975 Pontiac repainted. She felt "traumatized" when her washing machine went on the blink and she wound up charging a new one on her Sears charge card. Both she and her children go without health insurance coverage, since she cannot afford the $95 premium each month. Nor does she feel she can buy life insurance protection on herself, just as her husband did not believe he could afford to buy coverage beyond the group protection he had.

Since agents recommend whole life nine out of ten times, we can surmise he was never told that he could buy far more coverage with term insurance at a relatively modest premium. Under the present system, his decision not to divert money from an already tight budget was understandable.

"[The life insurance benefit of just under $100,000] seems like a lot, but when it's divided yearly, it's not that much," she said. "Many people don't think of how much income they get in a year and what is needed to replace it," she said.

In contrast to this widow, Elliot Jones, the widow of a prominent Washington physician, had no life insurance and no dependents. Still, she finds she may have to give up her home because of the financial squeeze she is now experiencing.

"It's very hard," she said. "I've had to take boarders. . . . There are so many financial traps lying in wait for a widow. It's like tigers in the jungle."

Jones's husband, Dr. Michael J. Halberstam, was fatally shot in a burglary. Arriving home with his wife, he encountered a man who ordered him to lie on the floor. When Halberstam made a move toward him, the man shot him and the physician died on the way to the hospital.

In the year before his death, Dr. Halberstam made $110,000, including a $30,000 advance on a novel about a doctor who was the president's physician. Out of that income, the forty-eight-year-old doctor paid $10,000 toward the support of the two children he adopted during his first marriage. He also paid for renting the office where he practiced cardiology and internal medicine, and he helped support his mother.

"He hated money," Jones said. "He didn't know anything about it. We spent what we got. We ate out when we wanted to and traveled when we wanted to," she said.

Like most widows, Jones found she knew little about the family finances, which she'd been supplementing by working part-time as a researcher at the National Geographic Society. "He assumed he wouldn't die, like everybody else," she said. "He never mentioned life insurance. He didn't have a will until a year ago."

Now Jones has learned the utility bills alone total $300 to $500 a month, and the mortgage $1,400 a month. Recently, Jones was shocked to learn she owes more than $60,000 in estate taxes as well as the $30,000 advance her husband received from a publisher.

"When [her lawyers] called me about the taxes, I cried one night and got drunk the next night," Jones said. "It's money I owe on money I've never seen." (Surviving spouses have since become exempt from paying estate taxes unless they have very large assets.)

To stay afloat, Jones began working full-time at *National Geographic*, which pays her $18,000 a year. Friends take her out to dinner. She gets $600 a month from boarders who come and go. But Jones has not bought any clothes, had to cancel her subscription to the opera, and fears she will wind up selling her home. If she stays, she does not know where she'll find the money to replace the rotting porches.

She doesn't want to move to an apartment. "I love the house and the furniture in it," she said. "Our baby grand that I learned to play on I'd have to sell. Our big poster bed would never fit. I'd have to get rid of my dogs and cats.

"It requires the stamina of an athlete to have someone die," she said. "If I were totally free of financial worries, I don't know how much better I'd feel." But she said that when the estate is finally settled, the debts will come due. "There will be a day of reckoning," she said.

Unlike Jones, Diane Wayman has three children, ages nine, fourteen, and seventeen. Her husband, a *Life* magazine photographer, died of a heart attack while driving a baby-sitter home one evening. Ten years later, Wayman and her children are still suffering financially.

Wayman's husband had just lost his job when *Life* folded, and with it, his group life insurance coverage. He had been talking with an agent about purchasing an individual policy but had made no decision. Wayman does not know for certain what type of policy was being suggested, but it was likely the usual whole life. Laid off from his job, Wayman's husband was in no position to pay thousands of dollars a year for such a policy.

Now, the family lives on $1,200 a month in Social Security benefits plus the income Wayman brings in as a photographer.

Wayman, who was twenty-eight when her husband died, has managed to stay in their fashionable home, and her low-interest mortgage still costs just $370 a month. But she and her children wind up wearing clothes donated by friends and neighbors. They make do with a gas-guzzling 1971 Buick. They do not have the security of full health insurance coverage. When their appliances break down, they wait until they can scrape together enough money to call a repairman. For dinner, they often share a stir-fried chicken breast among the four of them.

"My daughter said she's dressed in the 1970s instead of the 1980s," said Wayman. "We shop two times a year at J. C. Penney's."

When Wayman throws a party, the guests bring the food. When Christmas rolls around, each child gets $100 for buying the clothing and other necessities that Wayman wishes she could provide as a matter of course.

"I tell my kids we live in one of the wealthiest neighborhoods in one of the richest nations in the world," she said. Yet she fears she won't be able to afford to send the children to college.

Just after Wayman's husband died, a life insurance agent visited her. He recommended that she buy a whole life policy. He also recommended a policy on her son, who was then eight years old.

She took his advice and bought $25,000 in coverage on herself and her son. "I ended up paying $350 a year for two years because of the scare tactics," she said. "The agent said [my son] might be my only source of support."

She later realized she had been "crazy" to buy whole life, which would have provided meager benefits for her children if she died.

And she came to see that paying premiums to insure the life of her child, who had no income to protect, made no sense at all. Dropping both policies, she bought one term insurance policy. Now she has twice as much coverage on her life for half as much in payments.

■

As Wayman's experience suggests, the fundamental problem with the life insurance industry is that it is selling a product that no one wants, and it is not selling the product that people do want. The maxim most often repeated by life insurance people is that life insurance is sold, not bought. By that they mean that people need to be coaxed to buy life insurance because they prefer to avoid thinking about their own deaths.

Said Jack E. Bobo, executive vice-president of the National Association of Life Underwriters, "People buy because they feel somebody understands their problems. But they don't really want to buy. Any excuse you give them to postpone it, they'll grab."

Certainly, there is some truth to that. Many people postpone writing wills. But writing a will requires considerably more soul-searching and is more difficult to arrange than buying a life insurance policy. Surely people do not want to face the possibility of a fire destroying their homes. Yet they buy fire insurance without any hesitation.

In any case, there is ample evidence that people will buy life insurance if the product is attractive. When employees are offered the option of buying additional low-cost group life insurance through their employer, they routinely elect to take it. They make that decision without protracted sales pitches from life insurance agents, without endless trips to their homes, and without emotional appeals.

Life insurance is "sold, not bought" because the product the industry is selling to individuals, as opposed to groups at work, doesn't make economic sense. People realize intuitively that paying $1,500 a year for $100,000 in coverage at the age of thirty-two, for example, is not a good deal. They are right. The chances of dying

at that age are just a little over 1 in 1,000. Yet they are charged perhaps $15 for every $1,000 of coverage. In other words, the price is
roughly fifteen times greater than the actual risk of dying.

Agents overcome people's natural resistance to paying so much
for so little protection—but at a cost. They have to spend up to a
week just trying to peddle one policy. They sell their personalities
instead of selling policies, raising the cost to everyone. It is a vicious
cycle: people do not buy because the price is not attractive; the price
is not attractive because people don't want to buy it as it is normally
sold.

In *Life Insurance Selling*, a trade publication, a highly successful
agent described the steps he goes through to make a sale: "On the
average, in order to have one appointment that my prospect keeps,
I must dial twelve telephone calls. One person in three is in, so I
will reach four prospects. I can make appointments with two of
those four. One of those two appointments will be canceled or
rescheduled, resulting in one kept appointment." Over all, he said,
"A new sale requires about twenty-seven hours of my work, making and rearranging appointments, fact-finding, closing, and traveling to and waiting for appointments."

"The system is wasteful in the sense that you expend a lot of
effort and pay people that don't bring in a lot of sales," said Minck
of the American Council of Life Insurance. "But you have to find
something that would be more successful."

One system that would be more successful is the one used by the
rest of the financial world: companies advertise and customers
come to them.

Since buying life insurance is normally done once or twice in a
lifetime, there is little point in setting up special offices to handle
the transactions. The best approach is to use the existing offices of
financial institutions.

There's nothing new about the concept. It's called savings bank
life insurance. Pioneered by Louis D. Brandeis, who was later to
become a U.S. Supreme Court justice, it was seen as an answer to
the high-priced industrial coverage. Rallying social reformers and

fighting off insurance industry opposition, Brandeis saw the Massachusetts legislature approve the plan in 1907.

Now as then, the life insurance industry opposes savings bank life insurance as a socialistic infringement on the free enterprise system. In fact, it is as capitalist as buying life insurance from a mutual life insurance company. It permits mutually owned savings banks to sell life insurance over the counter, just as they sell money orders, in three states. Through lobbying of state legislatures by agents and companies, savings bank life insurance has been confined to Massachusetts, New York, and Connecticut. It cannot be purchased by out-of-state residents, and it is limited to $50,000 or less in coverage.

"We have been effectively blocked from offering life insurance everywhere except Massachusetts, Connecticut, and New York," said Louis H. Nevins, senior vice-president of the National Association of Mutual Savings Banks. "The battle [to obtain permission to sell it] is not worth it," he said.

As a result, savings bank life insurance accounts for just 0.3 percent of the total premiums paid for life insurance in this country. Because of the restrictions on coverage, savings bank life insurance, while cheaper than standard life insurance, is not as low-priced as it would be if it could be sold in larger chunks.

Purchasing term insurance through the mail would be another alternative to the present system. Yet here again, the industry has circumscribed its availability, not through laws, but through brainwashing of agents, who are taught that term insurance and advertising are close to being sinful.

Agents who try to sell only term insurance find they are regarded as pariahs by the industry and treated with contempt by their colleagues. When ITT Life Insurance Corporation announced it would no longer sell whole life insurance, it ran ads in industry publications asking agents to fill in a coupon requesting information about the company's term insurance plans. A number of coupons came back with epithets and outright threats written on them. A sampling: "We shall be looking for you. N.Y. Life." "Can we trust people with ads that encourage twisting? No!" "Your company and its marketing stink. You are an insult to the industry." "Get out of the insurance business!" "B.S. You termite!" "We at Metropolitan tell how ITT prostitutes our profession!"

What was ITT Life's crime? To sell life insurance and just life insurance, with no gimmicks and no investment values tacked on to confuse people.

There is no question that consumers respond to this approach. ITT Life has been doubling and tripling its sales. But old habits die hard. A San Mateo, California, agent, described to a 1983 meeting of the Million Dollar Round Table in Dallas, Texas, how he sold term insurance through the mails. He said he placed fourteen advertisements in local newspapers over a period of nine months. The ads brought in eighty-eight term policies with total annual premiums of $96,000. The agent, who achieved success selling whole life, found it remarkable that applicants actually arranged to have a medical examination on their own, without an agent there to prod them.

But after nearly thirty years in the insurance business, he told his audience, he had no desire to make a new career selling term insurance. Rather, he said, term sales can lead to sales of whole life and "other higher premium contracts."

"Let this business be a sideline," he advised. "By no means should you drop what you're doing in order to handle the mail order business as your sole source of income."

The best alternative to the present system would be an expansion of group insurance coverage. Equitable Life Assurance Society of the United States started group insurance in 1911, when it insured 125 employees of the Pantasote Leather Company. The arrangement eliminated the expense of selling policies individually. Commissions are far lower as a result. And companies, because they are usually more sophisticated than individual consumers, usually obtain competitive bids, lowering the prices still further. As a result, rates for group insurance are far more competitive than for other forms of life insurance.

Like savings bank life insurance, the availability of group insurance has been circumscribed by the insurance companies. Acting at the request of the industry, most states until just recently placed a cap on the amount of coverage that employees could obtain. Usually, the limit was 2.5 times an employee's annual salary, even if employees ponied up the entire cost of the additional coverage.

Like many of the laws passed by the state commissioners, this one was put there to protect the companies and agents, not the consumer. "The 2.5-times limit was developed because of the concern of agents who sell individual life insurance that larger amounts of group coverage would reduce their market," said Frank Johnston, vice-president of group regional operations at John Hancock Mutual Life Insurance Company of Boston, the nation's sixth-largest life insurance company.

While many states have now rescinded those laws, most employers remain unaware that they can offer enhanced coverage. Most insurance companies do nothing to tell them, and group coverage still accounts for only a fifth of the total life insurance premiums received.

Even with group insurance, consumers and companies can wind up paying more than they should. As we have seen, organizations may offer "group" rates that are not really group rates. And some group insurance, because the employer is not sophisticated enough to strike a good bargain, can actually be more expensive than standard life insurance sold to individuals.

An example of that is the group plan provided by the federal government to its employees. Known as the Federal Employees' Group Life Insurance program, or FEGLI, the plan covers some 2.4 million federal workers. Since 1954, when the plan was started, the rates have been negotiated with Metropolitan Life Insurance Company, which administers the plan on behalf of most of the life insurance companies in the country that share in the underwriting.

The federal government obtains no competitive bids when buying the insurance for its employees. Instead, any company that offers group life insurance gets a piece of the pie.

The program has so many unusual features that it is virtually impossible to compare it with other policies, even with the help of a computer. However, it's clear from the Computone Systems, Inc. data that the basic FEGLI program, at most comparison points, is far more expensive than term insurance policies sold to individuals.

For example, a man who bought a policy at age thirty-two would have obtained, by the age of sixty-nine, ten times more in benefits for the same price from Metropolitan's individual term policy than he would have from the FEGLI program. This is so even though the federal employee, because he is retired, has stopped making payments for FEGLI insurance.

By the age of eighty, a federal employee would do better with the FEGLI program, but people have no need for life insurance at that age, since a retired person has no income that will be cut off in the event of death.

"We think the rates are high, too," said Donald Devine, director of the federal Office of Personnel Management, which buys the policy on behalf of federal workers. "I think you've correctly identified a problem; we're looking at it."

■

The reason the life insurance industry does not work for consumers is that it is not accountable. Supermarkets are accountable because their prices are understandable. If customers feel the prices are too high, they will go elsewhere. In life insurance, there is no way to tell what the price is. Even the federal government, with all its computers and accountants, gets fooled.

If the companies are not accountable to the marketplace, they are, in theory at least, accountable to the regulators, to their directors, and to their owners. Yet, as we have seen, there is little the regulators can or will do to change the system, according to many of the regulators themselves.

"If you're embarking on a totally new direction [as a regulator], you'd have to sell it to the state legislature, and everybody will say you have been working too hard or drinking [after the industry gives its views], and you've had it," said Montgomery, the District's deputy insurance superintendent.

"[The system] hasn't been changed because the answers aren't easy, and the influence of the industry is heavy," Montgomery continued. "They want to avoid any form of rate regulation. There's a lack of expertise in the insurance departments to deal with it. If you asked me if I could be instrumental in bringing about change to some extent, we could convince the NAIC to review it. If you got a bunch of industry people [on the committee], you'll end up where you are now. It's hard to find people unrelated to the industry who have the expertise and imagination to do it."

If the regulators won't change the system, the directors are certainly in no position to do so. As a rule, they know as much about life insurance as the man on the street. As in most other types of companies, they are selected by management, which provides the board with all the information it ever gets about the company, as we shall see later in this chapter.

Nor do the directors bring particularly diverse backgrounds to their tasks. Invariably, the boards of life insurance companies, like the officers of those same companies, consist of white, Anglo-Saxon males. In that respect, life insurance companies are no different from banks or other financial institutions.

One might think that the owners of mutual companies would change the system. Mutual companies, after all, are owned by their policyholders and should therefore be run on their behalf. Many started specifically as alternatives to the abuses of stockholder-owned companies. Since mutual companies control two-thirds of the assets of the industry, their actions should pull the rest of the industry along, or so one might think.

But policyholders do not have enough of a stake in a mutual company to justify the effort required to seek reforms. Their relationship to the companies is really that of customers, not owners. Unlike large stockholders in publicly owned companies, no one individual ever holds more than one percent of the policies issued.

Originally eleemosynary societies, the mutual companies now compensate their employees handsomely and compete for business just as strenuously as do profit-making companies. In one year, the mutually owned Equitable paid fifty-four sales managers $100,000 to $200,000 each. In its sleek New York headquarters building, Equitable subsidizes employees' lunches served by Stouffer's to the tune of $1.1 million a year. And the company pays $40 an hour to a private company that waters indoor plants. Beck, the cigar-chomping chairman of the mutually owned Prudential, makes $728,880 a year—hardly the compensation of a missionary.

Because of their diffuse ownership, the mutual companies have no more incentive to bring down costs than the stockholder-owned companies. "Some of the mutual companies are run for the agency force [agents] and home offices," said Robert T. Jackson, chairman and chief executive officer of Phoenix Mutual Life Insurance Company of Hartford, Connecticut.

Phoenix Mutual happens to be one of the lower-cost companies, as symbolized by Jackson's office, which is darkened to conserve electricity and has plain, black plastic ashtrays. In contrast, the office of John H. Filer, chairman and chief executive officer of Aetna Life & Casualty Company, a stockholder-owned company about a mile from Phoenix Mutual in downtown Hartford, is decorated with oriental rugs and a grandfather clock. But a look at Acacia Mutual Life Insurance Company of Washington shows that mutual companies can be just as high-priced as stockholder-owned companies.

Founded in 1866, Acacia is one of the oldest mutual life insurance companies and one of the 125 largest life insurance companies in America. It once included on its board the late J. Edgar Hoover, director of the FBI. Since he never attended a meeting during his fifteen years as a director, Hoover eventually had to resign when an insurance examiner, in 1964, drew attention to the fact that he neither attended meetings nor owned an Acacia policy, as required by Acacia's bylaws governing directors.

Today, Acacia's board includes the presidents or chairmen of some of the largest banks and savings and loan associations in Washington. Highly respected in their fields and well-versed in finance, they meet once a month in Acacia's African mahogany-paneled board room, just across the street from the Capitol. At these meetings, they review the company's sales, investment, and operating policies to make sure they are in the interests of the policyholders.

With such an impressive board, one might expect Acacia's investment returns to be unusually high. In fact, Acacia's overall yield on investments, after deducting its expenses, was recently a mere 7.7 percent, compared with an industry average of 8.9 percent. While Acacia argues that it invests in certain lower-yielding notes because they are taxed at lower rates, Acacia's yield on stocks was just 5.3 percent. Since investment income represents more than a third of life insurance revenues, the result of those low returns is that Acacia's prices tend to be among the highest in the country.

"I don't think the directors knew it was a high-cost company, or that the investment returns were low," said William Simpson, a former senior vice-president and chief actuary of Acacia. "Things are always presented [by management] in rosy terms. They were sort of 'yes' men," he said.

According to Simpson, policyholders are not informed of these investment results in any meaningful way. On rare occasions when a policyholder shows up at one of Acacia's annual policyholder meetings, "The top management scurries around. They want to know, 'Who's this fellow?' [Going to policyholders' meetings is] sort of frowned on," he said.

Unlike Acacia, Prudential, with eighty times more money than Acacia, does not hold an annual meeting. Prudential informs its twenty-six million policyholders with their bills that they may request a form so they can vote for directors. In a recent election, only 230 policyholders, mostly employees, actually did so.

The right to vote is of little value if policyholders cannot communicate with other policyholders. Only through communication can a group be formed to unseat existing management. In theory, such a rump group might begin selling life insurance that is more in the interests of consumers.

After purchasing a Metropolitan policy in 1975, Lawrence M.

Cohen noticed that premium bills said policyholders could vote for directors of the giant company in annual elections. In 1978 Senate hearings, Cohen described how he tried to obtain a list of Metropolitan Life Insurance Company's policyholders so he could run himself as a director of the mutual company.

"This was sufficiently vague to spark my interest in finding out how and by whom these independent nominations could be made and how I could make such nominations," he told Sen. Howard M. Metzenbaum (D–Ohio), then chairman of the Senate Judiciary's antitrust subcommittee. As an executive assistant to the mayor of Utica, New York, from 1974 to 1978, Cohen had participated in presenting Metropolitan with a proclamation saying the city government is proud to have the company in the Utica area. He said he felt Metropolitan was a good company and wanted to be associated with its management.

"Thus followed a series of communications between the vicepresident of Metropolitan and myself as to the composition of the board of directors and how they were nominated and elected," he told the subcommittee.

Researching the law, Cohen found that he could run himself for the board if the New York State Insurance Department granted his request to obtain a list of policyholders. The department could only grant the request if Cohen obtained the signatures of twenty-five policyholders and appeared at a hearing before the insurance superintendent. If Cohen obtained the list, he would then have to obtain the signatures of a tenth of one percent of the policyholders to make an independent nomination for the board.

"In any event, in the summer of 1976, I drew up what I considered to be a valid petition," Cohen, who is not a lawyer, said. "I solicited the required number of signatures of policyholders and submitted the petition to the Metropolitan Life Insurance Company and to the New York State Insurance Department. Soon afterward, however, I was notified in a telephone call and then in writing by the New York State Insurance Department that there was an error in the heading of the petition, and it was therefore invalid."

The following year, Cohen tried again, this time using the correct heading. A hearing was granted for September 1977. "I was notified that I could bring witnesses with me and have an attorney present. At that time, however, I saw no reason to bring any witnesses. The law seemed clear that the only decision required at the hearing was whether I was entitled to the list of eligible voters," he said.

"As it turned out, the hearing was much more elaborate than I expected. Metropolitan had a battery of witnesses and attorneys who testified against me. They filed several affidavits which argued that I should not be entitled to the list, even though my petition was valid, because (a) I could not prove mismanagement of the company, and (b) it would be too costly to prepare a list of the eligible voters."

The insurance company told Cohen the list would cost $10 million to compile, would run to over 450,000 pages, and would weigh 6,000 pounds. Cohen argued that no election—including presidential elections—would ever be held if cost were taken into account.

At the hearing, Cohen was reminded that he had the right to have an attorney present, and that the hearing could be postponed so he could obtain one. "At this point, after seeing what Metropolitan had mounted against me, I decided a postponement would be in my best interest, so I agreed to the adjournment," Cohen testified.

In the next few months, however, Cohen became ill and could not travel back to New York. After he was told that the deadline for soliciting signatures for the next election had passed, he withdrew his petition and never tried to run again. When he asked for permission to speak at the annual meeting, he was told there is no annual meeting.

Referring to the lack of an annual meeting, Richard R. Shinn, then chairman and chief executive officer of Metropolitan, said in an interview, "I see no problem with that." He said Metropolitan, the second-largest company in the business, has other ways of communicating with policyholders and finding out what they want.

"We get hundreds of letters from customers asking questions or raising things. We are very careful about how we respond to them. We have a central organization that analyzes very carefully any complaints or suggestions or any comments that come from the policyholders," Shinn said.

In contrast to Metropolitan, Northwestern Mutual Life Insurance Company, the tenth largest in the business, mails proxies to each of its 1.7 million policyholders so they can vote on directors. The company holds an annual meeting, and it appoints a committee of five policyholders to act as examiners each year on behalf of the rest of the policyholders. The committee is changed each year, so the members acquire no vested interest in their positions. They receive a fee of $500 a day plus their expenses. Usually, the committee gives the company a clean bill of health. But Northwestern credits the committees' suggestions with the fact it was one of the first companies to cut costs by using computers to store data on policyholders.

While there is no easy way to make mutual companies more accountable, Northwestern at least is making an effort in the right direction.

■

The industry's own solution to growing criticism of its practices has been to create the impression that it now offers "competitive" policies.

"The life insurance industry today is in the midst of the most competitive stage in its history," says a statement prepared by the American Council of Life Insurance for use by its member companies. "Many companies are introducing new policies at reduced prices. All this leads to the conclusion that the cost disclosure system as a function of competition is working and is doing so to the benefit of the consumer."

Expanding on that theme, Dean E. Wolcott, Aetna Life & Casualty Company's senior vice-president for the life insurance division, said in an interview, "The marketplace is a great entity and a great force, and I continue to come back with renewed confidence about what the buyer decides, what the voter decides when you are talking about elections. . . .

"It seems to me that the consumer *en masse* is pretty intelligent and . . . whether it is over a beer at Piggy's [a Hartford, Connecticut, bar] across the street, or whether it is an office communication, rumors and conversations, or over lunch, or whether it is with an agent. . . . All those kinds of things interact in the marketplace," said Wolcott. "The consumer over the last few years has said, 'Hey, you know, I've got a better place to put my money than in cash value [whole life] insurance.' They voted, with or without a lot of index[es] that they don't understand. . . .

"I think," Wolcott continued, "the mass of people out there said, 'Hey, I want something different, and I want to continue to buy insurance,' but they have put their money elsewhere, because they think it is a better deal. And," Wolcott concluded, "they're probably right."

There is, of course, much to be said for the intelligence of consumers. They are wary of life insurance and life insurance salesmen, who rank in public opinion polls just above used-car salesmen in trustworthiness. A recent Gallup poll found a third of the public ranks the "honesty and ethical standards" of insurance agents "low or very low," while only nine percent had that opinion of bankers. As we have seen, the agents themselves are often the victims of misleading information presented by their companies.

But the point here is that the companies and agents are smarter, as demonstrated by Aetna's own statistics on new sales of life insurance. They show that, conversations at Piggy's notwithstanding, two out of three of Aetna's new premium dollars are for whole life policies.

If people have come to realize that whole life is a bad buy, you can't prove it by Aetna's customers—or by the rest of the industry's. Remarkably, four out of five new premium dollars industrywide continue to go for whole life.

While there is no easy solution to making sure life insurance companies are accountable, two things are certain: Most other companies sell products whose prices are easier to understand; and most companies that sell financial products come under far more stringent regulation than do life insurance companies.

In the life insurance industry, the confusion begins with the name of the product. The industry does not sell life insurance, it sells death insurance. The terminology used by the industry is arcane, and almost every definition has an exception. Just reading a policy requires a life insurance lexicon. Such terms as "paid-up insurance," "non-forfeiture options," and "extended term insurance" are used as if consumers actually know what they mean.

Often, the terminology is misleading. A life insurance dividend is really not a dividend but a refund of an overcharge of premiums. Mutual companies are usually defined as companies that return profits to policyholders in the form of dividends, while stockholder-owned companies pay dividends to stockholders. Yet that is not necessarily the case. Some stockholder companies sell policies that also pay dividends.

Whole life insurance, as usually defined, is life insurance that has cash-in values and premiums that do not go up as the policyholder gets older. But some whole life policies have increasing premiums, and some term insurance has level premiums. What's more, whole life is also referred to as "cash value" or "permanent" insurance. Even policyholders' ages are subject to differing interpretations. Some companies base their rates on a policyholder's age at his last birthday. Others base them on his age at his next birthday. Those differences alone can make it difficult to compare the prices.

Referring to the different names applied to the same policies, Minck of the American Council of Life Insurance said, "The differences are in the eye of the person naming the contract."

The confusion arises because the state regulators, among other things, have never bothered to standardize the terms and conditions, just as they have never required consistent price disclosure.

The industry is not unaware of the value of this massive confusion. Speaking at a Million Dollar Round Table meeting in 1983, Richard S. Schweiker, president of the American Council, warned,

"We can't assume that we are safe from scrutiny because of seemingly impenetrable jargon or forms or actuarial tables."

"The whole idea is to make it more complicated so people can't compare the price," said James P. Gibbons, Jr., president of the holding company that owns Consumers United Life Insurance Company.

The companies have made life insurance so bewildering that they have confused themselves. Ostensibly, the purpose of the life insurance industry is to sell life insurance. Yet the life insurance industry looks upon selling life insurance alone—which is all term insurance really is—with contempt. Somewhere along the line, the industry that collects $50 billion a year from American consumers lost sight of what it was doing. It got sidetracked from selling life insurance into selling low-yielding investments.

The problem with that is there are plenty of other industries that sell high-yielding investments, from mutual funds to bank certificates of deposit. When the life insurance industry competes against these other industries fairly—with discernible prices—it usually flounders.

The sale of Individual Retirement Accounts (IRAs) is but one example. When IRAs first became available, it took only a short time to see which institutions could sell them most efficiently and at the best price. INSURERS CLOBBERED IN IRA SALES RACE was the headline over a *National Underwriter* article in August 1983, describing how banks had obtained fifty-nine percent of new IRAs, compared with life insurance companies' twelve percent share of the market. In other words, when consumers know what the prices are, they opt to buy from other institutions.

Without a viable product, even some of the most honorable agents in the business turn to dissembling to put bread on the table. The abuses are so flagrant that they find their way into trade publications as recommended practices: "Suppose a prospect declares, 'Life insurance is a bad investment,'" advised an article in the December 1982 issue of *Life Insurance Selling*, an industry publication. "If the agent answers this objection with any kind of reply . . . he will have reinforced the objection. . . . If the agent ignores the objection, it is not reinforced. The probability of additional objections from the prospect therefore diminishes."

Another article from the February 1984 issue of the same publication advises, "The agent should nod his head (very slightly) when he makes a point and asks the prospect for agreement. . . . The agent will find the prospect nodding in agreement, and the agent will have control. With some practice, the agent can have a roomful of prospects nodding along in unison."

When nodding fails, some agents turn to derision and fear. A Northwestern Mutual customer who decided to drop her whole life policy and buy term insurance elsewhere got a letter from her Milwaukee-based Northwestern agent accusing her of being "very insecure," since she had listened to another agent's advice. The letter continued, "It's horrible when someone puts their trust and confidence in someone else and develops a very nice relationship with them and that relationship is broken. . . . In the future, when you die and your children need liquidity, you will be very sorry that you did not continue your permanent [whole life] insurance program with Northwestern Mutual." "Judi," the letter closed, "after thinking about what you have done to both me and your sons, I am asking that we never say another word to each other."

The American Council argues that the industry must be doing something right if the average cost of life insurance has gone down by over twenty-two percent in the last twenty years. Indeed, it has, and in the last one hundred years, the cost of life insurance has plunged even more dramatically. But that is because people are living longer and because investment returns have increased. In the last twenty years, the death rate has plummeted by twenty-two percent, while investment income has soared by more than one hundred percent. The reduction in rates has not begun to take into account these savings to the companies.

The fact is that the life insurance industry is only slightly more competitive than it was in the past and that little has changed since the days of Elizur Wright, Massachusetts' first insurance commissioner. In *Traps Baited with Orphan*, Wright lamented in 1877, "Our system of providing for the orphan, if not fallen down, has fallen into disrepute. The fault is not so much in the men as in the system. It leads into temptation. It would corrupt angels. It seems, in some respects, specially contrived for the propagation of rogues and enormous leeches."

In 1905, the Armstrong committee investigation found that the companies' costs were high because agents were obtaining commissions of forty percent to fifty percent of the first year's premium, that many new policies soon lapsed, that poor people paid too much for industrial life insurance, and that the companies accumulated far too much in surplus funds—money that should be returned to policyholders. Rather than stopping the abuses, the regulators conducted examinations that focused almost exclusively on the solvency of the companies, the investigation found.

Today, the companies continue to charge the poor more than the affluent. Rather than reducing commissions, the companies actually pay percentage commissions that are twice as high as those that were paid in 1905. The state insurance commissioners, at lavish meetings paid for by the industry, have been planning to scuttle many of the disclosure requirements put into effect because of the Armstrong commission's recommendations.

Instead of accumulating excessive sums in their surplus accounts, the companies now accumulate the money in reserve accounts by making unrealistic assumptions about investment returns and death rates. Instead of encouraging competition among the companies, the regulators, through antirebate laws, prohibit agents from reducing their own commissions so the consumer might pay less. Through "anti-twisting" laws, they stifle competition even further by making it difficult for a company to replace a policy of a competing company with its own.

In a quote that could as well have been lifted from a report of a congressional investigating committee today, the Armstrong report said, "The business of the Mutual, the Equitable, and the New York Life has grown beyond reasonable limits. . . . Notwithstanding the fact that they have long since passed the point where further enlargement can benefit their policyholders, they have resorted to every effort to obtain new business, regardless of the expense which is reflected in diminishing dividends.

"Fearful of losing prestige," the Armstrong report continued, "the chief concern of each has been to keep up with the others. Extravagant commissions have been paid, and these have been supplemented by liberal bonuses and prizes. Clubs have been formed, conventions held, and money lavishly expended for the entertainment of agents to excite them to their utmost endeavor.

"Notwithstanding their theoretical rights, policyholders have had little or no voice in the management.... the officers of these companies have occupied unassailable positions and have been able to exercise despotic power," while the directors of the companies, the report said, were mere "figureheads."

Turning to industrial insurance, the report summarized the abuses as aptly as one could hope to do today: "The most serious evils ... to wit, the excessive premiums, the enormous lapse rate, and the hardships of the agents, seem to be inherent in the system. A great reform could be accomplished if the expense of solicitation and collection could be avoided by the establishment of branch offices where insurance might be obtained by the thrifty poor who desire it."

The report pinpointed what continues to be the chief reason the price of a policy cannot be discerned: It is the multiplicity of types of policies "designed to attract customers either by catchy titles or by supposed liberality of provision." The report recommended that the insurance laws permit just four basic types of policies written in clear English.

Finally, the report pointed out that few of the abuses would have occurred if the regulators had exercised their powers in a courageous fashion.

Today, the companies continue to reward agents with trips to Hawaii and England. While this creates an appearance of competition, it is more mirage than reality. "It's [competition] more self-induced than imposed by the marketplace. There should be a clustering of prices. Instead, there is a great divergence of prices for the same product," according to William A. White, chief actuary of the New Jersey State Insurance Department.

Rather than offering the consumer a more competitive product, the industry is selling the same old whole life policy under different names, providing the consumer with little protection for the dollar. Life insurance agents continue to push it because they get paid more to sell it. The consumer has no way of knowing because agents are not required to disclose their commissions. Nor can they determine the price of what they are buying or compare it with other prices. The companies insist that they are not selling investments and should not have to disclose the true rate of return. Where once the companies advertised their prices when they were getting started in the 1800s, they now run ads that feature pictures of smiling agents.

Since 1905, the laws permitting only four policies have been snipped from the books, and companies now offer hundreds of policies that perplex the customer. Instead of regulating courageously, the insurance commissioners today largely rubber-stamp the laws that are drafted by the industry. Even the name used for universal life, touted as offering high yields, is not new. A policy called universal life was introduced in 1866. It was the first policy to guarantee payment of cash surrender values. That universal life policy, like the universal policy offered today, was a whole life policy.

"The business isn't that different from what it ever was," said Paul Buckley, the president of the Million Dollar Round Table, without suggesting any criticism. "It's just the playing field that's bigger. The players are still the same, but instead of playing at Elliot Field in Auburn, Maine, we're playing in Fenway Park or Yankee Stadium."

■

There is no reason why you should have to consult a book to learn how to tell the price of what you are buying, nor can this book offer anything more than rudimentary guidelines. When buying auto insurance, you can call an agent and get a quote on the telephone. When shopping for a mortgage loan, you can call a bank and get the current interest charge. When buying life insurance, you must wait weeks to obtain a price in the mail, and then it may not be an accurate one. In buying life insurance, there is much more needed to have accurate comparisons, since the price differences among companies could amount to as much as one-hundred percent or more.

"I believe the consumers have a right to know precisely what they are buying," Sen. Howard M. Metzenbaum (D–Ohio), then chairman of the Senate Judiciary Committee's antitrust subcommittee, stated at hearings on life insurance cost disclosure. "I believe that a buyer of insurance, just like the buyer of a TV set or refrigerator, should have the right to examine all models available and to look at all the price tags. I believe that is a fundamental and elementary proposition in the free enterprise system," he said.

In the opinion of many life insurance regulators and executives, that ideal will never be achieved so long as the industry is regulated by the states. According to these industry people, the state regulatory departments, with their limited budgets, closeness to the industry, and piecemeal approach, cannot hope to regulate effectively the affairs of companies that count their assets in the billions of dollars.

There is no reason why they should. Even more than banks and savings and loan associations, life insurance companies are nearly all engaged in interstate commerce. For the most part, they sell the same product in every state, and their practices are uniform nationally. Yet the insurance companies are regulated by the states, while banking institutions—through the Federal Deposit Insurance Corporation, the Comptroller of the Currency, and the Federal Reserve Board—are regulated in nearly all cases by the federal government. If trading on the country's stock exchanges were regulated by each of the fifty states, the stock market would be in chaos. Yet that is the situation that prevails in the insurance industry.

These days, it is not fashionable to advocate more regulation, and there is good reason for that. From the airline to the trucking industries, regulation by the federal government has meant less competition and higher prices rather than the other way around. But there are models of effective federal regulation, and the SEC is one of them. Through vigorous enforcement of disclosure laws, the SEC keeps the securities markets operating competitively and honestly. For all the angst the commission sometimes causes, no one in the financial world is calling for its abolition.

Indeed, rather than taking an antibusiness viewpoint, many who favor federal regulation believe that is the only way to permit the industry to operate effectively in a free market. Without understandable prices and honest disclosure, the competitive forces of capitalism cannot work.

No less a friend of corporate America than William F. Baxter, who recently resigned as the Justice Department's assistant attorney general for antitrust, believes repeal of the McCarran-Ferguson Act, giving the companies an exemption from federal regulation, should be considered. "I don't see any reason for the insurance industry to be treated any differently than any other industry," he said at a farewell news conference upon his return to teaching law at Stanford University. "It certainly needs to be examined."

For all the well-known problems with federal regulation, life insurance executives who have had experience with federal banking regulators say they tend to be tougher and more professional, if only because they are paid better and are further removed from the people they regulate and therefore less susceptible to political pressures. A bureaucrat in Washington hardly knows who John Filer, head of Aetna, is. In Hartford, where Aetna is based, the insurance commissioner had better know who he is. "They don't want national regulation because it's much harder to move Congress and the federal government than the states," said Gibbons of Consumers United Life Insurance Company.

The industry view is that there is already too much regulation and that the problem is the bad state regulators as opposed to the good ones. If the good ones predominated, everything would be fine. "The problem is a simple one of money," said Minck of the American Council. "Some of the departments still do a good job of it. You certainly can't expect someone who has four people in his department and pays them $18,000 a year to do a very good job. Most of the commissioners I've met have been well-motivated. If the state legislatures won't vote for adequate budgets for the departments, you are not going to have a department that is doing an adequate job."

That is true, and one reason is the vast duplication of effort and resulting waste created by fifty insurance departments that look into the affairs of companies that, in most cases, do business in all fifty states. A 1979 study by the General Accounting Office found the cost of maintaining fifty separate insurance departments actually exceeds the annual budgets of the SEC and the Federal Trade Commission combined. This cost of $122 million a year is passed on to policyholders in the form of state taxes levied on insurance premiums.

In the guise of keeping costs low, the present system actually raises the total cost to policyholders and wastes millions of dollars. Distributing the work of regulating to fifty state departments when one government agency could do the job more efficiently, makes no sense by anyone's philosophy. And paying so much money for regulation that doesn't work makes even less sense.

The problems with state regulation are so apparent that many industry leaders, publicly or privately, are beginning to call for federal regulation. Richard M. Best, chairman and chief executive officer of Security Mutual Life Insurance Company of Binghamton, New York, said the system of state regulation actually works to the disadvantage of the companies, because they must obtain approvals from fifty states. He has suggested a system of dual regulation, giving companies a chance to choose between federal or state regulation.

"The business has changed so much in the past few years we really do need federal regulation," Best said. "It's difficult for departments to maintain staffs to cope with the problems that come before them. I don't think we should have fifty departments that maintain that staff," he said, noting that the cost of regulation is borne by the policyholders.

The realities are that there can be no groundswell of support for change so long as consumers have no knowledge of how much they are overpaying. The agents, who are more the pawns of the companies than the villains, are hardly in a position to seek change. The ultimate responsibility for the way the game is played lies with the companies. If the companies finally decide it is too cumbersome to deal with fifty state regulatory departments, they might ask for federal regulation themselves. But if you were paying out $.41 for every $1.00 you received, would you want to change the system?

So the industry that has more money than any other financial industry except banking can be expected to continue to collect billions a year from unsuspecting consumers, who spend an average of a week a year working to pay for their policies. The industry will continue to present to the public the illusion that it is selling life insurance, while it is really engaged primarily in selling investments with shockingly low returns. It will continue, in particular, to take advantage of the poor and the aged, to pry into our private lives without justification, and to prepare computer comparisons and sales pitches that mislead.

The money will swell the companies' already excessive reserves and be used for unnecessary commissions to agents. The regulators will continue to pass bills drafted by the industry at functions paid for by the industry. And the widows and orphans who need life insurance protection will continue to lose at the life insurance game, receiving, in the end, an average benefit that is barely enough to cover funeral costs.

"It's a massive income transfer program," said Gibbons of Consumers United Life Insurance Company. "The companies overcharge and rely on high pressure tactics and confusion. The agents sell overpriced policies that don't give people the real death protection they need. The money and the power end up in a small number of hands in the top management of life insurance companies," Gibbons said, adding that the only way consumers ultimately can win at the life insurance game is through federal regulation.

APPENDIXES

HOW TO BUY LIFE INSURANCE

While the difficulties may seem insurmountable, they should not deter you from buying life insurance. If you have dependents, it is as necessary as fire insurance or auto insurance. (If you don't have dependents, you don't need life insurance.) While there is no way you can be sure of getting a good buy, there are certain steps that can help you win at the life insurance game.

You should first determine the amount of coverage you want. You should consider such factors as how much can be obtained from investing the death benefit; future needs, such as college educations for your children; liabilities, such as outstanding mortgages or rental payments; and other possible sources of income, including Social Security benefits and your spouse's salary. You should purchase one large policy that will provide enough to take care of these needs over time, replacing any existing smaller policies.

To try to get a good price, you should call an agent from one of the larger mutual companies, such as New York Life Insurance Company, Equitable of New York, Metropolitan, Phoenix Mutual Life Insurance Company, or New England Mutual Life Insurance

Company. While not as low as they should be, the prices of these companies are lower than at many other companies.

When talking with the agent, you should speak confidently and use as much jargon as possible. Using a coverage level of, say, $100,000 for comparison purposes, you should tell the agent, "I would appreciate it if you would mail me a ledger statement showing the values over twenty years for $100,000 [or whatever amount you want to buy] in yearly renewable term insurance." The coverage must be referred to as yearly renewable term insurance. You should also refer to a ledger statement. And you should ask the agent to include with the statement the interest-adjusted index figures mandated by regulators for comparison purposes.

Asking for these figures on the telephone will not help. The agents usually will not have them, will not know what they are, or will provide figures that do not represent the actual coverage being compared.

After you have made your request, the agent will ask your age, whether you are a smoker or nonsmoker, and whether you want additional benefits such as "waiver of premium." Do not buy it. This particular fringe benefit will pay insurance premiums should you become disabled. You should already have disability insurance where you work; buying additional insurance to cover premiums that cost a few hundred dollars a year is extremely costly.

The agent will probably say he wants to come out to deliver the ledger statement at your home. Tell him frankly and firmly that it would be a waste of his time. The same procedure should then be repeated with two other companies. When the ledger statements arrive in the mail, the policy with the lowest interest-adjusted figures should be purchased.

There are any number of pitfalls that could arise. For example, the agent may quote a price for a different type of coverage that is misleadingly cheap. In fact, it could lead to higher costs in later years. Or the prices of the companies cited here could change. Frequently, one company will include an optional feature that another company does not include, or the ages will be off. These differences are common occurrences and are enough to make the comparisons invalid. But if you need life insurance coverage, you have no choice but to buy what is readily available.

Once the policy arrives, you should cash in any whole life policies forgotten in drawers or safe-deposit boxes, and invest the proceeds at a good rate of return.

TOTAL WEALTH

Life insurance companies have more money than any other institutions except those engaged in banking. Because people place funds with life insurance companies for longer periods, the companies have more flexibility in investing the money than do banking institutions.

RANK	INSTITUTION	ASSETS (in billions)
1.	Commercial banks	$1,399.9
2.	Savings and loan associations	714.0
3.	Life insurance companies	563.1
4.	Private, non-insured pension funds	360.1
5.	State and local retirement funds	263.8
6.	Money market funds	229.3
7.	Finance companies	219.1
8.	Property casualty companies	201.5
9.	Mutual savings banks	180.5
10.	Credit unions	83.6
11.	Security brokers and dealers	81.0
12.	Foundations and endowments	79.4
13.	Open-end taxable investment funds	75.4
14.	Municipal bond funds	48.7

RANK	INSTITUTION	ASSETS (in billions)
15.	Mortgage corporations	17.7
16.	Real estate investment trusts	5.8
	TOTAL	$4,522.9

Data as of December 31, 1982, from "1983 Prospects for Financial Markets," Salomon Brothers, Inc. Final data from the American Council of Life Insurance show total life insurance industry assets stand at $588 billion.

TOP 20 LIFE INSURANCE COMPANIES

Two-thirds of the $588 billion in assets of the 2,100 life insurance companies in the country are owned by the 20 largest companies. Four of the five largest companies are mutual companies, marked below with an asterisk. Teachers Insurance, while not a mutual, is owned by a nonprofit organization.

RANK	COMPANY	ASSETS (in billions)	NET INVEST-MENT INCOME (in billions)
1.	*Prudential, Newark	$66.7	$3.8
2.	*Metropolitan, New York	55.7	4.3
3.	*Equitable, New York	41.1	2.4
4.	Aetna, Hartford	31.3	1.6
5.	*New York Life, New York	23.1	1.6
6.	*John Hancock, Boston	21.7	1.4
7.	Travelers, Hartford	17.4	1.4
8.	Connecticut General, Bloomfield	15.7	1.1
9.	Teachers Insurance, New York	13.5	1.3
10.	*Northwestern Mutual, Milwaukee	13.3	0.9
11.	*Massachusetts Mutual, Springfield	11.2	0.8
12.	Bankers Life, Des Moines	10.0	0.8
13.	*Mutual of New York, New York	8.8	0.6
14.	*New England Mutual, Boston	8.0	0.6

Appendix

RANK	COMPANY	ASSETS (in billions)	NET INVESTMENT INCOME (in billions)
15.	*Mutual Benefit, Newark	7.3	0.5
16.	*Connecticut Mutual, Hartford	6.3	0.4
17.	Lincoln National, Fort Wayne	4.9	0.3
18.	State Farm Life, Bloomington, Illinois	4.3	0.3
19.	*Penn Mutual, Philadelphia	4.0	0.3
20.	Continental Assurance, Chicago	3.7	0.2

THE LIFE INSURANCE DOLLAR

$1.00 in Income Comes from:

Premiums	.61
Investment income	.39

$1.00 is Spent for:

Death benefits	.14
Cash surrender payments	.18
Other benefits	.09
TOTAL BENEFITS	.41

Increases in reserves	.14
Agent commissions	.10
Other expenses	.24
Federal taxes	.03
Other taxes, fees	.02
Profit	.07

The life insurance dollar is based on total 1982 income and expense of standard, individual life insurance policies reported by life insurance companies to state regulators and compiled by the American Council of Life Insurance, which is the source of the data. The figures may not add to one hundred cents due to rounding. The profit or net gain of mutual companies is retained by the companies, while stockholder-owned companies distribute a portion of the profit in the form of dividends to stockholders. Dividends paid to policyholders, an overcharge of premiums, have been subtracted from both premiums and expenses.

PREMIUMS RECEIVED AND BENEFITS PAID OUT BY STATE

Life insurance companies received total income in 1982 of $166 billion, including investment income and premiums from health insurance and annuities.

Individual and group life insurance premiums accounted for $50 billion of that sum, including $8 billion in payments from policyholders in foreign countries.

By investing the life insurance premiums alone, the companies made $20 billion. They returned $8 billion of their total income from life insurance operations to policyholders as dividends. They paid out $15 billion as death benefits (about half of that under group insurance plans) and $11 billion in cash upon surrender of life insurance policies.

Here are the amounts that the companies received and paid out by state:

STATE	PREMIUMS RECEIVED (in millions)	DEATH BENEFITS PAID (in millions)	CASH PAID (in millions)
Alabama	$713	$246	$160
Alaska	71	25	11
Arizona	465	165	124
Arkansas	300	104	77
California	3,873	1,472	1,032
Colorado	607	190	151
Connecticut	727	267	207
Delaware	155	54	32
District of Columbia	204	96	29

STATE	PREMIUMS RECEIVED (in millions)	DEATH BENEFITS PAID (in millions)	CASH PAID (in millions)
Florida	1,842	709	511
Georgia	1,056	358	243
Hawaii	211	61	54
Idaho	146	48	42
Illinois	2,372	855	641
Indiana	1,016	342	279
Iowa	634	178	173
Kansas	483	152	111
Kentucky	518	195	117
Louisiana	873	284	152
Maine	161	50	51
Maryland	808	326	197
Massachusetts	1,046	372	274
Michigan	1,499	648	447
Minnesota	708	215	200
Mississippi	342	117	79
Missouri	895	322	213
Montana	126	43	31
Nebraska	353	102	88
Nevada	144	67	33
New Hampshire	162	52	43
New Jersey	1,585	636	448

Appendix

STATE	PREMIUMS RECEIVED (in millions)	DEATH BENEFITS PAID (in millions)	CASH PAID (in millions)
New Mexico	209	70	44
New York	3,433	1,296	861
North Carolina	1,076	357	273
North Dakota	120	31	36
Ohio	2,036	742	620
Oklahoma	551	195	109
Oregon	382	138	117
Pennsylvania	2,209	867	813
Rhode Island	189	62	59
South Carolina	556	186	124
South Dakota	127	37	35
Tennessee	786	279	199
Texas	2,720	956	633
Utah	226	75	62
Vermont	83	27	22
Virginia	991	377	236
Washington	617	214	191
West Virginia	279	107	50
Wisconsin	802	274	228
Wyoming	88	30	19

1982 data from the American Council of Life Insurance

LARGEST REAL ESTATE INVESTMENTS

PRUDENTIAL INSURANCE COMPANY OF AMERICA

1. Empire State Building, New York
2. New York Hilton, New York
3. Hyatt Regency, Chicago
4. Poydras Plaza, New Orleans
5. Prudential/Tenneco Building, Houston
6. First International Plaza Building, Dallas
7. Prudential Center, Boston
8. Prudential Building, Chicago
9. Embarcadero Center, San Francisco
10. Alcoa Twin Towers, Los Angeles

METROPOLITAN LIFE INSURANCE COMPANY

1. Pan Am Building, New York
2. Warren Place, Tulsa
3. Corporate Woods, Overland Park, Kansas
4. One Metropolitan Plaza, San Francisco
5. Dewey Square, Boston
6. One South Wacker, Chicago
7. Allied Center, Houston
8. Allied Bank Plaza, Houston
9. Georgia Pacific Building, Atlanta
10. Oakbrook Center, Oak Brook, Illinois

EQUITABLE LIFE ASSURANCE SOCIETY OF THE UNITED STATES

1. Equitable Building, New York
2. Gateway III, Chicago
3. Corning Glass Building, New York
4. Marriott Hotel, Anaheim
5. Northland Shopping Center, Southfield, Michigan
6. Marriott Hotel, Los Angeles
7. Military Circle Shopping Center, Norfolk, Virginia
8. Peachtree Dunwoody Pavilion, Atlanta
9. Mandell Building, Chicago
10. Ford City Complex, Chicago

AETNA LIFE & CASUALTY COMPANY

1. Amoco Tower, Denver
2. Royal Orleans-Sonesta, New Orleans
3. Citadel Mall, Colorado Springs
4. ENI Office, Bellevue, Washington
5. Ashford VI, Houston
6. Southwest Financial Plaza, Phoenix
7. North Arkansas Mall, Fayetteville
8. RBA Associates, Santa Monica
9. Biltmore, Phoenix
10. Empire Park, Denver

NEW YORK LIFE INSURANCE COMPANY

1. Pillsbury Center, Minneapolis
2. Texas Commerce Bank Building, Houston
3. Park Avenue Plaza, New York

4. Wells Fargo Building, Los Angeles
5. 1600 Market Street, Philadelphia
6. Southland Center, Dallas
7. Atrium Plaza Office Building, Seattle
8. Seafirst Fifth Avenue Plaza, Seattle
9. One Allen Center, Houston
10. Two Houston Center, Houston

The above data comes from each of the life insurance companies listed.

LIFE INSURANCE DATES

1500s   First life insurance policies are issued on the lives of captains of ships whose cargoes were insured. Previously, the Greeks and Romans had organized guilds that paid death benefits to members' families to cover burials.

1583   Earliest recorded life insurance policy is issued on the life of William Gybbon of London for a twelve-month period. The insurance company disputes the claim when he dies within the year, but a court rules it must be paid.

1660s   Lorenzo Tonti, an Italian physician and banker, popularizes life insurance through the tontine policy, which provides great benefits to remaining survivors of a pool.

1699   First British life insurance company, the Society of Assurance for Widows and Orphans, is established separately from other organizations. Membership is limited to 2,000.

1759   First life insurance company in this country is established. Now called the Presbyterian Ministers' Fund, it continues to operate in Philadelphia.

1762   The Equitable Society of England issues the first policy insuring an individual for the whole of his life, so long as the premiums are paid each year.

1789   Professor Edward Wigglesworth of Harvard University prepares the first computation in this country of required reserves based on death statistics.

1830   New York Life Insurance and Trust Company, the first company to employ agents, is established. It was later merged with the Bank of New York.

1835   New England Life Insurance Company, the first

mutual life insurance company in this country, is chartered in Boston. It begins business in 1843.

1840   The New York State legislature advances the cause of life insurance by enacting a law protecting life insurance death benefits from the claims of creditors.

1848   The Penn Mutual Life Insurance Company of Philadelphia is one of the first companies to pay a cash value upon surrender of a policy. The first life insurance policy loans are also granted.

1849   New York State passes the first general insurance law.

1851   New Hampshire establishes the first regulatory body to examine the affairs of insurance companies.

1852   After working on them for nine years, Elizur Wright completes tables of policy reserves and values, which are published the next year.

1858   Wright becomes Massachusetts' first insurance commissioner.

1859   New York State establishes the first insurance department.

1861   Massachusetts is the first state to require that policies pay cash values or other benefits if surrendered before death.

1868   Equitable Life Assurance Society of the United States begins selling tontine policies to boost sales.

1869   U.S. Supreme Court holds insurance is not a transaction in interstate commerce, affirming the industry's exemption from federal regulation.

1875   Industrial insurance aimed at the poor is introduced in this country by Prudential Insurance Company of America.

1905   The Armstrong investigation exposes a litany of abuses in the life insurance industry, leading to a body of laws that governs the industry to this day.

1909   New York State requires standard life insurance policy forms in an effort to make life insurance more comprehensible.

1911   First group life insurance policy is issued by Equitable Life Assurance Society of the United States.

1939   Temporary National Economic Committee begins an investigation of the life insurance business.

1944   U.S. Supreme Court reverses itself, holding insurance is subject to federal regulation because it is a transaction that crosses state lines.

1945   Congress, at the request of the industry, passes the McCarran-Ferguson Act, exempting insurance of all types from federal regulation and from the provisions of the federal antitrust laws so long as the business is regulated by state law.

American Council of Life Insurance and other sources.

MORTALITY RATES

In determining life insurance rates, life insurance companies begin with mortality tables which show the chances of dying at particular ages. Most companies continue to use a 1958 table that shows death rates substantially higher than current death rates. According to this table, the chances of a twenty-five-year-old dying are almost 2 in 1,000. The actual chance is about 1¼ in 1,000.

The exception to this pattern is in the first few months of life, when the standard table shows a lower death rate than the actual death rate. Few life insurance policies are purchased on infants' lives, however.

A more recent table, while showing lower death rates, still shows death rates that are higher than the actual rates.

DEATHS PER 1,000

AGE	TABLE	ACTUAL
0	7.1	13.2
1	1.8	.9
2	1.5	.7
3	1.5	.5
4	1.4	.4
5	1.4	.4
6	1.3	.3
7	1.3	.3
8	1.2	.3
9	1.2	.2

DEATHS PER 1,000 (continued)

AGE	TABLE	ACTUAL
10	1.2	.2
11	1.2	.2
12	1.3	.3
13	1.3	.4
14	1.4	.5
15	1.5	.7
16	1.5	.9
17	1.6	1.0
18	1.7	1.1
19	1.7	1.2
20	1.8	1.2
21	1.8	1.3
22	1.9	1.3
23	1.9	1.3
24	1.9	1.3
25	1.9	1.3
26	2.0	1.3
27	2.0	1.3
28	2.0	1.3
29	2.1	1.3
30	2.1	1.3
31	2.2	1.3

DEATHS PER 1,000 (continued)

AGE	TABLE	ACTUAL
32	2.3	1.3
33	2.3	1.4
34	2.4	1.5
35	2.5	1.6
36	2.6	1.7
37	2.8	1.8
38	3.0	2.0
39	3.3	2.1
40	3.5	2.3
41	3.8	2.5
42	4.2	2.8
43	4.5	3.1
44	4.9	3.4
45	5.4	3.7
46	5.8	4.1
47	6.4	4.5
48	7.0	4.9
49	7.6	5.5
50	8.3	6.0
51	9.1	6.6
52	10.0	7.2
53	10.9	7.8

DEATHS PER 1,000 (continued)

AGE	TABLE	ACTUAL
54	11.9	8.4
55	13.0	9.0
56	14.2	9.7
57	15.5	10.5
58	17.0	11.5
59	18.6	12.6
60	20.3	13.9
61	22.2	15.2
62	24.3	16.5
63	26.6	17.8
64	29.0	19.0
65	31.8	20.3
66	34.7	21.7
67	38.0	23.4
68	41.7	25.5
69	45.6	27.9
70	49.8	30.5
71	54.2	33.2
72	58.7	36.1
73	63.3	38.8
74	68.1	41.7
75	73.4	44.7

DEATHS PER 1,000 (continued)

AGE	TABLE	ACTUAL
76	79.2	48.1
77	85.7	51.9
78	93.1	56.2
79	101.2	61.2
80	110.0	67.0
81	119.4	73.5
82	129.2	80.8
83	139.4	89.2
84	150.0	98.6

Mortality table from the American Council of Life Insurance; death rates from Metropolitan Life Foundation's Statistical Bulletin.

INDEX

Index

Index

Whole life insurance (*cont'd*).
 vs. term, 15, 16, 22–23;
  commission paid for, 22, 27,
  31, 36, 39, 45, 46, 47; by
  Metropolitan, 24; by
  Prudential, 21–22; taxation of,
  24; and time value of money,
  23–24
 vs. universal life, 57, 62, 64
 see also Decreasing term
  insurance; Deposit term
  insurance; Industrial life
  insurance
Widows:
 case histories of, 228–33

 as victims of life insurance
  game, 10, 228
Will, Charles A., 140
Williams (A. L.) organization, 98–
 104
Williams, Art, 99
Williams, Virginia E., 65–66, 67,
 75–77
Wilson, John D., 74
Wolcott, Dean E., 244–45
Wolff, Thomas J., 15
Woodside, William S., 100
Wright, Elizur, 189–90, 248–49

Yunich, David L., 168